COUNTRY

Guide to Rural England

THE SOUTH
OF ENGLAND

Bedfordshire, Berkshire, Buckinghamshire,
Gloucestershire, Hampshire, Hertfordshire,
Isle of Wight, Oxfordshire and Wiltshire

By David Gerrard

© Travel Publishing Ltd

First Published: 2001
Second Edition: 2004
Third Edition: 2006
Fourth Edition: 2008

COUNTRY LIVING GUIDES:

East Anglia	Scotland
Heart of England	The South of England
Ireland	The South East of England
The North East of England	The West Country
The North West of England	Wales

PLEASE NOTE:

All advertisements in this publication have been accepted in good faith by Travel Publishing and they have not necessarily been endorsed by *Country Living* Magazine.

All information is included by the publishers in good faith and is believed to be correct at the time of going to press. No responsibility can be accepted for errors.

Editor:	David Gerrard
Printing by:	Latimer Trend, Plymouth
Location Maps:	© Maps in Minutes ™ (2008) © Collins Bartholomews 2008 All rights reserved.
Walks:	Walks have been reproduced with kind permission of the internet walking site: www.walkingworld.com
Walk Maps:	Reproduced from Ordnance Survey mapping on behalf of the Controller of Her Majesty's Stationery Office, © Crown Copyright. Licence Number MC 100035812
Cover Design:	Lines & Words, Aldermaston
Cover Photo:	River Windrush and Burford Church, Oxfordshire © www.britainonview.com
Text Photos:	Text photos have been kindly supplied by the Pictures of Britain photo library © www.picturesofbritain.co.uk and © Bob Brooks, Weston-super-Mare

Foreword

From a bracing walk across the hills and tarns of The Lake District to a relaxing weekend spent discovering the unspoilt hamlets of East Anglia, nothing quite matches getting off the beaten track and exploring Britain's areas of outstanding beauty.

Each month, *Country Living Magazine* celebrates the richness and diversity of our countryside with features on rural Britain and the traditions that have their roots there. So it is with great pleasure that I introduce you to the *Country Living Magazine Guide to Rural England* series. Packed with information about unusual and unique aspects of our countryside, the guides will point both fair-weather and intrepid travellers in the right direction.

Each chapter provides a fascinating tour of the South of England area, with insights into local heritage and history and easy-to-read facts on a wealth of places to visit, stay, eat, drink and shop.

I hope that this guide will help make your visit a rewarding and stimulating experience and that you will return inspired, refreshed and ready to head off on your next countryside adventure.

Susy Smith

Susy Smith
Editor, Country Living magazine

PS To subscribe to *Country Living Magazine* each month, call 01858 438844

Introduction

This is the fourth edition of *The Country Living Guide to Rural England – The South* and we are sure that it will be as popular as its predecessors. David Gerrard, a very experienced travel writer has completely updated the contents of the guide and ensured that it is packed with vivid descriptions, historical stories, amusing anecdotes and interesting facts on hundreds of places in Bedfordshire, Berkshire, Buckinghamshire, Gloucestershire, Hampshire, Hertfordshire, The Isle of Wight, Oxfordshire and Wiltshire. In the introduction to each village or town we have also summarized and categorized the main attractions to be found there, which makes it easy for readers to plan their visit.

The advertising panels within each chapter provide further information on places to see, stay, eat, drink and shop. We have also selected a number of walks from walkingworld.com (full details of this website may be found to the rear of the guide) which we highly recommend if you wish to appreciate fully the beauty and charm of the varied rural landscapes and coastlines of the South of England.

The guide however is not simply an 'armchair tour'. Its prime aim is to encourage the reader to visit the places described and discover much more about the wonderful towns, villages and countryside of the South of England in person. In this respect we would like to thank all the Tourist Information Centres who helped us to provide you with up-to-date information. Whether you decide to explore this region by wheeled transport or on foot we are sure you will find it a very uplifting experience!

We are always interested in receiving comments on places covered (or not covered) in our guides so please do not hesitate to use the reader reaction forms provided at the rear of this guide to give us your considered comments. This will help us refine and improve the content of the next edition. We also welcome any general comments which will help improve the overall presentation of the guides themselves.

For more information on the full range of travel guides published by Travel Publishing please refer to the order form at the rear of this guide or log on to our website (see below).

Travel Publishing

Did you know that you can also search our website for details of thousands of places to see, stay, eat or drink throughout Britain and Ireland? Our site has become increasingly popular and now receives monthly over 160,000 visits. Try it!

website: www.travelpublishing.co.uk

Contents

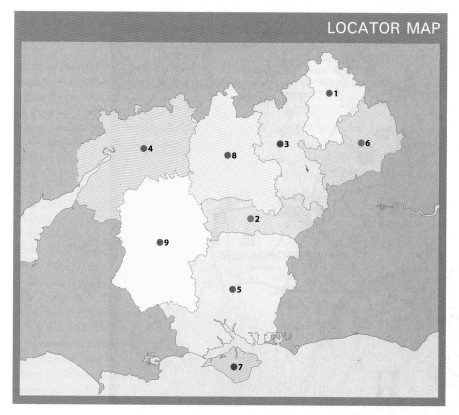

LOCATOR MAP

Luton

🏠 Luton Hoo   🏛 Luton Museum and Art Gallery

🏛 Stockwood Craft Museum   🏚 Someries Castle

The largest town in Bedfordshire and perhaps best known for Luton Airport, Vauxhall cars – and, for those with long memories of radio days, the Luton Girls Choir. Although the town has expanded rapidly from a market town in the early 19th century to a major industrial centre by the mid-20th century, it still boasts more than 100 listed buildings and three Conservation Areas.

Luton first began to prosper in the 17th century on the strength of its straw plaiting and straw hat-making industries. These activities are amongst those featured at the **Luton Museum and Art Gallery**, housed within a delightful Victorian mansion in Wardown Park, a traditional town park with tennis and bowls. The park was opened to the public in the early years of the reign of Edward VII, but not the house, which was first a restaurant and then, during the First World War, a military hospital. It was not until 1931 that the town's museum and art gallery, originally housed in the library, moved here. As well as featuring a re-creation of a Victorian shop and pub, the museum is also home to a range of collections covering the hat trade, costume, local history, archaeology and childhood. As lace-making was one of the two main cottage industries in Bedfordshire, visitors will not be surprised to learn that the museum also has the largest collection of lace anywhere in the country outside London.

Visitors can also take a step back in time by seeking out **Stockwood Craft Museum and Gardens**. Occupying a Georgian stable block, the museum has a collection of Bedfordshire craft and rural items enhanced by frequent craft demonstrations. The walled garden is equally impressive and the Period Garden includes knot, medieval, Victorian, cottage, Dutch and Italian sections. The Hamilton Finlay Sculpture Garden showcases six pieces of sculpture by the internationally renowned artist Ian Hamilton Finlay in a lovely natural setting. The Mossman Collection of over 60 horse-drawn vehicles, the largest of its kind on public display in Britain is also housed here. The story of transport comes into the 20th century in the Transport Gallery, whose exhibits include bicycles, vintage cars and a model of the Luton tram system. Replicas of some of the vehicles on display here have found their way into such films as *Ben Hur* and *Out of Africa*.

Just to the south of the town is the magnificent house **Luton Hoo**, originally designed by Robert Adams and set in 1,500 acres of parkland landscaped by Capability Brown. Construction of the house began in 1767, though it was extensively remodelled in 1827 and again in 1903, when the interior was given a French style for Sir Julius Wernher, who installed his fabulous art collection in the

Someries Castle, Luton

house. Luton Hoo is now a private hotel and is no longer open to the public.

Just southeast of Luton is **Someries Castle**, the remains of a fortified medieval manor house dating from the middle to late 15th century. The earliest surviving brick building in the county, both the gatehouse and chapel have survived and are still a very impressive sight. The original castle on this site belonged first to the de Someries family and then to the Wenlocks, and the house, of which only a romantic ruin remains, may have been built for the Lord Wenlock who died at the Battle of Tewkesbury in 1471, when the Yorkist victory ended the Wars of the Roses.

Around Luton

SLIP END
1 mile S of Luton on the B4540

🐾 Woodside Animal Farm

Woodside Animal Farm is home to more than 200 different breeds and there are

hundreds of animals and birds to see and feed. The farm's many attractions include a walk-through monkey house, red squirrel enclosure, alpaca family, fabulous flamingos and hand-reared racoons. There are indoor and outdoor picnic and play areas, crazy golf, pony and tractor rides, a bouncy castle, farm shop, craft shop and coffee shop.

WHIPSNADE
5 miles SW of Luton off B489

🐾 Whipsnade Tree Cathedral 🐾 Wild Animal Park

This small village with a charming, simple church is surrounded by common land on which stands **Whipsnade Tree Cathedral** (National Trust, see panel below). After the First World War, a local landowner, Edmund Kell Blyth, planted a variety of trees that have grown into the shape of a medieval cathedral, with a nave, transepts, cloisters and chapels. Designed as a memorial to friends of Blyth killed in the war, it's a curiously moving place. During the summer, services are held here.

To the south of the village can be seen the

Whipsnade Tree Cathedral

Whipsnade Tree Cathedral Trustees,
c/o Chapel Farm, Whipsnade,
Dunstable, Bedfordshire LU6 2LL
Tel: 01582 872406
website: www.nationaltrust.org.uk

Situated on the edge of Whipsnade Village Green the **Tree Cathedral** combines a range of different varieties of trees and shrubs laid out to the plan of a cathedral. There is a nave, transepts, chancel, cloisters and four chapels and an outer cloister walk enclosing a wide area with a dew pond as its focal point

Owned by the National Trust the Tree Cathedral is managed by trustees and cared for and maintained by volunteers. The planting continues in order to maintain the principle features for future generations.

There is an annual inter-denominational service held each year in June. There is a small car park signposted from the B4540 in Whipsnade.

white silhouette of a lion cut into the green hillside, which is reminiscent of the much older White Horse at Uffington. A magnificent landmark, the lion also advertises the whereabouts of **Whipsnade Wild Animal Park**, the country home of the Zoological Society of London. Whipsnade first opened its doors in 1931, attracting over 26,000 visitors on the first Monday, and in the years since, it has grown and developed and continues to provide fun and education for thousands of visitors each year. There are 2,500 animals on show in the park's 600 acres, and behind the scenes Whipsnade is at the forefront of wild animal welfare and conservation, specialising in the breeding of endangered species such as cheetahs, rhinos and the scimitar-horned oryx. There are daily demonstrations - penguin feeding, sea lions, free-flying birds - and other attractions include a railway safari, Discovery Centre, Children's Farm and Adventure Playground. Feeding time for the animals is always a popular occasion, while humans who feel peckish can make tracks for the Café on the Lake or (in summer) the Lookout Café, or graze on ice cream and snacks from the many refreshment kiosks in the park.

Dunstable Downs

DUNSTABLE
2 miles W of Luton on the A505

🏠 Church of St Peter   🝔 Dunstable Downs

Dunstable is a bustling town that grew up at the junction of two ancient roads, Icknield Way and Watling Street, and was an important centre in Roman Britain, when it was known as Durocobrivae. The town's finest building is undoubtedly the **Priory Church of St Peter**,

all that remains of a Priory founded by Henry I in 1131; only the nave actually dates from that time. It was at the Priory that Archbishop Cranmer's court sat in 1533 to annul the marriage of Henry VIII and Katherine of Aragon.

On the B4541 Dunstable-Whipsnade road, **Dunstable Downs** commands some of the finest views over the Vale of Aylesbury. Designated a Site of Special Scientific Interest and a Scheduled Ancient Monument, it has much to attract the visitor, including a Countryside Centre with interpretive displays and gifts, circular walks and a picnic area; it's a popular spot with hang-gliders and kite-flyers, and a refreshment kiosk is open all year round. South of Dunstable Downs at the junction of the B4541 and B4540, Whipsnade Heath is a small area of woodland containing fungi and some unusual plants.

TOTTERNHOE
6 miles W of Luton off the A505

🍃 Totternhoe Knolls

This attractive village is situated below **Totternhoe Knolls**, a steeply sloped spur of chalk that is now a nature reserve known nationally for its orchids and its butterflies.

🏠 historic building   🏛 museum and heritage   🏛 historic site   🝔 scenic attraction   🍃 flora and fauna

On the top of the spur are the remains of a motte-and-bailey castle dating from Norman times, with commanding views of the surrounding countryside.

BILLINGTON
8 miles W of Luton on the A4146

🐾 Mead Open Farm

Mead Open Farm is home to a variety of traditional and rare farm animals and offers a particularly wide range of attractions for children, including an indoor play barn, activity house, sandpit, indoor pets corner and ride-on toys. There's also a tearoom and shop, and a number of daily activities and weekly events.

LEIGHTON BUZZARD
9 miles W of Luton on A505

🏛 All Souls Church   ⚲ Greensand Ridge Walk

The town's interesting name tells a lot about its history: Leighton is Old English and refers to a centre for market gardening, whilst the Buzzard is a reference not to the bird of prey, but to a local clergyman, Theobald de Busar, the town's first Prebendary. The town's past prosperity as a market centre is reflected in the grandeur of its fine Market Cross, a 15th century pentagonal structure with an open base and statues under vaulted openings all topped off by pinnacles. The market is still held here every Tuesday and Saturday.

The spire of **All Saints Church** is over 190 feet high and is a local landmark. This big ironstone church dates from 1277 and it contains a number of endearing features in the form of graffiti left by the medieval stonemasons: one shows a man and a woman quarrelling over whether to boil or bake a simnel cake. Seriously damaged by fire in 1985, the church has been carefully restored

Leighton Buzzard Railway

*Page's Park Station, Billington Road,
Leighton Buzzard, Bedfordshire LU7 4TN
Tel: 01525 373888 Fax: 01525 377814
website: www.buzzrail.co.uk*

One of England's premier narrow gauge heritage railways, **Leighton Buzzard Railway** was established in 1919 to carry sand from the quarries, which had opened up to supply the demand for sand during the First World War, in the north of the town through to the town's railway sidings and canal wharf. Built using war surplus materials and equipment, the line, since 1968, has carried a passenger service, mostly steam hauled, from Page's Park to Stonehenge Works in the countryside near the village of Heath and Reach.

Operated by volunteers of the Leighton Buzzard Narrow Gauge Railway Society, the trains pass through a modern housing estate before emerging into rolling countryside with views of the Chiltern Hills in the distance. The railway is now the home of the largest collection of narrow gauge locomotives in Britain and, of the 50 here, some 12 are steam driven. The oldest engine dates from 1877 whilst the newest is a diesel locomotive built especially for the line in 1999. The return journey takes just over an hour and the railway operates on Sundays and Bank Holiday weekends between March and October.

THE CROSS KEYS

Pulloxhill, nr Flitton, Bedfordshire, MK45 5HB
Tel: 01525 712442
e-mail: www.ukeventsandtents.co.uk

Veteran hosts Peter and Sheila Meads took over **The Cross Keys** 38 years ago, earning them the proud title of longest serving landlord and landlady of the Charles Wells Brewery. They have the warmest of welcomes for their customers and with such a wealth of experience behind the bar, the 17th century Cross Keys has a solid reputation as one of the best-loved pubs in the region.

Behind its Grade II listed frontage, the bar with its beams, inglenook fireplace and friendly staff; all contribute to the cosy, relaxed ambience for enjoying a drink or a meal. The comfortable 50-seat restaurant serves traditional English food every lunchtime and evening. Peter makes an exceptional effort to source only local ingredients while food is prepared fresh in the kitchen satisfying appetites with an enjoyable home-cooked meal. The excellent wine list is a great complement to the fine food on offer.

Also the pub boasts a flower-decked patio and a large rear garden, providing a popular spot for the whole family to enjoy.

An offshoot of the Cross Keys is a company run by Peter's son, called UK Events and Tents, specialising in marquee hire for use at weddings, parties and corporate events.

---

tombs and monuments to the de Grey family of Wrest Park.

SILSOE

3 miles SE of Ampthill off A6

🏛 Wrest Park

Although the manor of Wrest has been held by the de Grey family since the late 13th century, the house standing today dates from the 1830s. Built for the 1st Earl de Grey from the designs of a French architect, it follows faithfully the style of a French chateau of the previous century. Parts of the house at **Wrest Park** are open to the public, but the real glory is the gardens, which extend over 90 acres. They are a living history of English gardening from 1700 to 1850 and are the work of Charles Bridgeman, with later adaptations by Capability Brown. The layout remains basically formal, with a full range of garden appointments in the grand manner - there is a Chinese bridge, an artificial lake, a classical temple, and a rustic ruin.

Wrest Park, Silsoe

Toddington Manor Gardens

those travelling the nearby M1 who think only of the service station of the same name. However, the village is an attractive place, with cottages and elegant houses grouped around the village green. Unfortunately, all that remains of **Toddington Manor** is a small oblong building with a hipped roof, which is believed to be the Elizabethan kitchen of the large quadrangular house that was built here around 1570. Toddington is a place that makes much of its folklore and is host to Morris dancers in the summer, and mummers who tour the village providing traditional entertainment at Christmas. Local legend has it that a witch lives under Conger Hill - which is actually a motte that would, at one time, have had a castle on top - and, on Shrove Tuesday, the children put their ears to the ground to listen to her frying pancakes.

RIDGMONT
4 miles W of Ampthill on the A507

Part of the Woburn Estate, this is a typical estate village where the owners of the land (in this case the Bedford family) provided the houses and other buildings. Here the workers lived in gabled, redbrick houses. The church, designed by George Gilbert Scott, was also built at the expense of the estate.

WOBURN
6 miles W of Ampthill on the A4012

🏛 Woburn Abbey 🦌 Wild Animal Kingdom
🚶 Aspley Woods

First recorded as a Saxon hamlet in the 10th century, and again mentioned in the Domesday Book, Woburn grew into a small market town after the founding of the Cistercian Abbey here in 1145. All but destroyed by fire in 1720, this pretty village has retained many of the pleasant Georgian

Two buildings of particular interest are the Baroque Banqueting House, designed by Thomas Archer, which forms a focus of the view from the house across the lake, and the Bowling Green House, dating from about 1740 and said to have been designed by Batty Langley, who was best known as a writer of architectural books for country builders, but built little himself. Immediately beside the house is an intricate French-style garden, with an orangery by the French architect Cléphane, flowerbeds, statues, and fountains. The village of Silsoe itself boasts more than 130 listed buildings.

TODDINGTON
5 miles S of Ampthill on A5120

🏛 Toddington Manor

Situated on a hill above the River Flitt, this village is often overlooked, particularly by

of Milton Keynes from **Aspley Woods**, one of the largest areas of woodland in Bedfordshire, set between Woburn and Woburn Sands. The woods offer peace, tranquillity and miles of tracks for walking.

MARSTON MORETAINE
3 miles NW of Ampthill off the A421.

🔾 Forest Centre

Forest Centre and Millennium Country Park offers a splendid day out in the countryside for all the family. The 600 acres of wetland and woodland are home to a wide variety of wildlife, and the park provides excellent walking and cycling; bikes can be hired from the Forest Centre, which also has an interactive Discover the Forest exhibition, café bar, art gallery, gift shop, free parking and children's play area.

Biggleswade

Set on the banks of the River Ivel, which was once navigable through to the sea, Biggleswade was an important stop on the Great North Road stagecoach routes and several old inns have survived from that period. The town also has another link with transport, it was the home of Dan Albone (1860-1906), the inventor of the modern bicycle. He produced a number of variants, including a tandem and a ladies cycle with a low crossbar and a skirt guard, but is best known for his racing cycle, which in 1888 set speed and endurance records with the intrepid CP Mills in the saddle. Dan Albone's inventiveness was not confined to bicycles, as he also developed the Ivel Agricultural Tractor, the forerunner of the modern tractor.

Around Biggleswade

SHEFFORD
5 miles SW of Biggleswade on the A507

🔾 Hoo Hill Maze

The small town of Shefford grew up, as the name suggests, around a sheep ford across the Rivers Hitt and Flitt and enjoyed a brief status as an inland port on the Ivel Navigation. This waterway was built primarily to bring coal from Kings Lynn by way of the River Ouse. In North Bridge Street a wall plaque marks the house of the pastoral poet Robert Bloomfield, a poor farm labourer and shoemaker who found fame when he published *The Farmer's Boy* in 1800. The poet, who died, as he had lived, in extreme poverty, is buried in the churchyard at nearby Campton.

In Hitchin Road, the **Hoo Hill Maze**, constructed with hedges more than 6 feet high, stands in an orchard with a picnic site and plenty of space for children to romp.

Shefford is also the starting point of the 21-mile-long cycle route, the Jubilee Way, a circular route that passes through undulating landscape and picturesque villages.

LOWER STONDON
6 miles S of Biggleswade off the A600

🏛 Transport Museum

Lower Stondon attracts visitors from near and far to its renowned **Transport Museum** and garden centre. The museum, on the A600 next to Mount Pleasant golf course, contains a marvellous collection of several hundred exhibits covering all forms of transport – from motorcycles to helicopters, from a Jowett Javelin and a Bedford Dormobile to a London bus – and covers the period from the early 1900s to the recent past. The centrepiece of the collection is a full size replica of Captain Cook's barque, *Endeavour*, in which he undertook one of his most important journeys in 1768. The replica was built using the original plans. Guided tours of the museum are available and there's a café selling light refreshments.

SANDY
3 miles N of Biggleswade on A1

🦅 The Lodge

The sandy soil that gave the town its name helped it rise to fame as a market gardening centre in the 16th century. The 14th-century Church of St Swithun contains an interesting statue of Captain Sir William Peel, third son of Sir Robert Peel, famous Prime Minister and founder of the Police Force, who was one of the first recipents of the Victoria Cross for heroic action in the Crimean War.

A little way southeast of the town, at **Sandy Lodge**, is the national headquarters of the Royal Society for the Protection of Birds and a nature reserve set in over 350 acres of open heath and woodland. As well as offering a great deal to those interested in birds, the formal gardens surrounding the mansion house are a delight. They were first created in the 1870s and restored in the 1930s by Sir Malcolm Stewart and are well worth visiting in their own right. Also on the site is a newly developed wildlife garden.

BLUNHAM
5 miles N of Biggleswade off the A1

This quiet rural village was the home of the poet John Donne while he was rector here from 1622 until his death in 1632, a post he held while also Dean of St Paul's in London. While he was convalescing here after a serious

---

SEDDINGTON NURSERY

Great North Road, Seddington, Sandy, Bedfordshire SG19 1NZ
Tel: 01767 680983   Fax: 01767 690951
e-mail: sales@seddingtonnursery.com
website: www.seddingtonnursery.com

Michael and Lynda Scott at **Seddington Nursery**, share your passion for the garden. For nearly 25 years, they have been providing plants, products, advice and inspiration to gardeners.

It is the friendly relaxing atmosphere, guarantee of quality and excellent customer service that make this nursery so popular with its customers. Seddington Nursery and Garden Centre, has as the title suggests, its roots as a Nursery before expanding into a Garden Centre. The Nursery was originally built in 1924 and has played its part during the Second World War growing food for the war effort. Nowadays a large selection of the plants on show are still grown on site in the greenhouses, but the demand for larger and more exotic hardy species has meant that plants are sourced from literally all continents. B.B.Q.'s here are another main feature for this site offering sound advice, huge choice and great value.

Should your thoughts turn to food on site is the Coffee Cabin. Whether you require a snack or a meal with Coffee of Wine we are able to cater for you. Sunday Lunches are available from 12.00pm - 3.00pm. Booking is advisable for this Home made speciality.

WOODVIEW FARM SHOP

Mill Hill, Potton Road, Gamlingay,
Cambridgeshire SG19 3LW
Tel: 01767 650200
Mobile: 07815 093052

For many people the weekly food shop has become a bit of a chore. A quick trip to the supermarket may fill the cupboards but does it really tease the taste buds and excite the senses? **Woodview Farm Shop** does all this and more.

When it comes to diversity, ranges include all the everyday essentials you can't live without as well as dozens of treats and delicacies you might find difficult to find elsewhere. Better still, being able to find so many products with just a single journey makes this farm shop the natural choice both for your convenience and the environment's health.

From irresistible handmade cakes by local ladies, delicious golden honey, free-range eggs from the farms own flock, fresh fruit & vegetables, butcher's shop, cheese counter to the delectable treats in the delicatessen, you'd be hard pushed to find a more irresistible shop.

Choose between succulent cuts of beef, lamb & pork, beautifully presented game & poultry, burgers & sausages made on the premises, and as if that wasn't enough there is an excellent selection of cooked meats. From traditionally prepared hams, roast topside of beef to traditional faggots and scotch eggs, you'll quickly realise that there is something to suit the most conservative of tastes to the much more adventurous!

Woodview Farm Shop is very much a family run business and is a constant hive of activity with fresh meat being prepared in front of you. Owner, Geoff Titmus and his family have lived on Woodview Farm for over 15 years, but only in the last year have they re-opened the farm shop. Already it is proving highly successful and important to the local community.

As a family business committed to tangible values (quality, traceability and freshness), Geoff and his sons (Manager, Rob and Butcher, Jason) make it their business to hand pick every product sold. What's more, their passion for great food is matched by only by their passion for good old-fashioned service – they value every one of their customers, and it definitely shows. So helpful and informative are the staff that nothing is too much trouble for them. Not only will, Jason and his team of butchers, cut and prepare meat to your specification, they can also give good cooking advice and menu suggestions for when you're entertaining. Don't forget there's a good butcher behind every excellent menu!

🏛 historic building 🏛 museum and heritage 🏚 historic site ⚜ scenic attraction 🌳 flora and fauna

ASTERBY & CHALKCROFT NURSERY

The Ridgeway, Blunham, Bedfordshire, MK44 3PH
Tel: 01767 640148
website: www.asterbyplants.co.uk
e-mail: sales@asterbyplants.co.uk

At **Asterby & Chalkcroft Nursery** we specialise in just plants. We grow something like 3000 different sorts, so there's a lot to choose from.

Here you will find Trees, Shrubs, Perennials, Conifers and Climbers. In Spring we grow some 300 varieties of Summer Bedding, and in Autumn, a big selection of Pansies plus other plants for the Winter Garden. All at what we hope are very reasonable prices.

The Nursery started in 1992, and moved here to Blunham in 1999. It is run by Edwin, Simon, and his wife Eva – she's the one whose brains you need to borrow for plant advice.

We have a website, where you can look up to see if we do any particular plant. But much better if you can visit and look at the actual plants in person.

We are open every day from 10.00am to 5.00pm, 7 days a week. Closed mid-December to the beginning of February.

illness in 1623 he wrote *Devotions*, which contains the immortal lines "No man is an island, entire of itself, and Never send to know for whom the bell tolls; it tolls for thee". Donne divided his time between London and Blunham, where he stayed in the house opposite the parish church. Inside can be seen some fine Norman work, interesting bosses and the chalice Donne presented to the church in 1626.

Another building of interest is the Old Vicarage, constructed of startling yellow and orange bricks in 1874.

MOGGERHANGER

3 miles NW of Biggleswade off the A603

🏛 Moggerhanger Park

Grade I-listed **Moggerhanger Park** was designed by Sir John Soane, architect of the Bank of England, and is set amidst 33 acres of gardens and parkland originally landscaped by Humphry Repton. Guided tours of this fine Georgian house are available daily during the summer months; the restaurant and tearooms are open all year round.

OLD WARDEN

3 miles W of Biggleswade off B658

🏛 Shuttleworth Collection 🦢 Swiss Garden

🦅 Bird of Prey Conservation Centre

This charming village of thatched cottages along a single street has developed its unique character as a result of the influence of two local families. In the early 18th century, Sir Samuel Ongley, a London merchant, ship-owner, and former director of the South Sea Company, bought this country seat for himself and his family, who stayed here for

📖 stories and anecdotes 🐦 famous people 🎨 art and craft 🎭 entertainment and sport 🚶 walks

River Great Ouse, Bedford

Mound, all that remains of a fortress built here shortly after the Battle of Hastings but destroyed in 1224. A timber-framed building has been constructed on top of the mound, which commands a spectacular view over the River Great Ouse.

The **Church of St Peter de Merton**, Saxon in origin, boasts a fine Norman south doorway that was not actually intended for this building but was brought here from the Church of St Peter in Dunstable. St Peter's is not Bedford's main church: this is **St Paul's Church** in the centre of St Paul's Square, a mainly 14th- and 15th-century building, with some interesting monuments and brasses, and a stone pulpit from which John Wesley preached in 1758. Outside the church is a statue of one of the best-known sons of Bedford, John Howard, an 18th-century nonconformist landowner who denounced the

attractive features of the town. Bedford was already a thriving market place before the Norman Conquest, and a market is still held on Wednesday and Saturday each week. There's also a farmer's market once a month and, in the summer months, a gourmet and speciality food market on Thursdays, and a flower and garden market on Fridays.

The town's oldest visible structure is **Castle**

Cecil Higgins Art Gallery

Castle Lane, Bedford, Bedfordshire MK40 3RP
Tel: 01234 211222 Fax: 01234 327149
website: www.cecilhigginsartgallery.org

The Cecil Higgins Art Gallery is situated in pleasant gardens leading down to the river embankment and is a recreation of an 1880s home, with superb examples of 19th century decorative arts. Room settings include items from the Handley-Read collection and the famous Gothic bedroom containing works by William Burges.

In an adjoining gallery are housed renowned collections of watercolours, prints and drawings (exhibitions changed regularly – ring for details), and there are also ceramics, glass and the Thomas Lester Lace Collection.

A self-service coffee bar is on hand for refreshments and the gallery shop sells a range of souvenirs. Tours can be arranged for groups if booked in advance and there is a programme of lunchtime lectures & demonstrations (call for details).

🏛 historic building 🏛 museum and heritage 🏛 historic site 🐿 scenic attraction 🌱 flora and fauna

appalling conditions in jails and prison ships. His name lives on in the Howard League for Penal Reform.

Bedford's most famous son, John Bunyan was born just south of the town, in Elstow, but lived – and was twice imprisoned – in Bedford in the 1660s and 1670s. The son of a tinsmith, Bunyan followed the same trade as his father and so was able to travel the countryside more than most people of that time. In the 1650s, Bunyan met John Gifford, the then pastor of the Independent Congregation, which held its meetings at St John's Church. It was their lengthy discussions that led to Bunyan's conversion and he was baptised shortly afterwards by Gifford in a backwater that leads off the Great Ouse. In 1660, Bunyan was arrested for preaching without a licence. He was to spend 12 years in goal, time he put to good use by writing *Grace Abounding*, his spiritual autobiography. But it was during a second imprisonment, in 1676, that he began writing his most famous work, *The Pilgrim's Progress*. This inspired allegory of the way to salvation still entrances even non-believers with the beauty and simplicity of its language. Following his release from prison in 1672, Bunyan was elected pastor of the Independent Congregation.

The **Bunyan Meeting Free Church** was constructed in 1849 on the site of the converted barn where Bunyan used to preach. The magnificent bronze doors, with illustrations from *The Pilgrim's Progress*, were given to the church by the Duke of Bedford in

God, Gold & Kings Exhibition, Bedford Museum

1676. Adjacent to the church is the **Bunyan Museum**, which graphically tells the story of the man as well as the times through which he lived. Among the many displays are the jug in which his daughter Mary brought him soup whilst in prison, his chair, his tinker's anvil, and the violin and flute that he made in prison.

Another tribute to Bunyan in the town is **Bunyan's Statue**, which was presented to the town in 1874 by the Duke of Bedford. Made of bronze, the statue is the work of Sir JE Boehm; around the pedestal of the 9ft figure, which weighs more than three tons, are three bronze panels depicting scenes from *The Pilgrim's Progress*.

Beside the river and running through the heart of the town are the Bedford Embankment Gardens, which provide a year-round display of plants. Close by is also the **Priory Country Park**, an area of 206 acres with a diverse habitat, which represents the flood meadows, reed beds and woodland that once surrounded the town. In Park Road North, Hill Rise Wildlife Area is a site for nature conservation specialising in butterflies amphibians and small mammals.

For an insight into the history of the town and surrounding area, the **Bedford Museum** is well worth a visit. Among the many interesting displays is a piece of wall that shows the construction of the wattle walls that were an essential building technique in the 14th century.

Housed within the unlikely combination of a Victorian mansion and an adjoining modern gallery, the **Cecil Higgins Art Gallery** (see panel on page 20) was started in 1949 by a wealthy Bedford brewery family. It is currently closed for refurbishment, but it is scheduled to re-open in 2009. Its treasures include an internationally renowned collection of watercolours, prints, and drawings, as well as some fine glass, ceramics, and furniture. The permanent display includes works by Turner, Gainsborough, Picasso and Matisse, and a needle panel entitled Bunyan's Dream. This was designed by Edward Bawden in 1977 to commemorate the tercentenary of the publication of *The Pilgrim's Progress*, the 350th anniversary of John Bunyan's birth and the Queen's Silver Jubilee. Other contemporary work can be seen at the **RCA Gallery**, which showcases the visual arts, including film, photography and animation.

A building with more modern connections is the Corn Exchange in St Paul's Square, from where Colonel **Glenn Miller** frequently broadcast during the Secons World War. A bust of the bandleader who gave the world *In the Mood* and *Moonlight Serenade* stands outside the Exchange, and in 1994 a plaque was unveiled on the 50th anniversary of his mysterious disappearance over the English Channel. East of Bedford, Clapham Twinwood Control Tower is the last place where Miller was seen alive. A small museum is open at weekends and Bank Holidays in the summer.

Around Bedford

ELSTOW
1 mile S of Bedford off the A6

🏛 Abbey Church   🏠 Moot Hall

John Bunyan connections are everywhere in the picturesque village of Elstow. The cottage where he was born in 1628 no longer stands, but its site is marked by a stone erected in Festival of Britain Year, 1951. The **Abbey Church of St Helena and St Mary** has two renowned stained glass windows, one depicting scenes from *The Pilgrim's Progress*, the other scenes from the Holy War. Here, too, are the font where Bunyan was christened in 1628 and the Communion Table used when he attended service. Bunyan's mother, father and sister are buried in the churchyard. The church also tells the story of the ill-fated R101

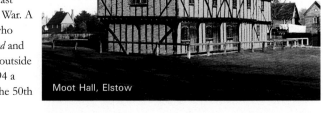

Moot Hall, Elstow

🏛 historic building   🏠 museum and heritage   🏚 historic site   🌿 scenic attraction   🌱 flora and fauna

airship (see under Cardington), and there's a handsome memorial in the churchyard.

Elstow's notable buildings include a charming row of Tudor cottages and **Moot Hall**, which was built in the 15th century. It served as a place for hearing disputes and as a store for equipment for the village fair. Restored by Bedfordshire County Council, it is now a museum depicting life in 17th-century England with particular reference to Bunyan.

CARDINGTON
1 mile E of Bedford off the A603

🏛 Hangars

The Whitbread brewing family is closely connected with Cardington. The first Samuel Whitbread was born in the village in 1720, and it was another Whitbread, also Samuel, who restored the church and endowed the red-brick almshouses of 1787 overlooking the green.

But Cardington is best known for the two giant **Hangars** that dominate the skyline. Built in 1917 and 1927 to construct and house the airships that were once thought to be the future of flying, they are best known as the birthplace of the R100 and the R101. The R101 first took off from Cardington in October 1929 with 52 people on board for a five-hour flight over the southeast. The passengers enjoyed a four-course lunch in the luxurious dining saloon and were amazed at the airship's quietness - they could hear the sounds of traffic and trains below. In July 1930, the R101 started her maiden flight across the Atlantic and tied up in Montreal after an uneventful flight of 77 hours. In October of that year the world's biggest airship left the hangars at Cardington for her first trip to India. Disaster struck not long into the journey when the R101 crashed into a

hillside near Beauvais in France. Forty-four people, including the Air Secretary Lord Thomson of Cardington, died in the crash, which was believed to have been caused at least in part by lashing rain that made the ship dip suddenly. The Church of St Mary contains memorials to both Samuel Whitbreads, and in the churchyard extension is the tomb of those who perished in the R101 disaster.

WILDEN
4 miles NE of Bedford off the A421

🍃 Wild Britain

Wild Britain has quickly become one of the county's leading family attractions. It stands in 10 acres of land untouched by modern farming practices and specially selected by its founder Andrew Green. Some 60 varieties of wildflowers flourish here, an irresistible attraction for 60 species of butterfly. The Wondrous World exhibit displays the variety of life found in rain forests. Other attractions include an adventure playground, tearoom and gift shop.

STEVINGTON
4 miles NW of Bedford off A428

🏛 Post Mill

This is a typical English village with a church that was here at the time of the Domesday survey, a village cross decorated with capitals and a large finial, and a Holy Well that attracted visitors in the Middle Ages. It is claimed that it never freezes or dries up.

However, the most important building in the village is the **Post Mill**, the only one of the county's 12 remaining windmills that still retains its sails. Dating from the 1770s, the mill continued to operate commercially until 1936, having been rebuilt in 1921. Extensively restored in the 1950s, it is in full working

After the Civil War, the town's clothing industry declined. However, the 18th century saw the construction of turnpike roads and Newbury became a busy coaching stop on the road from London to Bath. The town further opened up to travellers and the needs of carriers with the completion of the **Kennet and Avon Canal** in 1810. Newbury Lock, built in 1796, was the first lock to be built along the canal and it is also the only one to have lever-operated ground paddles (the sluices that let in the water), which are known as 'Jack Cloughs'.

Back in the centre of the town, in the Market Square is the **West Berkshire Museum**, housed in two of the town's most historic buildings, the 17th-century cloth hall and the adjacent 18th-century granary, a store once used by traders travelling the canal. The history of the canal is explained, and other exhibits include crafts and industries, the two Battles of Newbury (1643 and 1644) during the Civil War, the story of Greenham Common and local archaeology.

Those arriving in Newbury from the south will pass the Falkland Memorial, which has nothing to do with the 1980s conflict in the South Atlantic. It is in fact a memorial to Lord Falkland, who was killed at the first battle of Newbury. To the east of the town lies **Newbury Racecourse**, which stages top-quality flat and National Hunt racing throughout the year.

Around Newbury

HAMPSTEAD NORREYS
6 miles NE of Newbury on the B4009

🌱 The Living Rainforest

Just to the north of the village lies **The Living Rainforest**, an education and conservation charity devoted to the raising of awareness about the world's rainforests. Here, at the indoor rainforest inside a giant glasshouse, the temperature never falls below 70°F. Visitors can walk through the humid and shadowy jungles of the lowland tropical forests, the cool, orchid-festooned and ferny cloud forests, and the Amazon with its amazing flowers and wonderful bromeliads. There is also a unique collection of spectacular and rare plants, tranquil pools, the sounds of the tropics, and rainforest animals, including a pair of Goeldi's monkeys, marmosets, tree frogs, iguanas and Courtney the dwarf crocodile. Also on site are a shop selling plants and gifts, and a teashop.

DONNINGTON
1 mile N of Newbury on the B4494

🏰 Castle

Despite being so close to the town of Newbury, Donnington has managed to retain its village identity and atmosphere. To the west of the village, and visible from the road, is Donnington Grove House. Built in 1759 and designed by the architect John Chute, this was the home, in

Kennet and Avon Canal, Newbury

surrounded by woodland. The common comprises several different habitats, including woodland, heathland and bog, and it supports a correspondingly wide variety of plant and animal life. It is a particularly important area for ground-nesting birds such as the nightjar and woodlark. The site has many footpaths and tracks and an area set aside for picnics.

WICKHAM
6 miles NW of Newbury on the B4000

🏛 Church of St Swithin

This ancient village with its typical Berkshire mix of brick and flint, thatch and tile is most notable for its **Church of St Swithin** that stands atop a hill with grand views across the Kennet valley. It has a Saxon tower – unique in the county – but it is the interior that is truly remarkable because of the elephants in the north aisle. Made of papier-mâché and gilded, they were purchased at the Paris Exhibition of 1862 and intended for the rectory. They were too large however so they now appear to support the spectacular wooden roof of the church.

HUNGERFORD
9 miles W of Newbury on the A4

🏛 Bear Hotel 🐾 Tutti Day

Although not mentioned in the Domesday Book, by the Middle Ages this old market town was well established. The manor of Hungerford had some distinguished lords, including Simon de Montfort and John of Gaunt. Hungerford's heyday came in the 18th century when the turnpike road from London to Bath was built, passing through the town. By 1840, the town had eight coaching inns serving the needs of travellers and its prosperity continued with the opening of the Kennet and Avon Canal. The building of the

Donnington Castle

the late 18th century, of the Brummell family; Beau Brummell, the instigator of the Bath Society, lived here as a child.

However, most visitors to the village come to see **Donnington Castle** (English Heritage), a late-14th century defence that was built by Sir Richard Abberbury. Once a magnificent structure, only the twin-towered gatehouse survives amidst the impressive earthworks. The castle had its most eventful period during the Civil War when it was the scene of one of the longest sieges of the conflict. Charles I's troops were held here for 20 months and it was during this period that most of the castle was destroyed.

WINTERBOURNE
3 miles N of Newbury off the B4494

🌱 Snelsmore Common Country Park

Just south of the village lies **Snelsmore Common Country Park**, a heathland site

CROWN NEEDLEWORK

115 High Street, Hungerford, Berkshire RG17 0LU
Website: www.hungerfordberks.co.uk
Tel: 01488 684011   Fax: 01488 686416

Crown Needlework is a specialist needlework shop located halfway along Hungerford's High Street, opposite the Town Hall and next to the Three Swans Inn.

The comprehensive thread stock includes full ranges of embroidery threads including Appletons, Paterna, Anchor, DMC, Madeira, Coats and Caron. Materials range from 6 count canvas to 36 count Linen, and include Aida, Evenweave, Hardanger and Binca. All materials can be cut to customers' individual requirements. There is a large selection of printed canvases, charts, publications and kits for (amongst others) Cross Stitch, Tapestry, Trammed, Bargello, Hardanger, Blackwork, and Embroidery. Other items include magnifiers, simulated daylight lamps, frames and hoops, aperture cards, ribbons, braids, shisha mirrors, beads (including full Mill Hill range), bell pull ends, sewing baskets, boxes and organisers; plus many more too numerous to mention. It's definitely not a 5-minute store - more an Aladdin's Cave!

The Bossom family and staff are very experienced in many aspects of embroidery and stitching, and are always willing to offer help and advice. Crown Needlework is open from 10am to 5pm Tuesday to Saturday (also by appointment Sunday and Monday).

JANE CORBETT

9 Bridge Street, Hungerford, Berkshire RG17 0EH
Tel/Fax: 01488 686321
website: www.janecorbett.com

Couture Milliner **Jane Corbett** designs and creates unique hats and head dresses to suit each individual client, their outfit and the occasion. Each piece is handmade using traditional millinery techniques. Jane specialises in hand dyeing silks, staws and feathers to exactly colour match clients outfits. For Jane, it is the personal service to her clients that makes her business such a pleasure.

Jane's exquisite little shop in Hungerford is an absolute delight to walk in to. One client said, "it is like shopping in Paris as it used to be!"

"My hats are a labour of love and so was the setting up of the shop itself; the shop has an eclectic mix of furniture and display cabinets and I have decorated the walls with hand painted designs."

Alongside Jane's hats and head dresses, she has a fabulous collection of clothing; own label, retro restyle and gorgeous vintage pieces. She has also introduced a collection of beautiful vintage handbags and jewellery which have been carefully selected by Jane herself. The results are truly unique works of art!

railway took much of that trade away and the town reverted to its early, gentle lifestyle. However, several of the old coaching inns have survived, notably **The Bear Hotel**. Although it has an impressive Georgian frontage, the building actually dates back to 1494, making it one of the oldest buildings in the town.

An event of great historical importance occurred in December 1688 when William of Orange arrived to stay at The Bear to negotiate with the Commissioners of King James II concerning the future of the monarchy. The result was the Glorious Revolution of 1689, generally accepted as the beginning of true Parliamentary democracy as William and his wife Mary were invited to take the throne by a Protestant Parliament.

As well as still holding a weekly market, the town also continues the ancient tradition

known as the Hocktide Festival or **Tutti Day** (tutti meaning a bunch of flowers). Held every year on the second Tuesday after Easter, the festival was originally used as a means of collecting an early form of council tax. During the colourful event, two men carrying a six-foot pole decorated with ribbons and flowers go around each household collecting the tax. To ease the burden of their visit, the men share a drink with the man of the house, give him an orange, and kiss his wife before collecting their penny payment. Today, however, though the visits are still made, no money is collected but the kisses are still required.

Hungerford lies at the centre of the North Wessex Area of Outstanding Natural Beauty, designated as such in 1972. It stretches from the River Thames in the east to Devizes in the west, Wantage in the north and Andover in the south.

THE CLOCKMAKER

Wessex Place, 127 High Street, Hungerford, Berkshire RG17 0DL
Tel: 01488 682277
e-mail: theclockmaker@btconnect.com   website: www.clockmaker.info

Hungerford is a small historic town set in the midst of an Area of Outstanding Natural Beauty on the western fringe of Berkshire. It is here, on the high street, that you will find **The Clockmaker**, a shop dedicated to the creation of something we cannot live without – the telling of time.

Founder and Owner Chris Bessent starting working with these intricate timepieces in the late 70's as an apprentice for a Rolex agency jewellers in Wiltshire. During his time here he discovered a real passion for clocks and went on to run workshops in various parts of the country before starting his own business producing handmade clocks of the highest quality, each one an individual work of art. Chris and his team are focused on matching the needs of their customers with no job too big or too small. Whether it's a watch battery that needs replacing or the restoration of a much treasured long case clock you can be assured that your item will be carefully and lovingly taken care of. The staff work with master cabinet makers, conservators of fine art and decorative art specialists, ensuring that every aspect of the work receives the closest attention.

Chris' passion for restoration also extends to barometers and with the concentration on quality, all creations be it repair or restoration, come with a 3 year guarantee. There is customer parking available in the courtyard.

of Reading Gaol whilst staying in Paris in 1898.

Though the town developed during the Middle Ages as a result of a flourishing woollen industry, it was during the 18th century with the coming of both the turnpike roads and the opening of the Kennet and Avon Canal that the town boomed. By the 19th century, Reading was known for its three Bs: beer, bulbs and biscuits. As the trade of the canal and River Thames increased, the movement of corn and malt explains the growth of the brewing trade, and the leaders in the bulb trade were Sutton Seeds, founded here in 1806 but now just a memory. The world renowned biscuit-making firm of Huntley & Palmer began life here in 1826, when Joseph Huntley founded the firm, to be joined, in 1841, by George Palmer, inventor of the stamping machine.

The Story of Reading, a permanent exhibition at the **Museum of Reading**, is the ideal place to gain a full understanding of the history of the town, from the earliest times to the present day. Here, too, can be seen the world's only full-size replica of the Bayeux Tapestry, made in the 19th century and featuring Edward the Confessor, once Lord of the Royal Manor in Reading, as a central figure. As a contrast to the museum's displays depicting the life of the town in the 20th century, the Silchester Gallery is devoted to describing the day-to-day life at Calleva Atrebatum, the Roman town of Silchester, using Roman artefacts unearthed there during early excavations. This museum, one of the most go-ahead in the country, has special events and changing exhibitions throughout the year, so every visit will reveal something new and exciting to see.

In 1925 Reading Extension College became a university in its own right. Lying to the south of the town centre in Redlands Road, the **Museum of English Rural Life** (see panel on page 35) is the national centre for the history of food, farming and the countryside. The centre has one of the country's finest collections of artefacts relating to daily life and work in the countryside, an extensive library and archives, and more than 750,000 photographic images of rural life.

Around Reading

SONNING
3 miles NE of Reading off the A4

This pretty little village leading down to the Thames is a popular spot to visit, especially on summer weekends. In 1399, after he had been deposed, Richard II brought his young bride Isabella here to be looked after in the palace of the Bishops of Salisbury. Her ghost is said to appear on the paths beside the river. On Grove Street stands Turpin's, a

River Thames, Sonning

house thatbelonged to the aunt of Dick Turpin and provided occasional refuge for the notorious highwayman. Behind the wall of the old bishop's palace is Deanery Gardens, a house built in 1901 to the design of Sir Edwin Lutyens.

WOODLEY
3 miles E of Reading off the A329

🏛 Museum of Berkshire Aviation

At Woodley Airfield the **Museum of Berkshire Aviation** (see panel below) celebrates the contribution the county has made to the history of aviation. The exhibits include Spitfires and reconstructed Miles & Handley Page aircraft, which are shown along with fascinating pictorial records and archives.

HURST
4½ miles E of Reading off the A321

🖴 Dinton Pastures Country Park

This attractive, scattered village is home to a Norman church, well endowed with monuments, and a row of fine 17th-century almshouses. The village bowling green is said to have been made for Charles II.

Just to the south lies **Dinton Pastures Country Park**, a large area of lakes, rivers, hedgerows and meadows rich in wildlife. Until the 1970s, this area was excavated for sand and gravel, but the former pits are now attractive lakes and ponds; one of them has been stocked for coarse fishing and the largest is set aside for canoeing and windsurfing.

WOKINGHAM
6 miles SE of Reading on the A329

This largely residential town has, at its centre, an old triangular market place with a matching triangular Town Hall built in 1860. In the mainly Victorian town centre is a sprinkling of attractive Georgian houses and shops, and the medieval parish church of All Saints. The most attractive building, however, is Lucas Hospital, built of mellow red brick and rather like a miniature Chelsea Hospital. It was originally built in 1666 as almshouses and a chapel, by Henry Lucas, a mathematician and MP for Cambridge University. Today, the hospital still cares for

Museum of Berkshire Aviation

Mohawk Way (off The Bader Way), Woodley, nr Reading, Berkshire RG5 4UE
Tel: 0118 944 8089
e-mail: MuseumBerksAv@gmail.com
website: www.museumofberkshireaviation.co.uk

Berkshire's dynamic contribution to aviation history is graphically re-captured at the museum. Run as a charitable trust, the museum is at the historic site of Woodley Airfield - once the centre of a thriving aircraft industry. Miles and Handley Page aircraft built at Woodley are being re-constructed and exhibited along with fascinating pictorial records and priceless archives. The museum welcomes group visits and runs an active educational programme for schools, linked to National Curriculum requirements, demonstrating the development of aviation techniques.

🎭 stories and anecdotes　🕊 famous people　🎨 art and craft　🎗 entertainment and sport　🚶 walks

BARN ELMS TROUT FISHERY

Barn Elms Farm, Dark Lane, Bradfield, Reading,
Berkshire RG7 6DF
Tel: 0118 974 4744
e-mail: barnelms@btopenworld.com
website: www.barnelmsfishery.co.uk

Barn Elms Trout Fishery is a spring-fed chalk stream lake
situated on a 350-acre working farm in the idyllic Pang
Valley where there is an abundance of aquatic life and
many beautiful mature trees. Although 7 acres in extent
and with an average depth of 8 feet, it is an intimate
lake shaped like a four-leaved clover with nooks and
crannies suitable for novices and experienced fishermen
alike. The nymph and the dry fly on floating lines prove
to be the best method of fishing here.

The lake is stocked weekly with energetic fighting
Rainbow and Brown Trout. These are predominantly 2lbs
in weight with 10% of the weekly stocking being up to
8lbs. There is a comfortable Fishing Hut on site with tea
and coffee-making facilities. Here, fish must be weighed and recorded on the cards supplied.

Day tickets for 2, 3 or 4 fish, or for the season are available - no pre-booking is required for
day tickets. Car parking is available on site. There are fully flushing loos and good disabled
access. The fishery is open from 9am to dusk, March to early December, but is closed on
Wednesdays for charity/corporate/club bookings.

THE QUEEN'S HEAD

Southend Road, Bradfield, Berkshire RG7 6EY
Tel: 0118 9744332
e-mail: info@queens-bradfield.co.uk
website: www.queens-bradfield.co.uk

Occupying a sturdy Victorian building dating back to the
1850s, **The Queen's Head** at Bradfield has a warm
down-to-earth charm and customers receive a warm
welcome from owners Andrew Loupekine and Laura
Maton, both of them local people. The restaurant at The
Queen's Head, with its duck egg blue walls, mix 'n'
match wooden chairs, eclectic bric a brac and an open
fireplace, is a major attraction for discerning diners.

Andrew is the chef and his traditional British menu is
a hit with the locals and visitors alike. You'll find
Devilled Lamb's Kidneys, and Wood Pigeon with bacon
and black pudding amongst the starters. As a main
course how about Whole Roast Sea Bream with Fennel Salad and new potatoes, or Fillet of Beef
with seared foie gras and sauté potatoes? In good weather, you can enjoy the fine fare in the
neat and peaceful garden where there's also a children's play area. To accompany your meal,
the bar offers a comprehensive choice that includes Fuller's real ales and more than a dozen
wines available by the glass. The Queen's |Head is open all day, every day, but the kitchen is
closed from 2.30pm to 6pm but you can still enjoy afternoon tea and cakes.

FINCHAMPSTEAD
8 miles S of Reading off the A327

⚷ Finchampstead Ridges

To the east of the village are **Finchampstead Ridges**, a popular spot for walkers that offers wonderful views across the Blackwater Valley. Simon's Wood has a varied mixture of conifers and broad-leaved trees, and in the wood and on the heath are siskin and flycatchers, dragonflies, damselflies and a wide range of invertebrates and lichens.

ALDERMASTON
9 miles SW of Reading on the A340

🏫 St Mary's Church ⚷ Aldermaston Wharf

🛶 Kennet & Avon Canal Visitor Centre

It was in this tranquil village, in 1840, that the William pear was first propagated by John Staid, the then village schoolmaster. First known as the Aldermaston pear, a cutting of the plant is believed to have been taken to Australia where it is now called the Bartlett pear.

Still retaining much of its original 12th-century structure, and with a splendid Norman door, the lovely **St Mary's Church** provides the setting for the York Mystery Cycle, nativity plays dating from the 14th century, which are performed here each year. Using beautiful period costumes and contemporary music, including a piece written by William Byrd, the cycle lasts a week and the plays attract visitors from far and wide. Another old custom still continued in the village is the auctioning of the grazing rights of Church Acres every three years. Using the ancient method of a candle auction, a pin - in this case a horseshoe nail - is inserted into the tallow of a candle one inch from the wick. The candle is lit while bidding takes place and

the grazing rights go to the highest bidder as the pin drops out of the candle.

Outside, under a yew tree in the churchyard, lies the grave of Maria Hale, formerly known as the Aldermaston witch. She was said to turn herself into a large brown hare and although the hare was never caught or killed, at one time a local keeper wounded it in the leg, and from then on it was observed that Maria Hale had become lame.

Close to the village is a delightful walk along the Kennet and Avon Canal to **Aldermaston Wharf**. A Grade II-listed structure of beautifully restored 18th-century scalloped brickwork, the wharf houses the Aldermaston Visitor Centre, where the canalman's cottage contains an exhibition on the canal and information on its leisure facilities.

WOOLHAMPTON
9 miles W of Reading on the A4

This tranquil village (see walk on page 38) on the banks of the Kennet and Avon Canal had a watermill at the time of the Domesday Survey of 1086 and was mentioned again in 1351, when the manor and mill were owned by the Knights Hospitallers. The present mill, built in 1820 and extended in 1875, was powered by a brook that runs into the Kennet. It was last used in 1930 and has since been turned into offices.

BEENHAM
9 miles W of Reading off the A4

🐺 UK Wolf Conservation Trust

Set in 6,000 acres of beautiful woodlands, the **UK Wolf Conservation Trust** proves that wolves are not the big, bad, dangerous animals of nursery rhymes and legend. There are wolves here you can actually stroke and which

fine plasterwork, pictures and furniture, and the rooms open to the public include the Octagon Room and a decorative Shell Room. If the name Basildon seems familiar, it is probably as a result of the notepaper: the head of the papermaking firm of Dickinson visited the house and decided to use the name for the high quality paper his firm produced.

ALDWORTH
11 miles NW of Reading on the B4009

⌂ Aldworth Giants

The parish Church of St Mary is famous for housing the **Aldworth Giants** - the larger than life effigies of the de la Beche family, which date back to the 14th century. The head of the family, Sir Philip, who lies here with eight other members of his family, was the Sheriff of Berkshire and valet to Edward

II. Though now somewhat defaced, the effigies were so legendary that the church was visited by Elizabeth I. Outside, in the churchyard, are the remains of a once magnificent 1,000-year-old yew tree that was damaged in a storm.

Nearby, at **Little Aldworth**, is the grave of the poet Laurence Binyon who wrote the famous lines: "At the going down of the sun and in the morning, we shall remember them." Opposite the Bell Inn is one of the deepest wells in the country. Topped by great beams, heavy cogs, and wheels, it is some 327 feet deep.

Windsor

⌂ Castle ⌂ Guildhall ⌂ St George's Chapel
⌂ Frogmore House ❦ Savill Garden
❧ Racecourse ❧ Smith's Lawn ❧ Legoland
⚘ Windsor Great Park ⚘ Long Walk
❧ Windsor Wheel

This old town grew up beneath the walls of the castle in a compact group of streets leading from the main entrance. Charming and full of character, this is a place of delightful timber-framed and Georgian houses and shop fronts, with riverside walks beside the Thames, and a wonderful racecourse. The elegant **Guildhall**, partly built by Wren in the 17th century, has an open ground floor for market stalls, while the council chambers are on the first floor. Concerned that they might fall through the floor on to the stalls below, the council members requested that Wren put in supporting pillars in the middle of the market hall. As his reassurances that the building was sound fell on deaf ears, Wren complied with their wishes but the pillars he built did not quite meet the ceiling - thereby proving his point!

Windsor Castle

⌂ historic building 🏛 museum and heritage ⌂ historic site ⚘ scenic attraction ❦ flora and fauna

A regular and magnificent spectacle that takes place at 11am Monday to Saturday in the summer months, weather permitting, is the **Changing of the Guard**. The correct term for the ceremony is actually Guard Mounting, when the new guard exchanges duty with the old guard. The Guard is provided by the resident regiment of Foot Guards in their full-dress uniform of red tunics and bearskins. They march up to and from the Castle accompanied by the Guards Band playing traditional military marches as well as popular songs.

The greatest attraction here is, of course, **Windsor Castle**, one of three official residences of the Queen (the others are Buckingham Palace and Holyrood House in Edinburgh). The largest castle in the country, and a royal residence for over 900 years, it was begun in the late 11th century by William the Conqueror as one in a chain of such defences

that stood on the approaches to London. Over the years its role changed from a fortification to a royal palace; various monarchs added to the original typical Norman castle, the most notable additions being made by Henry VIII, Charles II and George IV. Various parts of the castle are open to the public, in particular the state apartments with their remarkable collection of furniture, porcelain and armour. Carvings by Grinling Gibbons are to be seen everywhere, and the walls are adorned with a plethora of masterpieces, including paintings by Van Dyck and Rembrandt. The Gallery shows changing displays from the Royal Library, including works by Leonardo, Michelangelo and Holbein. On a somewhat smaller scale, but nonetheless impressive, is Queen Mary's Dolls' House. Designed by Sir Edwin Lutyens for Queen Mary, this is a perfect miniature palace, complete with working lifts and lights and running water.

THE ROYAL ADELAIDE HOTEL

46 Kings Road, Windsor, Berkshire, SL4 2AG
Tel: 01753 863916
e-mail: info@theroyaladelaide.com
website: www.theroyaladelaide.com

The historic 4* **Royal Adelaide Hotel** is an elegant Georgian hotel in Windsor located opposite the Long Walk to Windsor Castle and offers exceptional service and accommodation at affordable prices. The hotel is located in a quiet residential area just a gentle stroll from Windsor Castle, the River Thames and the fashionable shops, restaurants and art galleries of Windsor and Eton. The Royal Adelaide Hotel was built for the consort of William IV, Queen Adelaide and has been a hotel for over 100 years. However this elegant hotel combines British royal history with 21st century luxury. All the bedrooms offer, air conditioning, flat screen TV,

WIFI internet access, iron and ironing board, tea/coffee making facilities, direct dial telephone, hairdryer, room service, newly refurbished bathrooms, many with both bath and shower, and complimentary car parking is available on a first come, first served basis.

The Head Chef in the Garden Restaurant provides a varied and interesting menu that changes with the seasons, ensuring that the food on offer is always at its best. Open for Full English breakfast, Light bites, A la carte dining, and Sunday lunches. Alternatively a light bite, afternoon tea or a quiet drink is available at any time in our comfy bar - an ideal meeting place for family, friends or business colleagues.

River Thames, Windsor

century manor house in Home Park, has over the years acted as a second, more relaxed royal residence than the nearby castle. It was bought in 1792 for Queen Charlotte, consort of George III, and later became a favourite retreat of Queen Victoria, who remarked that "all is peace and quiet and you only hear the hum of the bees, the singing of the birds". She and Prince Albert built a mausoleum in the grounds to house the remains of the Queen's mother, the Duchess of Kent, and their own - both Victoria and Albert are at rest here. (The mausoleum is closed throughout 2008.) The former library now contains furniture and paintings from the Royal Yacht *Britannia*. The house is surrounded by 30 acres of picturesque gardens containing masses of spring bulbs and some fine specimen trees.

Built on a 1-to-12 scale, it took three years to complete, and 1,500 craftsmen were employed to ensure that every last detail was correct; the house was presented to the Queen in 1924.

In November 1992, a massive fire swept through the northeast corner of the castle and noone in the country at the time will forget the incredible pictures of the great tower alight. Following five years of restoration, the damaged areas were re-opened to the public.

Within the castle walls is the magnificent **St George's Chapel**. Started by Edward IV in 1478, and taking some 50 years to finish, the chapel is not only one of the country's greatest religious buildings, but also a wonderful example of the Perpendicular Gothic style. It is the last resting place of 10 monarchs, from Edward IV himself to Henry VIII with his favourite wife Jane Seymour, Charles I, George V with Queen Mary, and George VI, beside whom the ashes of his beloved daughter Princess Margaret were laid in February 2002 and the body of his wife, the Queen Mother, in April 2002. It is also the Chapel of the Most Noble Order of the Garter, Britain's highest order of chivalry.

Frogmore House, a modest early 18th-

To the south of the town stretches the 4,800-acre **Windsor Great Park**, a remnant of the once extensive Royal Hunting Forest, and a unique area of open parkland, woodland, and impressive views. Within the park, at Englefield Green, is the **Savill Garden** (see panel opposite), created by Sir Eric Savill when he was Deputy Ranger, and one of the finest woodland gardens to be seen anywhere. A garden for all seasons, its attractions include colourful flowerbeds, secret glades, alpine meadows and a unique temperate house. The gateway to the garden is the iconic **Savill Building**. Inspired by the shape of a leaf, the building's roof has a gold award-winning grid shell design and was created from sustainable resources from the forests within Windsor Great Park. The building contains a visitor centre, shopping, a boutique plant centre and a terraced restaurant.

The **Long Walk** stretches from the Castle to Snow Hill, some three miles away, on top of which stands a huge bronze of George III on horseback, erected there in 1831. The three-mile ride to nearby Ascot racecourse was created by Queen Anne in the early 1700s. On the park's southern side lies **Smith's Lawn**, where polo matches are played most summer weekends. Windsor Great Park is also the setting for the Cartier International competition, polo's highlight event held every July, and the National Carriage Driving Championships.

The Savill Garden

Visitor Services - The Savill Building, Wick Lane, Englefield Green, Surrey TW20 0UU
Tel (shop and restaurant): 01784 435544
e-mail: enquiries@theroyallandscape.co.uk
website: www.theroyallandscape.co.uk

The south-east corner of Windsor Great Park is a rich and picturesque area of gardens, lakes and woodland. It has been a place of recreation, associated with royalty, for over a thousand years. **The Savill Garden**, perhaps the best known feature of this landscape, is a magical world, a woodland garden created by the master landscaper Sir Eric Savill. The gateway into The Royal Landscape is The Savill Building, opening its doors in the early summer of 2006. This spectacular visitor centre offers a level of service on a par with the royal status of the Park.

The Savill Garden is one of Britain's great woodland gardens - a domain of shady paths and sudden discoveries. Its 35 acres of trees and shrubbery, ponds and streams, lawns, meadows and formal beds protect some of the world's most beautiful decorative plants. Developed under the patronage of Kings and Queens, The Savill Garden was created by Sir Eric Savill, grand master of the woodland garden, in the 1930s. Since then, the garden has grown, with the encouragement of the Royal Family, many of whom are keen gardeners.

In the Spring, the woodland is a riot of colour, with rhododendrons, azaleas, camellias and magnolias. In Summer, the formal gardens come into their own, with the brilliant colours of the long borders and royal roses. Autumn in The Savill Garden is as spectacular, with the trees ablaze with red and gold. Winter is a time of quiet beauty, with the more subtle colours of bark and branches.

The well-stocked shop carries a wide range of articles, in keeping with the character of the gardens and of The Royal Landscape. A small but interesting plant centre features plants chosen by the Windsor gardens staff. The Savill Building offers information on the Garden, The Royal Landscape and the Park as a whole, an exhibition area and modern conference room.

📖 stories and anecdotes 🦅 famous people 🎨 art and craft 🖌 entertainment and sport 🚶 walks

To the southwest, set in 150 acres of parkland, is **Legoland Windsor**, where a whole range of amazing Lego models is on display, made from over 20 million bricks. Designed for children aged two to 12 – and their families – the site also offers more than 50 rides, shows and attractions including a 3-D cinema and the Jungle Coaster with twists and turns travelling at up to 60km per hour.

In a pleasant setting close to the River Thames, **Royal Windsor Racecourse** is one of the most attractive in the country. Though less grand than neighbouring Ascot, its Monday evening meetings always bring a good crowd, but many regret the decision to give up the jumping fixtures.

From mid-July to early November, the town is graced with the **Windsor Wheel**, a smaller brother of the London Eye. Weighing 365 tonnes and 60 metres high, the Wheel provides a spectacular 360 degree view of the surrounding area. There are 36 capsules seating up to six adults and two children, and the ride lasts approximately 12 minutes.

Around Windsor

ASCOT
6 miles SW of Windsor on the A329

🐾 Racecourse 🌱 Englemere Pond

A small village until 1711 when Queen Anne moved the Windsor race meeting to here and founded the world famous **Ascot Racecourse**. Its future was secured when the Duke of Cumberland established a stud at Windsor in the 1750s, and by the end of the century the meetings were being attended by royalty on a regular basis. Today, Royal Ascot, held every June, is an international occasion of fashion and style with pageantry and

tradition, and the very best flat-racing spread over five days.

To the west of the town is **Englemere Pond**, a Site of Special Scientific Interest and also a local nature reserve. Once part of the royal hunting ground, which surrounded Windsor Castle and is still owned by the Crown Estate, the main feature is the shallow acidic lake, which offers a wide range of habitats from open water to marsh, for the many species of plants, birds, animals and insects found here.

BRACKNELL
7 miles SW of Windsor on the A329

🌳 Windsor Forest 🌳 Look Out Discovery Park

Designated a new town in 1948, Bracknell has developed quickly from a small village in poor sandy heathland, with some 3,000 inhabitants, into a large modern town of around 60,000 residents. It boasts one of the first purpose-built shopping centres in the country - opened in the 1960s. As well as boasting a number of high tech companies, Bracknell is also the home of the Meteorological Office.

The centrally located Bill Hill is a very prominent landmark, seen from many parts of the town. At the top of the hill, a circular mound of earth is visible, hollowed out at the centre, which is all that remains of a Bronze Age round barrow. Used throughout that period, these burial mounds, which may cover either individuals or groups, are the most common prehistoric monuments in the country.

What remains of the great royal hunting ground, **Windsor Forest** (also called Bracknell Forest) lies to the south of the town and has more than 30 parks and nature reserves and some 45 miles of footpaths and bridleways. Of particular interest in the area is

Lookout Discovery Park, Bracknell

the **Look Out Discovery Park**, an interactive science centre that brings to life the mysteries of both science and nature. In the surrounding 2,600 acres of Crown Estate woodland there are nature trails and walks to points of interest, as well as the inappropriately named Caesar's Camp. Not a Roman fort, this camp is an Iron Age hill fort built more than 2,000 years ago although, close by, runs the Roman link road between London and Silchester. Known locally as the Devil's Highway, it is said to have acquired the name because the local inhabitants thought that only the Devil could have undertaken such a prodigious feat of engineering.

TWYFORD
10 miles W of Windsor on the A4

At Twyford, the River Loddon divides into two separate streams from which the town

takes its name – 'double ford'. With its watery location it's not surprising that there have been several mills here. A miller is mentioned in a document of 1163, although the first mill is dated 1363. There was a silk mill here until 1845, and a flour mill until 1976 when it was destroyed by fire. The replacement modern mill lacks the traditional appeal, but it does continue the milling tradition in the town.

BINFIELD
8 miles SW of Windsor on the B3034

🐦 Pope's Wood

Binfield is famous as the boyhood home of the poet Alexander Pope. The family moved here after his father had amassed a fortune as a linen draper, and the boy Pope sang in the local choir and gained a local following for his poems about the Windsor Forest and the River Loddon. To the south of the village is **Pope's Wood**, where the poet is said to have sought inspiration. Other connections include the artist John Constable, who sketched the parish church while here on his honeymoon, and Norah Wilmot, who was one of the first lady racehorse trainers to be allowed to hold a licence in her own name, having been forced to train for years in the name of her head lad. The Jockey Club abandoned this archaic ruling as recently as 1966.

WARGRAVE
10 miles W of Windsor on the A321

🏛 Hannen Mausoleum 🏛 Druids' Temple

This charming village developed as a settlement in the 10th century at the confluence of the Rivers Thames and Loddon on an area of flat land in a wooded valley. The peace that generally prevails here was disturbed in 1914 when suffragettes burnt down the church in protest at the vicar's

Chalfont St Giles

🏛 Chiltern Open Air Museum   ⚜ Milton's Cottage

Among the various ancient buildings of interest in this archetypal English village there is an Elizabethan mansion, The Vache, which was the home of friends of Captain Cook. In the grounds is a monument to the famous seafarer. However, by far the most famous building in Chalfont St Giles is **Milton's Cottage**. John Milton moved to this 16th-century cottage, found for him by his former pupil Thomas Ellwood, in 1665 to escape the plague in London. Though Milton moved back to London in 1666, he wrote *Paradise Lost* and began work on its sequel, *Paradise Regained*, while taking refuge in the village. The only house lived in by the poet to have survived, the cottage and its garden have been preserved as they were at the time Milton was resident. The building is now home to a museum that includes collections of important first editions of Milton's works and a portrait of the poet by Sir Godfrey Kneller.

Another fascinating and unusual place to visit in the village is the **Chiltern Open Air Museum** (see panel below), which rescues buildings of historic or architectural importance due to be demolished from across the Chilterns region and re-erects them on its 45-acre site. The 30-odd buildings rescued by the museum are used to house and display artefacts and implements that are appropriate to the building's original use and history. Also on the museum site is a series of fields farmed using medieval methods where, among the historic crops, organic woad is grown, from which indigo dye is extracted for use in dyeing demonstrations.

Madame Tussaud, famous for her exhibitions in London, started her waxworks here in the village, and another well-known resident was Bertram Mills of circus fame. His tomb stands beside the war memorial in the churchyard of St Giles.

Around Chalfont St Giles

JORDANS
1 mile S of Chalfont St Giles off the A40

This secluded village reached down a quiet country lane is famous as the burial place of

Chiltern Open Air Museum

Newland Park, Gorelands Lane, Chalfont St. Giles, Buckinghamshire HP8 4AB
Tel: 01494 871117
web site: www.coam.org.uk

Visit **Chiltern Open Air Museum** in the parish of Chalfont St Peter, explore more than 30 rescued historic buildings and roam through 45 acres of beautiful woods and parkland.

Don't miss the chance to stroll along the woodland walk and relax at Wood End Cafe, where you can purchase light refreshments. The Museum organises a wide range of hands-on activities, demonstrations and special events for all the family to enjoy throughout the season. During the school holidays there are a series of themed weeks, special activities and demonstrations that focus on one aspect of the history of the buildings.

🏛 historic building   🏛 museum and heritage   🏚 historic site   ⚜ scenic attraction   🌱 flora and fauna

William Penn, Quaker and founder of Pennsylvania. He and members of his family are buried in the graveyard outside the Quaker meeting house, which is among the earliest to be found in the country and has been described as the Quaker Westminster Abbey. In the grounds of nearby Old Jordans Farm is the **Mayflower Barn**, said to have been constructed from the

Mayflower Barn, Jordans

timbers of the ship that took the Pilgrim Fathers to America.

CHALFONT ST PETER
2 miles S of Chalfont St Giles on the A413

🦅 Hawk & Owl Trust

Now a commuter town, Chalfont St Peter dates back to the 7th century and, as its name means 'the spring where the calves come to drink', there is a long history here of raising cattle in the surrounding lush meadows. First mentioned in 1133, the parish Church of St Peter was all but destroyed when its steeple collapsed in 1708. The building seen today dates from that time as it was rebuilt immediately after the disaster.

Housed in a barn at Skippings Farm is the **Hawk and Owl Trust's National Education and Exhibition Centre**. Dedicated to conserving wild birds of prey in their natural habitats, the Trust concerns itself with practical research, creative conservation and imaginative educational programmes.

STOKE POGES
6 miles S of Chalfont St Giles off the A355

🦅 Gray Monument

The ploughman homeward plods his weary way
And leaves the world to darkness and to me.

It was in the churchyard of this surprisingly still rural village that Thomas Gray was inspired to pen his *Elegy Written in a Country Churchyard*. He often visited Stoke Poges to see his mother and aunt who lived in a large late-Georgian house built for the grandson of the famous Quaker, William Penn. He was seated beside his mother's tomb when he wrote the classic poem. To the east of the church is the imposing **Gray Monument**, designed by James Wyatt and erected in 1799. The Church of St Giles itself is very handsome and dates from the 13th century, but perhaps its most interesting feature is the unusual medieval bicycle depicted in one of the stained glass windows. Dating back to the 1600s, the window depicts a naked man with a horn

productions, including BBC-TV's 2008 production of *Cranford*.

Of the various members of the Dashwood family, it was Sir Francis who had most influence on both the house and the village. West Wycombe house was originally built in the early 1700s but Sir Francis boldly remodelled it several years later as well as having the grounds and park landscaped by Thomas Cook, a pupil of Capability Brown. Very much a classical landscape, the grounds contain temples and an artificial lake shaped like a swan, and the house has a good collection of tapestries, furniture and paintings.

Hewn out of a nearby hillside are **West Wycombe Caves** (see panel below), which were created, possibly from some existing caverns, by Sir Francis as part of a programme of public works. After a series of failed harvests, which created great poverty and distress amongst the estate workers and tenant farmers, Sir Francis employed the men to extract chalk from the hillside to be used in the

construction of the new road between the village and High Wycombe.

The village **Church of St Lawrence** is yet another example of Sir Francis' enthusiasm for remodelling old buildings. Situated within the remnants of an Iron Age fort on top of a steep hill, the church was originally constructed in the 13th century. Its isolated position, however, was not intentional as the church was originally the church of the village of Haveringdon, which has long since disappeared. Dashwood remodelled the interior in the 1760s in the style of an Egyptian hall and also heightened the tower, adding on the top a great golden ball where six people could meet in comfort and seclusion.

The **Dashwood Mausoleum** near the church was built in 1765; a vast hexagonal building without a roof, it is the resting place of Sir Francis and other members of the Dashwood family. Sir Francis had a racier side to his character. As well as being remembered as a great traveller and a successful politician,

The Hell-Fire Caves

West Wycombe Caves, High Wycombe, Buckinghamshire HP14 3AJ
Tel: 01494 533739
website: www.hellfirecaves.co.uk

The **Hell-Fire Caves** at West Wycombe offer a totally unique experience. The Caves are owned by Sir Edward Dashwood, a direct descendent of Sir Francis Dashwood, who originally excavated them in the 1750's on the site of an ancient quarry. Throughout the 1700's and 1800's, the caves, which are quarter of a mile underground, were reputed to have hosted the Hell-Fire Club whose membership included some of Britain's most senior aristocrats and statesmen.

Today, the caves are a popular tourist attraction and a wonderful insight into our history. A tour of the caves includes a long winding passage that leads past various small chambers to the Banqueting Hall, down over the River Styx to the Inner Temple, which is about 300 feet beneath the church at the top of the hill. The Caves are scattered with statues in costume and a commentary with sound effects are included throughout the tour.

🏠 historic building 🏛 museum and heritage 🏛 historic site 🝔 scenic attraction 🌱 flora and fauna

he was the founder of the Hell-Fire Club. This group of rakes, who were also known as the Brotherhood of Sir Francis or Dashwood's Apostles, met a couple of times a year to engage in highly colourful activities. Though their exploits were legendary and probably loosely based on fact, they no doubt consumed large quantities of alcohol and enjoyed the company of women. Traditionally, the group meetings were held in the caves, or possibly the church tower, though between 1750 and 1774, their meeting place was nearby Medmenham Abbey.

HUGHENDEN

2 miles N of High Wycombe off the A4128

🏛 Hughenden Manor 🌲 Bradenham Woods

This village is famous for being the home of Queen Victoria's favourite Prime Minister, Benjamin Disraeli; he lived here from 1848 until his death in 1881. He bought **Hughenden Manor** (National Trust) shortly after the publication of his novel *Tancred*. Though not a wealthy man, Disraeli felt that a leading Conservative politician should have a stately home of his own. In order to finance the purchase, his supporters lent him the money so that he could have this essential characteristic of an English gentleman. The interior is an excellent example of the Victorian Gothic style and contains an interesting collection of memorabilia of Disraeli's life as well as his library, pictures and much of his furniture. The garden is based on the designs of Disraeli's wife Mary Anne; the surrounding park and woodland offer some beautiful walks. Disraeli, who was MP for

CARMEN LADIES FASHIONS

7 Park Parade, Shopping Centre, Western Dean, Hazlemere, Buckinghamshire HP15 7AA
Tel: 01494 716555

This ladies fashion clothing store has a range of clothes on offer for ladies of 30 and above, from seasonal general day wear, to evening and cruise wear, from t-shirts to posh frocks. Whatever your style, **Carmen Ladies Fashion** has it all.

They sell fashionable tops, knitwear, trousers, skirts, shirts, crops and even some leisure items. Exclusive hand crafted jewellery can be found here, made by a local designer to suit individual tastes, giving it a truly unique look. An alterations service is also available for that personal fitting.

This independent ladies fashion shop has been well established in the area for over 15 years now. It was refurbished by the new owners in early 2007 and a number of new suppliers have been introduced to provide new, more modern styles to mix with the traditionally popular ones. The staff have worked in the retail business for up to 15 years and have significant customer service experience, and you are bound to receive personal attention when required. Changing rooms are available for you to try on your choices. The shopping centre has free parking and offers a diverse number of local shops.

WELL HEELED OF WENDOVER

5 High Street, Wendover, Buckinghamshire HP22 6DU
Tel: 01296 622186

If visitors to Wendover notice that the townspeople are particularly well shod, it's probably because they've bought their shoes at **Well Heeled of Wendover**. Ron and Kate's popular shop at the bottom of the Chiltern Hills is filled with fine-looking yet practical shoes. It is a treasure trove of footwear that not only offers style and fashion but also most importantly comfort and fit.

Having been established for five years, the lovely owners pride themselves upon their product knowledge, knowing exactly where the shoes come from, how they are made, how they fit and how to care for them; an exemplary service.

The ladies' shoe range includes Gabor, Ara, Josef Seibel and HB. Mens shoes are selected from Loake, Barker and Rockport. The shoes are complemented by a range of leather goods, handbags, silver and costume jewellery. Shoes by Rainbow Club offer handmade bridal or special occasion satin shoes that can be dyed to match your exact requirements. The key phrase at Well Heeled of Wendover is 'personal service'. You will be looked after and given every assistance from fitting to style choice.

Aylesbury

🏛 County Museum 🦉 Roald Dahl's Children's Gallery

Founded in Saxon times and the county town since the reign of Henry VIII, Aylesbury lies in rich pastureland in the shelter of the Chilterns. Post-war development took away much of the town's character, but some parts, particularly around the market square, are protected by a conservation order. At various times in the Civil War, Aylesbury was a base for both Cromwell and the King, and this period of history is covered in the splendidly refurbished **County Museum & Art Gallery**. The museum, housed in a splendid Georgian building, also has an exhibit on Louis XVIII of France, who lived in exile at nearby Hartwell House. Also within the museum is the award winning **Roald Dahl Children's Gallery**, an exciting hands-on gallery for children that uses Dahl's characters to introduce and explain the museum's treasures.

Around Aylesbury

MENTMORE
6 miles NE of Aylesbury off the B488

🏛 Mentmore Towers

The village is home to the first of the Rothschild mansions, **Mentmore Towers**, which was built for Baron Meyer Amschel de Rothschild between 1852 and 1855. A splendid building in the Elizabethan style, it was designed by Sir Joseph Paxton, the designer of Crystal Palace, and is a superb example of grandiose Victorian extravagance. However, the lavish decoration hides several technologically advanced details for those times, such as central heating, and, as might be expected from Paxton, there are large sheets of glass and a glass roof in the design. In the late 19th-century the house became the home of Lord Rosebery and the magnificent turreted building was the scene of many glittering parties and gatherings of the most wealthy and influential people in the country. However, in the 1970s the house was put up for auction and, while the furniture and works of art were sold to the four corners of the world, the building was bought by the Maharishi Mahesh Yogi and became the headquarters of his University of Natural Law. In 2007, planning permission was granted for this spectacular building to be redeveloped as a hotel.

IVINGHOE
7 miles E of Aylesbury on the B488

🏭 Ford End Watermill 🔱 Ivinghoe Beacon

🚶 Ridgeway National Trail

As the large village church would suggest, Ivinghoe was once a market town of some importance in the surrounding area. In this now quiet village can be found **Ford End Watermill**, a listed building that, though probably much older, was first recorded in 1616. It is the only working watermill with its original machinery in Buckinghamshire and on milling days stone-ground wholemeal flour is on sale. The farm in which it stands has also managed to retain the atmosphere of an 18th-century farm. Limited opening times.

To the east lies the National Trust's **Ivinghoe Beacon**, a wonderful viewpoint on the edge of the Chiltern Hills. The site of an Iron Age hill fort, the beacon was also the

inspiration for Sir Walter Scott's *Ivanhoe*. The Beacon is at one end of Britain's oldest road, the **Ridgeway National Trail**. The other end is the World Heritage Site of Avebury in Wiltshire, and the 85-mile length of the Ridgeway still follows the same route over the high ground used since prehistoric times. Walkers can use the whole length of the trail (April to November is the best time) and horse riders and cyclists can ride on much of the western part.

PITSTONE
7 miles E of Aylesbury off the B489

🏭 Pitstone Windmill 🏛 Pitstone Green Museum

Though the exact age of **Pitstone Windmill** (National Trust) is not known, it is certainly one of the oldest post mills in Britain. The earliest documentary reference to its existence was made in 1624. It is open to the public on a limited basis. Also in the village is **Pitstone Green Museum**, where all manner of farm and barn machinery, along with domestic bygones, are on display. There are three model railways, a full size section of a Second World War Lancaster bomber and additional entertainment includes tractor rides, pottery

Pitstone Windmill

🎭 stories and anecdotes 🦅 famous people 🎨 art and craft 🏃 entertainment and sport 🚶 walks village in England, is even better known for its wonderful **Church of St Michael**, one of the finest Norman churches in the land, with spectacular zigzag atterns and a massive tower. Built between 1150-1180, this mighty building has remained virtually unaltered. In the 1970s, when neighbouring Cublington was being considered as the site for London's third airport, the government proposed to move it elsewhere stone by stone.

WING

12 miles SE of Buckingham on the A418

🏛 All Saints Church 🏛 Ascott

Wing's church faced the same threat as Stewkley with the proposed Cublington Airport development. **All Saints Church**, standing on a rise above the Vale of Aylesbury, retains most of its original Saxon features, including the nave, aisles, west wall, crypt and apse. The roof is covered in medieval figures, many of them playing musical instruments. This remarkable church also contains numerous brasses and

monuments, notably to the Dormer family who came to Ascott Hall in the 1520s.

Just east of the village, **Ascott** (National Trust) was bought in 1874 by Leopold Rothschild who virtually rebuilt the original farmhouse round its timber-framed core. The house contains a superb collection of fine paintings, Oriental porcelain and English and French furniture. The grounds are magnificent too, with specimen trees and shrubs, a herbaceous walk, lily pond, Dutch garden, an evergreen topiary sundial and two fountains, one in bronze, the other in marble, sculpted by the American artist Thomas Waldo Story.

THORNBOROUGH

3 miles E of Buckingham off the A422

This lively and attractive village is home to Buckinghamshire's only surviving medieval bridge. Built in the 14th century, the six-arched structure spans Claydon Brook. Close by are two large mounds, which were opened in 1839 and revealed a wealth of Roman

Stowe Landscape Gardens

Buckingham,
Buckinghamshire MK18 5DQ
Tel: 01494 755568
website: www.nationaltrust.org.uk

Stowe is a breathtakingly beautiful work of art, created by the leading architects, sculptors and gardeners of the 18th century.

In 1989 the largest and most celebrated landscape gardens in the world were handed to the National Trust. The gardens were overgrown, lakes silted up, temples and monuments crumbling. Now two-thirds underway, the restoration project has seen the gardens slowly return to their former glory.

Stowe has lots to offer all ages, from the perfect picnic spot to a fascinating tale of wealth, politics and power. With the changing seasons, continuing restoration and a calendar of events for all the family, each visit provides something new to see and do.

objects many of which are on display at the Old Gaol Museum in Buckingham. Though it was known that there was a Roman temple here, its location has not been found.

STOWE

3 miles N of Buckingham off the A422

🏛 Stowe School & Gardens

Stowe School is a leading public school that occupies an 18th-century mansion that was once the home of the Dukes of Buckingham. Worked upon by two wealthy owners who both had a great sense of vision, the magnificent mansion house, which was finally completed in 1774, is open to the public during school holidays. Between 1715 and 1749, the owner, Viscount Cobham, hired various well-known landscape designers to lay

out the fantastic **Stowe Landscape Gardens** (National Trust, see panel opposite) that can still be seen. Taking over the house in 1750, Earl Temple, along with his nephew, expanded the grounds and today they remain one of the most original and finest landscape gardens in Europe. Temples, alcoves and rotundas are scattered around the grounds, strategically placed to evoke in the onlooker a romantic and poetic frame of mind. It is one of the more intriguing quirks of fate that Lancelot Brown, always known as Capability Brown because he told his clients that their parks had capabilities, was head gardener at Stowe for 10 years. He arrived here in 1741 and began to work out his own style, a more natural style of landscape gardening, which was to take over where gardens like the one at Stowe left off.

BARRS NURSERIES

Windy Ridge, Bletchley Road, Thornborough,
Buckinghamshire MK18 2DZ
Tel: 01280 816855 website: www.barrsnurseries.co.uk

Barr's Nurseries is committed to enhancing the beauty and value of the Buckinghamshire landscape – one garden at a time. Established in 1985, owners Alison and Jim Barr first specialised in Fuchsias but quickly realised that their customers required a greater assortment of plants therefore they expanded their home-grown collection to include: herbs; shrubs; climbers; herbaceous perennials and a vast array of summer bedding and hanging basket plants. They also source beautiful, well grown; trees, roses, clematis, alpines, soft fruit and conifers from other British growers. Where possible all hardy plants are grown outside so that they have experienced the British weather before they reach your home.

Rest assured this is not a garden centre but a specialist Nursery. Alison, Jim and the staff take great pride in their expert knowledge, which enables them to help and advise customers in their choice and care of plants on offer.

Log on to the website and extend your visit; it is attractive, extremely informative and easy to navigate. Alison also keeps a blog that demonstrates her enthusiasm and passion for her work – an enjoyable read! The nursery is located on the A421 between Buckingham and Bletchley. Open six days and closed on Mondays, except Bank Holidays.

🎭 stories and anecdotes 🐦 famous people 🎨 art and craft 🎪 entertainment and sport 🚶 walks

and *God moves in a mysterious way*.

The house in which Cowper lived from 1768 to 1786 is now the **Cowper and Newton Museum**, a fascinating place that concentrates on Cowper's life and work, but also has some exhibits and collections concerned with the times in which he lived and the life of Olney. Each of the rooms of the large early 18th-century town house has been specially themed and there are numerous displays of Cowper's work, including the *Olney Hymns*. As we went to press, the museum was about to acquire the most important collection of Cowper-related material ever to come on the market – 170 letters, 24 books from Cowper's library, two miniatures by William Blake and many objects connected with Cowper's life. Cowper was also a keen gardener and the summerhouse, where he wrote many of his poems, can still be seen in the rear garden. Here he experimented with plants that were new to 18th-century England. Also at the museum is the nationally important Lace Collection, and items particular to the shoemaking industry, which was another busy local trade in the 19th and early 20th century.

When Cowper died in 1800 he was buried at East Dereham in Norfolk, but his associate, the reformed slave-trader, is interred in the churchyard of **St Peter and St Paul**, where he had been the curate. This church is a spacious building dating from the mid 14th century and its spire rises some 185 feet to dominate the skyline of Olney.

For more than 300 years Olney was a centre of lace-making by hand, using wooden or bone bobbins. When lace was at its most expensive, in the 1700s, only the well-to-do could afford to buy it, but the rise in

machine-made lace from Nottingham saw a fall in prices and a sharp decline in Olney lace. A revival of the trade was tried by Harry Armstrong when he opened the Lace Factory in 1928 but, although handmade lace is still produced locally, the factory only lasted until Armstrong's death in 1943.

Amongst the town's present day claims to fame is the annual **Pancake Race**. Legend has it that the first 'race' was run in the 15th century when a local housewife heard the Shriving Service bell ringing and ran to church complete with her frying pan and pancake.

Nearby **Emberton Country Park**, located on the site of former gravel pits, is an ideal place to relax. Not only are there four lakes and a stretch of the River Ouse within the park's boundaries but facilities here include fishing, sailing, and nature trails.

NEWPORT PAGNELL
3 miles NE of Milton Keynes on the A422

Modern development hides a long history at Newport Pagnell, which local archaeological finds indicate was settled in the Iron Age and during the Roman occupation. It was an important administrative centre, and in the 10th century the Royal Mint was established here. Lacemaking was once an important industry, and the town is also associated with the car-maker Aston Martin which started life in the 1820s as a maker of coaches for the nobility.

CHICHELEY
5 miles NE of Milton Keynes on the A422

🏛 Chicheley Hall

This attractive village is the home of **Chicheley Hall**, a beautiful baroque house that was built in the early 1700s for Sir John

Chester and which remains today one of the finest such houses in the country. Down the years it was used by the military and as a school, but in 1952 it was bought by the 2nd Earl Beatty and restored to its former state of grace. The earl's father, the 1st Earl, was a particularly courageous naval commander and, as well as receiving the DSO at the age of just 25, he was also a commander in the decisive battle of Jutland in 1916.

WILLEN
1 mile NE of Milton Keynes on the A509

The village Church of St Mary Magdalene, built in the late 17th century, is an elegant building in the style of Sir Christopher Wren. Willen is also home to another house of prayer, the Peace Pagoda and Buddhist Temple, opened in 1980. It was built by the monks and nuns of the Nipponsan Myohoji, and it was the first peace pagoda in the western hemisphere. In this place of great tranquillity and beauty, 1,000 cherry trees and cedars, donated by the ancient Japanese town of Yoshino, have been planted on the hill surrounding the pagoda in memory of the victims of all wars.

GREAT LINFORD
2 miles NE of Milton Keynes on the A422

🏛 Stone Circle

Situated on the banks of the Grand Union Canal, this village, which is now more or less a suburb of Milton Keynes, has a 13th-century church set in parkland, a 17th-century manor house, and a **Stone Circle**, one of only a few such prehistoric monuments in the county. Despite the encroachment of its much larger neighbour, the village has retained a distinctive air that is all its own.

The central block of the present manor house was built in 1678 by Sir William Pritchard, Lord Mayor of London. As well as making Great Linford his country seat, Pritchard also provided a boys' school and almshouses for six unmarried poor of the parish. The manor house was extended in the 18th century by the Uthwatt family, relatives of the Lord Mayor, and they used various tricks to give an impressive and elegant appearance to the building. The Grand Union Canal cuts through the estate, whose grounds are now a public park.

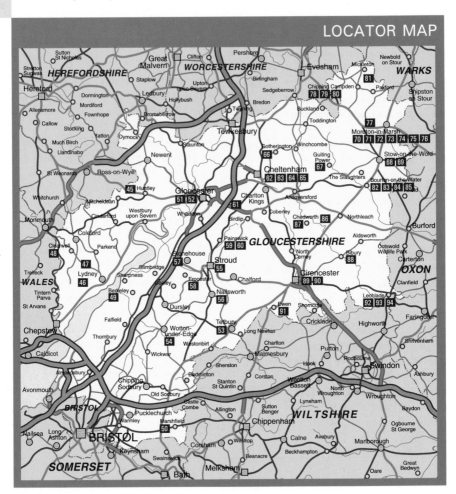

ADVERTISERS AND PLACES OF INTEREST

Accommodation, Food and Drink

Activities

🏚 historic building 🏛 museum and heritage 🏛 historic site 🔱 scenic attraction 🌱 flora and fauna

4 Gloucestershire

For many, Gloucestershire *is* the Cotswolds, the delightful limestone hills that sweep across the county from Dyrham in the south to Chipping Campden in the north. As well as providing some of the most glorious scenery and the prettiest villages in the country, the county is also home to the historic towns of Cirencester and Cheltenham. 'The most English and the least spoiled of all our countryside.' So wrote J B Priestley in 1933 in his *English Journey* and, more than 70 years later, his verdict would surely have been the same.

However, Gloucestershire is not all about the Cotswolds. To the west, on the River Severn, is the ancient city of Gloucester, while further down river is the Vale of Berkeley and historic Berkeley Castle. On the opposite bank of the river lies the Forest of Dean. Wild woodland, royal hunting ground, naval timber reserve, important mining and industrial region: the Forest has been all these, and today its rich and varied landscape provides endless interest for walkers, nature-lovers and historians. Bounded by the Rivers Severn and Wye, the area has been effectively isolated from the rest of England and Wales and so has developed a character all its own.

ADVERTISERS AND PLACES OF INTEREST

🎭 stories and anecdotes 🖼 famous people 🎨 art and craft 🎭 entertainment and sport 🏃 walks

Newent

🏛 Market House 🏛 Church of St Mary

🐦 Bird of Prey Centre 🜕 Castle Hill Farm

🐦 Three Choirs Vineyard

Capital of the area of northwest Gloucestershire known as the Ryelands, and the most important town in the Vale of Leadon, Newent stands in the broad triangle of land called Daffodil Crescent. The rich Leadon Valley soil was traditionally used for growing rye and raising the renowned Ryelands sheep, an ancient breed famed for the quality of its wool. The town was one of the county's principal wool-trading centres, and the wealth produced from that trade accounts for the large number of grand merchants' houses to be seen here. The most distinctive building in Newent is the splendid timber-framed **Market House**, built as a butter market in the middle of the 16th-century, its upper floors supported on 16 oak pillars that form an open colonnade. The medieval **Church of St Mary** has many outstanding features, including the shaft of a 9th-century Saxon cross, the 11th-century Newent Stone and the 17th-century nave. During the Civil War, Royalist troops had removed the lead from the roof to make bullets, an act that caused the roof to collapse during a snowstorm in 1674. A new nave was started after Charles II agreed to donate 60 tons of timber from the Forest of Dean. The church's 150ft spire is a landmark for miles around.

There aren't too many windmills in Gloucestershire, but at **Castle Hill Farm** just outside town, is a working wooden mill with great views from a balcony at the top.

A mile south of Newent is the **National Birds of Prey Centre** housing one of the largest and best collections of birds of prey in the world. The 110 aviaries are home to eagles, falcons, owls, vultures, kites, hawks, caracaras, secretary birds and buzzards. Between 20 and 40 birds are flown daily at the Centre, which is open every day from February to November. Also on site are a tearoom, children's play area, pets corner and picnic area.

On the road north towards Dymock, set in 75 acres of rolling countryside, the **Three Choirs Vineyard** is the country's largest wine producer. Unusually, there's also a brewery here, Whittington's, named after Dick Whittington who is believed to have been born in the nearby hamlet of Pauntley. The vineyard also has a restaurant, shop and offers bed and breakfast accommodation in rooms overlooking the rows of vines.

Market House, Newent

🏛 historic building 🏛 museum and heritage 🏚 historic site 🜕 scenic attraction 🐦 flora and fauna

Around Newent

DYMOCK
3 miles N of Newent on the B4216

🐦 Dymock Poets

Dymock boasts some fine old brick buildings, including the White House and the Old Rectory near the church and, outside the village, the Old Grange, which incorporates the remains of the Cistercian Flaxley Abbey.

At the heart of the village is the early Norman Church of St Mary, whose unusual features include a tympanum depicting the Tree of Life, a 13th-century stone coffin lid, stained glass by Kempe – and the last ticket issued at Dymock station, in 1959. A corner of the church is dedicated to the memory of the **Dymock Poets**, a group who based themselves in Dymock from before the First World War. The group, which comprised Lascelles Abercrombie (the first to arrive), Rupert Brooke, John Drinkwater, Wilfred Gibson, Edward Thomas and Robert Frost, sent out its *New Numbers* poetry magazine from Dymock's tiny post office. It was also from here that Brooke published his *War Sonnets*, including *The Soldier* (*'If I should die, think only this of me: That there's some corner of a foreign field that is forever England...'*). Brooke and Thomas died in the war, which led to the dissolution of the group. Two circular walks from Dymock take in places associated with the poets.

Many other literary figures are associated with the Forest. Dennis Potter, born at Coleford in 1935 the eldest son of a Forest coal-miner, is renowned for writing the screenplays for some of TV's most memorable programmes, including *Pennies*

Dymock Village

From Heaven and *The Singing Detective*. But he also wrote with passion about the Forest in *The Glittering Coffin* and *The Changing Forest: Life in the Forest of Dean Today*. Mary Howitt, born in Coleford in 1799, is known as a translator, poet and author of children's books. It was as a translator that she met a Danish story-teller called Hans Christian Andersen who asked Mary to translate his stories into English.

UPLEADON
2 miles N of Newent off the B4215

🏠 Church of St Mary the Virgin

The **Church of St Mary the Virgin** features some fine Norman and Tudor work, but is best known for its unique tower, half-timbered from bottom to top; even the mullion windows are of wood. The church has a great treasure in its Bible, an early example of the Authorised Version printed by King James' printer Robert Barker. This was the unfortunate who later issued an edition with a small but rather important word missing. The so-called Wicked Bible of 1631 renders Exodus 20.14 as 'Thou shalt commit adultery'.

🎭 stories and anecdotes 🐦 famous people 🎨 art and craft 📖 entertainment and sport 🔥 walks

around the Forest of Dean is Longhope, a pleasant settlement south of the A40 Gloucester to Ross-on-Wye road.

Longhope is the location of the **Harts Barn Crafts Centre**, situated in a hunting lodge built by William, Duke of Normandy, and housing an array of working crafts including jewellery, pine furniture, art gallery, handmade gifts, glassware, dried flowers and picture framing. There's also a tearoom.

Just to the north on the A40 is **Willow Lodge Gardens and Arboretum**. (see panel on page 91) The four acre garden and arboretum is open to the public most Sundays and Mondays from April to August.

NEWNHAM-ON-SEVERN
3 miles SW of Cinderford off the A4151

One of the gateways to the Forest, and formerly a port, Newnham lies on a great bend in the river. Its heyday was at the beginning of the 19th century, when a quay was built and an old tramway tunnel converted into what was perhaps the world's first railway tunnel. The village has many interesting buildings, which can be visited by following the Millennium Heritage Walk plaques installed by the parish council with funds provided by an open-air jazz concert.

LITTLEDEAN
1 mile W of Cinderford off the A4151

🏛 Littledean Hall

Places of interest here include the 13th-century church, the 18th-century prison and, just south of the village, **Littledean Hall** (private), reputedly the oldest inhabited house in England. The house has Saxon and Celtic remains in the cellars and is thought to have originated in the 6th century. It became a Royalist garrison during the Civil War.

RUARDEAN
4 miles NW of Cinderford on the A4136

🏛 Church of St John the Baptist   ♣ Ruardean Hill

A lovely old village whose **Church of St John the Baptist**, one of many on the fringe of the forest, has a number of interesting features. A tympanum depicting St George and the Dragon is a great rarity, and on a stone plaque in the nave is a curious carving of two fishes. These are thought to have been carved by craftsmen from the Herefordshire School of Norman Architecture during the Romanesque period around 1150. It is part of a frieze removed with rubble when the south porch was being built in the 13th century. The frieze was considered lost until 1985 when an inspection of a bread oven in a cottage at nearby Turner's Tump revealed the two fish set into its lining. They were rescued and returned to their rightful place in the church.

Ruardean was the birthplace in the 1840s of James and William Horlick, later to become famous with their Horlicks formula. Their patent for malted milk was registered in 1883, and the granary where the original experiments were carried out still remains in the village.

Ruardean Hill is 951 feet above sea level and from its summit, on a clear day, Herefordshire, the Black Mountains and the Brecon Beacons can all be seen.

Lydney

🎦 Dean Forest Railway & Norchard Railway Centre

🎦 Forest Model Village & Gardens

🏛 Roman Temple Site

♣ Lydney Park Spring Gardens

The harbour and the canal at Lydney, once an important centre of the iron and coal industries and the largest settlement between Chepstow and Gloucester, are well worth exploring, and no visit to the town should end without a trip on the **Dean Forest Railway**. A regular service of steam and diesel trains operates the 4¼ mile route through the Forest between Lydney Junction, St Mary's Halt, Norchard and Parkend. The fare covers unlimited travel for the day. At **Norchard Railway Centre**, headquarters of the line, are a railway museum, souvenir shop and details of restoration projects. Popular events throughout the year include Days Out with Thomas, Santa Specials and Steam Footplate Experience Courses.

A popular family tourist attraction is the **Forest of Dean Model Village & Gardens**, which features more than 50 detailed miniatures of local landmarks and buildings in five landscaped garden zones.

One of the chief attractions in the vicinity is **Lydney Park Spring Gardens and Roman Temple Site**. The gardens, which lie beside the A48 on the western outskirts, are a riot of colour, particularly in May and June, and the grounds also contain the site of an Iron Age hill fort and the remains of a late-Roman temple excavated by Sir Mortimer Wheeler in the 1920s. The nearby museum houses a

number of Roman artefacts from the site, including the famous Lydney Dog - dating from about 365 AD this is a bronze statuette which apparently represents a half-grown wolfhound - and a number of interesting items brought back from New Zealand in the 1930s by the first Viscount Bledisloe after his term there as Governor General. Also in the park are traces of Roman iron-mine workings and Roman earth workings.

Around Lydney

ALVINGTON
2 miles SW of Lydney on the A48

🦌 Wintour's Leap

In the churchyard at Alvington are the graves of the illustrious Wintour family, leading figures in the defeat of the Spanish Armada. Half a century after that event came Sir John Wintour's remarkable escape from Cromwell's men at what is now known as **Wintour's Leap**. Sir John was an adventurer, Keeper of the Forest of Dean and sometime secretary to Queen Maria Henrietta of the Netherlands. In 1644 he was at the head of a Royalist force defeated at Blockley, near Chepstow, by Parliamentary troops. Wintour is said to have

🎬 stories and anecdotes 🦌 famous people 🎨 art and craft 🎭 entertainment and sport 🚶 walks

escaped from the battlefield by riding up by the Wye and hurling himself and his horse into the river from the cliffs.

Coleford

📷 GWR Museum 🔾 Puzzle Wood

🍃 Perrygrove Railway

Coleford is a former mining centre, which received its royal charter from Charles I in the 17th century in recognition of its loyalty to the Crown. It was by then already an important iron processing centre, partly because of the availability of local ore deposits and partly because of the ready local supply of timber for converting into charcoal for use in the smelting process. It was in Coleford that the Mushet family helped to revolutionise the iron and steel industry. Robert Forester Mushet, a freeminer, discovered how spiegeleisen, an alloy of iron, manganese, silicon and carbon, could be used in the reprocessing of burnt iron and went on to develop a system for turning molten pig iron directly into steel, a process that predated the more familiar one developed by Bessemer.

Coleford, still regarded as the capital of the Forest of Dean, is a busy commercial centre with an interesting church and a number of notable industrial relics. The Forestry Commission is housed at Bank House and has information on all aspects of the Forest. There are miles of way-marked walks and cycle trails through the Forest, and the famous Sculpture Trail starts at Beechenhurst Lodge.

Coleford is also home to the **Great Western Railway Museum**, housed in an 1883 GWR goods station next to the central car park. Exhibits include several full-size steam locomotives, large scale model engines, original signal box and a wealth of railway memorabilia. There's also a craft shop and refreshment room.

Another treat for railway fans is the **Perrygrove Railway**, where a narrow gauge steam train takes a 1.5 mile trip through farmland and woods. In the evening, the Ghost Train journey through the dark woods promises a few scary surprises. There are also woodland walks, picnic and play areas, and light refreshments available.

Nearby is another visitor attraction, also on the B4228 just south of the town. This is **Puzzle Wood**, where 14 acres of pre-Roman open-cast ore mines have been redesigned as a family attraction, with paths forming an unusual maze, breathtaking scenery, wooden bridges, passageways through moss-covered rocks and lots of dead ends and circles. J R R Tolkien, author of *Lord of the Rings*, was a regular visitor to the Forest of Dean and reputedly based Middle Earth on Puzzlewood.

Around Coleford

STAUNTON
3 miles NW of Coleford on the A4136

🏛 Buck Stone and Suck Stone

Lots to see here, including a Norman church with two stone fonts and an unusual corkscrew staircase leading up past the pulpit to the belfry door. Not far from the village are several enormous mystical stones, notably the **Buck Stone** and the **Suck Stone**. The former, looking like some great monster, used to buck, or rock, on its base, but is now firmly fixed in place. The Suck Stone is a real giant, weighing in at many thousands of tons. There are several other stones in the vicinity, including the Near Harkening and Far Harkening down among the trees, and the **Long Stone** by the A4136 at Marion's Cross.

CANNOP
4 miles E of Coleford on the B4226

🏛 Hopewell Colliery ⚔ Cannop Valley

Cannop Valley has many forest trails and picnic sites; one of the sites is at Cannop Ponds, picturesque ponds created in the 1820s to provide a regular supply of water for the local iron-smelting works. Nearby is **Hopewell Colliery**, a true Forest of Dean free mine where summer visitors can see old mine workings and some of the old tools of the trade, then relax with a snack from the café.

PARKEND
3 miles SE of Coleford off the B4234

🐦 Nagshead Nature Reserve   🐾 Go Ape!

A community once based, like so many others in the area, on the extraction of minerals. In the early years of the 19th century, before steam engines arrived and horses did all the donkey work, Parkend became a tramroad centre and laden trams ran from coalpits, iron mines, quarries, furnaces and forges to river-borne outlets at Lydbrook and Lydney. New Fancy Colliery is now a delightful picnic area, with a nearby hill affording breathtaking views over the forestscape. Off the B4431, just west of Parkend, is the RSPB's **Nagshead Nature Reserve**, with hundreds of nest boxes in a woodland site with footpaths, way-marked

CLEARWELL CAVES

nr Coleford, Royal Forest of Dean, Gloucestershire GL16 8JR
Tel: 01594 832535   Fax: 01594 833362
e-mail: jw@clearwellcaves.com
website: www.clearwellcaves.com

Clearwell Caves are set in an Area of Special Landscape Value on the outskirts of the historic village of Clearwell. The caves are part of the last remaining working iron mine in the Forest of Dean and the last ochre mine in the UK. They are part of a natural cave system that became filled with iron ore around 180 million years ago.

Mining in the Forest of Dean is now believed to have begun over 7,000 years ago during the Mesolithic period (Middle Stone Age) as people migrated back into the area after the last Ice Age (10,000 years ago).

People were collecting ochre pigments, particularly red ochre which was very highly prized and had important decorative and ritual uses. Once the use of iron as a metal was established and certainly by the 1st century AD, there was a thriving iron industry here.

Large scale iron ore mining continued until 1945 and in its last year as a large scale mine it produced over 3,000 tons of ore. Today production of minerals rarely exceeds four tons per annum. Small scale ochre mining carries on, using traditional techniques which would often be familiar to even the earliest miners.

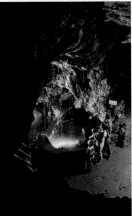

Visitors to the caves are offered a wide range of activities, from a leisurely and fascinating self-guided underground walk, descending for more than 100ft, to a more strenuous adventure caving trip – or even a Natural Paint workshop. The cave shop is a treat in itself with unusual gift ideas, books, souvenirs and a wide range of spectacular minerals and crystals from around the world. And of course you can buy the ochre mined here.

Don't forget to pay a visit to the tearoom. Here you'll find a good selection of freshly prepared lunches and refreshments, along with some very interesting mining artefacts displayed around the ceiling and walls. An unusual day out for all ages and a great underground experience. Clearwell Caves are open from 10am to 5pm, daily, from 14th February until 31st October. Visitors are still welcome during November but the caves are then being prepared for the Christmas Fantasy (open 1st - 24th December) so normal displays are interrupted.

trails and a summer information centre.

To the east of Parkend, **Go Ape!** Is an award-winning high wire forest adventure course with rope bridges, Tarzan swings and zip slides, all set high up in the treetops. Full and half-day packages are available.

CLEARWELL
1.5 miles S of Coleford off the A466

🏛 Clearwell Caves

Clearwell Caves (see panel opposite and walk on page 98) are part of the only remaining working iron mine in the Forest of Dean. This natural cave system became filled with iron ore around 180 million years ago and has been mined for at least 4,000 years. As a result, the cave complex now consists of many miles of passageways and hundreds of caverns. Visitors can take their own self-guided tour or participate in a more strenuous adventure caving trip. Other amenities on site include a gift shop, picnic area and tea room. A memorable visit can be completed by wandering down to Clearwell village with its lovely French Gothic-style church and the pretty surrounding countryside.

ST BRIAVELS
5 miles S of Coleford on minor roads

🏛 Castle

On the edge of a limestone plateau high above the Wye Valley, this historic village is named after a 5th-century Welsh bishop whose name appears in various forms throughout Celtic Wales, Cornwall and Brittany, but nowhere else in England. In the Middle Ages St Briavels was an important administrative centre for the royal hunting forest and also a leading manufacturer of armaments, supplying weapons and ammunition to the Crown.

The ample Church of St Mary the Virgin, Norman in origin, enlarged in the 12th and 13th centuries and remodelled by the Victorians, is the scene of a curious and very English annual custom, the St Briavels Bread and Cheese Ceremony. After evensong a local forester stands on the Pound Wall and throws small pieces of bread and cheese to the villagers, accompanied by the chant, 'St Briavels water and Whyrl's wheat are the best bread and water King John can ever eat'. This ceremony is thought to have originated more than 700 years ago when the villagers successfully defended their rights of estover (collecting wood from common land) in nearby Hudnalls Wood. In gratitude, each villager paid one penny to the church warden to help feed the poor, and that act led to the founding of the ceremony. The small pieces of bread and cheese were considered to bring good luck, and the Dean Forest miners would keep the pieces in order to ward off harm.

St Briavels Castle, which stands in an almost impregnable position on a high promontory, was founded by Henry I and enlarged by King John, who used it as a hunting lodge. Two sturdy gatehouses are

St Briavels Castle

🎭 stories and anecdotes 🕊 famous people 🎨 art and craft 🎵 entertainment and sport 🥾 walks

Frampton Manor

at Splatt Bridge and Saul
Bridge at Frampton, there
are splendid little bridge-
keeper's cottages with
Doric columns.

To the west of
Frampton, on a great bend
in the river, is the
Arlingham Peninsula,
part of the Severn Way
Shepperdine-Tewkesbury
long-distance walk. The
trail passes close to Wick
Court, a 13th-century
moated manor house. The
land on which the village of Arlingham
stands once belonged to the monks of St
Augustine's Abbey in Bristol who believed it
to be the point where St Augustine crossed
the Severn on his way to converting the
heathen Welsh tribes.

The Severn naturally dominated life
hereabouts and at Saul, a small village on the
peninsula, the inhabitants decorated their
houses with carvings of sailors, some of
which, in bright, cheerful colours, can be seen
today. The village lies at the point where two
canals cross. Two separate waterways, the
Stroudwater Navigation and the Thames &
Severn Canal, once linked the Severn and the
Thames, a route of 37 miles. The canals,
known collectively as the **Cotswold Canals**,
were abandoned in 1933 and 1954 respectively
but most of the route is intact, and since 1972
the Cotswold Canals Trust has worked in
partnership with local authorities on
restoration work. Continuing round the bend
in the river, Epney is the point from which
thousands of baby eels are exported each year
to the Netherlands and elsewhere to replenish
their own stocks.

outstanding example of a Georgian country
house, built in the Palladian style in the 1730s
and the seat of the Clifford family ever since.
Fine porcelain, furniture and paintings grace
the interior, and in the peacock-strutted
grounds an ornamental canal reflects a superb
Orangery in Dutch-influenced Strawberry Hill
Gothic. A unique octagonal tower was built in
the 17th century as a dovecote.

On the other side of the green is
Frampton Manor, the Clifford family's
former home, built between the 12th and 16th
centuries. This handsome timber-framed
house is thought to be the birthplace of Jane
Clifford, who was the mistress of Henry II
and bore him two children. The manor, which
has a lovely old walled garden with some rare
plants, is open by written appointment.

At the southern edge of the village stands
the restored 14th-century Church of St Mary
with its rare Norman lead font. The church
stands beside the Sharpness Canal, which was
built to allow ships to travel up the Severn
Valley as far as Gloucester without being at
the mercy of the estuary tides. The canal has
several swing bridges and at some of these, as

SLIMBRIDGE
4 miles S of Frampton on the A38

🐦 Wildfowl and Wetlands Centre

Slimbridge Wetland Centre was founded as a trust on the banks of the Severn in 1946 by the distinguished naturalist, artist, sailor and broadcaster Peter (later Sir Peter) Scott. He believed in bringing wildlife and people together for the benefit of both, and the Trust's work continues with the same aims. Slimbridge has the world's largest collection of ducks, geese and swans, and spectacular flamingoes among the exotic wildfowl. Land Rover or canoe safaris are available. Also at the centre are a tropical house, pond zone, a watery children's play area, wildlife art gallery, restaurant and gift shop, and there are magnificent views from the observation tower. Sir Peter died in 1989 and his ashes were scattered at Slimbridge, where he had lived for many years. A memorial to him stands at the entrance to the Centre.

BERKELEY
6 miles S of Frampton off the A38

🏰 Berekley Castle   🏛 Jenner Museum

🐦 Butterfly House & Plant Centre

⚓ Gloucester & Sharpness Canal

The fertile strip that is the Vale of Berkeley, bounded on the north by the Severn and on the south by the M5, takes its name from the small town of Berkeley, whose largely Georgian centre is dominated by the Norman **Berkeley Castle**. Said to be the oldest inhabited castle in Britain, with the same family resident from the start, this wonderful gem in pink sandstone was built between 1117 and 1153 on the site of a Saxon fort. It was here that the barons of the West met before making the journey to Runnymede to witness the signing of Magna Carta by King John in 1215. Edward II was imprisoned here for several months after losing his throne to his wife and her lover. He eventually met a painful death in the dungeons in the year 1327. Three centuries later the castle was besieged by Cromwell's troops and played an important part in the history of the Civil War. It stands very close to the Severn and once incorporated the waters of the river in its defences so that it could, in an emergency, flood its lands. Visitors passing into the castle by way of a bridge over a moat will find a wealth of treasures in the Great Hall, the circular keep, the state apartments with their fine tapestries and period furniture, the medieval kitchens and the dungeons.

The Berkeley family have filled the place with objects from around the world, including painted glassware from Damascus, ebony chairs from India and a cypress chest that reputedly belonged to Sir Francis Drake. Other exhibits include a four-poster bed with a solid wooden top and a set of bells once worn by the castle's dray horses and now hanging in the dairy. The castle is surrounded

Berkeley Castle

Gloucester Cathedral

the finest in existence, and the great east window, 72ft by 38ft, is the largest surviving stained-glass window in the country. It was built to celebrate the English victory at the Battle of Crécy in 1346 and depicts the coronation of the Virgin surrounded by assorted kings, popes and saints. The young King Henry III was crowned here, with a bracelet on his little head rather than a crown.

The old area of the city around Gloucester Cross boasts some very fine early buildings, including St John's Church and the Church of St Mary de Crypt. Just behind the latter, near the house where Robert Raikes of Sunday School fame lived, stands an odd-looking tower built in the 1860s to honour Hannah, the wife of Thomas Fenn Addison, a successful solicitor. The tower was also a memorial to Raikes.

Three great inns were built in the 14th and

Gloucestershire Wildlife Trust

Conservation Centre, Robinswood Hill Country Park, Reservoir Road, Gloucester, Gloucestershire GL4 6SX
Tel: 01452 383333 Fax: 01452 383334
e-mail info@gloucestershirewildlifetrust.co.uk
website: www.gloucestershirewildlifetrust.co.uk

The team of volunteers and staff take care of more than 70 nature reserves across Gloucestershire, each one a special place for wildlife. Staff and volunteers work all year round to maintain and enhance these important sites for wildlife. The reserves are home to some of the rarest wildlife in the county and are visited and enjoyed by thousands of people every year.

The conservation team protects the threatened wildlife in Gloucestershire by working with landowners, national organisations and local authorities. They work to ensure the future of threatened species such as the water vole, skylark and stag beetle and their habitats. The wild ranging events programme promotes understanding and enjoyment of wildlife and the environment.

They work to organise informative activity days, talks and guided walks for people of all ages and abilities. Children have fun and gain curriculum knowledge through exciting activities in schools, at the Conservation Centre on Robinswood Hill, and through Wildlife Watch club activities.

🏛 historic building 🏛 museum and heritage 🏛 historic site 🏞 scenic attraction 🌿 flora and fauna

The National Waterways Museum

Llanthony Warehouse, Gloucester Docks, Gloucester,
Gloucestershire GL1 2EH
Tel: 01452 318200 Fax: 01452 318202
website: www.nwm.org.uk

There's so much to see and do for all ages at the award-winning **National Waterways Museum** located in a splendid Victorian warehouse in historic Gloucester Docks. The Museum charts the fascinating 300-year story of Britain's inland waterways through interactive displays, touch-screen computers, working models and historic boats. Visitors can find out what made the waterways possible, from the business brains and design genius to the hard work and sweat of the navvies, and try their hand at designing and painting a narrow boat, building a canal and navigating a boat through a lock.

The Museum has a working blacksmith's forge, a floor of displays dedicated to waterway trade and cargoes, a marvellous interactive gallery and family room where weights and pulleys, water play areas, period costume, large jigsaw puzzles and brass rubbings bring history to life in a way that is both instructive and entertaining. The museum shop sells unusual gifts and souvenirs and refreshment is provided in the café. There are computerised information points throughout the Museum and visitors can even take to the water themselves on a 45-minute boat trip running along the adjacent Gloucester & Sharpness Canal between Easter and October. The National Waterways Museum is owned by the Waterways Trust, which preserves, protects and promotes the waterway heritage while giving new life to their future.

15th centuries to accommodate the scores of pilgrims who came to visit Edward II's tomb. Two of them survive. The galleried New Inn, founded by a monk around 1450, doubled as a theatre and still retains the cobbled courtyard. It was from this inn that Lady Jane Grey was proclaimed Queen. Equally old is the Fleece Hotel in Westgate Street, which has a 12th-century stone-vaulted undercroft. In the same street is Maverdine House, a four-storey mansion reached by a very narrow passage. Described as the finest and largest urban timber framed building in Britain, this was the residence and headquarters of Colonel Massey, Cromwell's commander, during the Civil War siege of 1643. Most of the region was in Royalist hands, but Massey survived a month-long assault by a force led by the king himself and thus turned the tide of war.

Gloucester Docks were once the gateway for waterborne traffic heading into the Midlands, and the handsome Victorian warehouses are always in demand as location sites for period films. Restaurants, bars, cafes and shops have sprung up and various river cruises are available from the Llanthony Warehouse quay. The docks are also home to several award-winning museums. The **National Waterways Museum** (see panel above) occupies three floors of a splendid Victorian warehouse and is entered by a lock chamber with running water. The museum tells the fascinating 300-year story of Britain's

📖 stories and anecdotes 🦜 famous people 🎨 art and craft 🎭 entertainment and sport 👣 walks

(clay) from which it takes its name, and once
the property of the French d'Abitot family,
was for a time the home of the actress Lily
Langtry, mistress of the Prince of Wales, later
King Edward VII. The link with the actress is
remembered in two streets in the village -
Drury Lane and Hyde Park Corner.

Tewkesbury Abbey

Tewkesbury

🏛 Abbey 🏛 John Moore Countryside Museum

🏛 Battle of Tewkesbury

A town of historic and strategic importance
close to the confluence of the Severn and
Avon rivers. Those rivers also served to
restrict the lateral expansion of the town,
which accounts for the unusual number of tall
buildings. (They also contributed to the
disastrous floods of summer 2007.)
Tewkesbury's early prosperity was based on
the wool and mustard trades, and the
movement of corn by river also contributed
to its wealth. Tewkesbury's main
thoroughfares, High Street, Church Street and
Barton Street, form a Y shape, and the area
between is a marvellous maze of narrow
alleyways and small courtyards hiding many
grand old pubs and medieval cottages. At the
centre of it all is **Tewkesbury Abbey**, the
cathedral-sized parish church of St Mary. One
of the largest and grandest parish churches in
the country, it was founded in the 8th century
and completely rebuilt in the 11th. It was once
the church of the Benedictine Abbey and was
among the last to be dissolved by Henry VIII.
In 1540, it was saved from destruction by the
townspeople who raised £453 to buy it from
the Crown. Many of its features are on a
grand scale - the colossal double row of
Norman pillars; the six-fold arch in the west
front; and the vast main tower, 132ft in height

and 46ft square, the tallest surviving Norman
main tower in the world. The choir windows
have stained glass dating from the 1300s, and
the abbey has more medieval monuments than
any besides Westminster. A chantry chapel
was endowed by the Beauchamps, an
influential family that married into another,
that of Richard Neville, Warwick the
Kingmaker. Other treasures include the 17th
century Milton Organ that is still in daily use.
There's a cathedral shop, and the refectory has
been restored to its original function as an
eating place although it is now licensed.

American visitors to the abbey may be
interested in a memorial plaque to Victoria
Woodhull Martin, a native of Ohio for which
she served as Congresswoman and then, in
1872, became the first woman to run for

President. When she failed to get elected and her second husband having died, she quit American politics and settled in Tewkesbury where, says her epitaph, 'she devoted herself unsparingly to all that could promote the great cause of Anglo-American friendship'. She died in 1927.

An excellent introduction to Tewkesbury and its history is provided at Out of the Hat, a recently opened heritage and visitor centre that occupies a former hat shop. The 17th-century building has been lovingly restored, renovated and enhanced. The Tourist Information Centre is on the ground floor, the two upper storeys incorporate interactive displays, games, information panels and much more.

Three museums tell the story of the town and its environs: the Little Museum, laid out like a typical old merchant's house; Tewkesbury Museum, with displays on the social history and archaeology of the area; and the John Moore Countryside Museum, a natural history collection displayed in a 15th-century timber-framed house. The museum commemorates the work of John Moore, a well-known writer, broadcaster and naturalist, who was born in Tewkesbury in 1907.

The Battle of Tewkesbury was one of the fiercest in the Wars of the Roses. It took place in 1471 in a field south of the town, which has ever since been known as Bloody Meadow. Following the Lancastrian defeat, those who had not been slaughtered in the battle fled to the abbey, where the killing began again. Abbot Strensham intervened to stop the massacre, but the survivors, who included the Duke of Somerset, were handed over to King Edward IV and executed at Market Cross. The 17-year-old son of Henry VI, Edward Prince of Wales, was killed in the conflict and a

plaque marking his final resting place can be seen in the abbey. One of the victors of the battle was the Duke of Gloucester, later Richard III. Tewkesbury was again the scene of military action almost two centuries later during the Civil War. The town changed hands several times during this period and on one occasion Charles I began his siege of Gloucester by requisitioning every pick, mattock, spade and shovel in Tewkesbury.

Around Tewkesbury

BREDON
4 miles NE of Tewkesbury on the B4080

🏠 Bredon Tithe Barn

Bredon Tithe Barn (National Trust) is a 14th-century structure built of Cotswold stone, with a splendid aisled interior that gives it the atmosphere of a church. Unusually, it has five porches, one of which has a rare stone chimney cowling.

DEERHURST
3 miles S of Tewkesbury off the A38

🏠 Odda's Chapel

Set on the eastern bank of the Severn, Deerhurst is a village whose current size and status belies a distinguished past. The church, with a distinct Celtic feel, is one of the oldest in England, with parts dating back to the 7th century, and its treasures include a unique double east window, a 9th-century carved font, a Saxon carving of the Virgin and Child and some fine brasses dating from the 14th and 15th centuries. One depicts the Cassey family, local landowners, and their dog, Terri.

Another Saxon treasure, 200 yards from the church, is **Odda's Chapel**, dedicated in 1056 and lost for many centuries before being

---

HORSE & GROOM

Bourton on the Hill, Moreton-in-Marsh,
Gloucestershire GL56 9AQ
Tel: 01386 700413   Fax: 01386 700413
e-mail: greenstocks@horseandgroom.info
website: www.horseandgroom.info

A Georgian building of honey coloured Cotswold stone, the Horse & Groom is bursting with character and enjoys spectacular views from its hill-top setting. The pub has a large garden together with convenient private parking.

Since buying the pub in 2005 brothers Tom & Will Greenstock have created a lively new venue for drinkers, diners and overnight guests. Their hard work has already rewarded them with an ever increasing following of loyal customers and commendations in leading guidebooks.

The bar provides a cosy, clean environment and offers a selection of beverages. As well as regularly changing ales, we are also pleased to offer the locally brewed 'Premium Cotswold Lager' and 'Cotswold Wheat Beer' from the Cotswold Brewing Co. Tom's wine list is short but highly selective.

Head chef Will's incredible passion and enthusiasm for food has already put the Horse & Groom firmly on the culinary map. With a host of local suppliers and the pub's own veg patch, Will and his team have the benefit of perfect produce with which to work their culinary magic. The blackboard menu allows complete flexibility and changes regularly.

There are five individually styled en-suite bedrooms, available on a bed & breakfast or an all-inclusive leisure break basis. The Deluxe Room tops the bill with a king size bed and incredible views over the village whilst the Garden Room has French doors opening onto the landscaped garden.

---

regular intervals during the day. Other attractions in the park include a gift shop, tearoom and garden centre.

A mile east of town on the A44 stands the Four Shires Stone marking the original spot where the counties of Gloucestershire, Oxfordshire, Warwickshire and Worcestershire met.

BLOCKLEY
7 miles N of Stow off the A44/A429

⚘ Mill Dene Garden

This pretty village was once a very busy place. Silk-spinning was the main industry and six mills created the main source of employment until the 1880s. As far back as the Domesday Book water mills were recorded here, and the village also once boasted an iron foundry and factories making soap, collars and pianos. The mills have now been turned into private residences and Blockley is a quieter place.

One of the chief attractions for visitors is **Mill Dene Garden**, set around a mill in a steep-sided valley. The garden has hidden

Mill Dene Garden, Blockley

🏛 historic building 🏛 museum and heritage 🏚 historic site ⚘ scenic attraction 🌱 flora and fauna

paths winding up from the mill pool, and at the top there are lovely views over the Cotswolds. Also featured are a grotto, a potager, a trompe l'oeil and dye plants.

CHIPPING CAMPDEN
10 miles N of Stow on the B4081

🏛 Market Hall 🖌 Cotswold Olimpicks

🎨 Old Silk Mill 🎨 Court Barn

The Jewel of the Cotswolds, full of beautifully restored buildings in golden Cotswold stone. It was a regional capital of the wool trade between the 13th and 16th centuries, and many of the fine buildings date from that period of prosperity. In the centre of town is the Jacobean **Market Hall**, built in 1627 and one of many buildings financed by the wealthy fabric merchant and financier Sir

Baptist Hicks. He also endowed a group of almshouses and built Old Campden House, at the time the largest residence in the town; it was burnt down by Royalists to prevent it falling into the hands of the enemy. All that survives are two gatehouses, the old stable block and the banqueting halls. The 15th-century Church of St James was built on a grand scale and contains several impressive monumental brasses, the most impressive being one of William Grevel measuring a mighty eight feet by four feet.

Chipping Campden has important links with the Arts and Crafts movement. CR Ashbee set up his Guild of Handicrafts here in 1902 with 150 workers imported from London's East End. His workshop in the **Old Silk Mill** in Sheep Street is now a small

---

THE DRESSER

1 Cambrook Court, High Street, Chipping Campden, Gloucestershire GL55 6AT
Tel: 01386 849109 e-mail: hangingsucess@aol.com

Located in a pleasant courtyard entrance just off the high street lays **The Dresser**. The only ladies fashion shop in this historic Cotswold town opened in 2007 and is owned and run by two sisters, Tricia Lewis and Elaine Harley.

The Dresser sets itself apart from high street fashion stores and aims to create a timeless wardrobe from a top selection of British designers including Margaret Howell, Marion Foale and Mr& Mrs McLeod, with shoes from Emma Hope. There are also a beautiful range of jewellery and bags available to accessorize any outfit.

ORIENTAL BAGS

Cambrook Court, High Street, Chipping Campden, Gloucestershire GL55 6AT
Tel: 01386 840178
e-mail: orientalbags@tiscali.co.uk website: www.orientalbags.co.uk

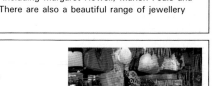

Oriental Bags - established in 2005 by Sarah Rabone, she relocated to Cambrook Court in Chipping Campden just off the High Street in December 2007. You will find the most unique collection of handbags limited to two per style-colour and prices range from £15.00 - £200. The bags are sourced ethically from 9 different countries and there is a bag for every women for any occasion.You will find delightful accessories from silk scarves to purses, parasols and pashminas.

🎬 stories and anecdotes 🎨 famous people 🎨 art and craft 🖌 entertainment and sport 🚶 walks

THE GUILD, CHIPPING CAMPDEN

The Old Silk Mill, Sheep Street,
Chipping Campden, Gloucestershire GL55 6DS

THE GALLERY @ THE GUILD

Tel. 07870 417144 website: www.thegalleryattheguild.co.uk

Attracted by the history of the building and Campden's
significant reputation in the Arts & Crafts movement, a
new cooperative of artists and artisans moved into the site of the Guild of Handicraft workshops
in 2005. **The Gallery @ The Guild** now draws on the work of over twenty local members who
present a diverse programme of exhibitions throughout the year. The members include fine
artists, ceramicists, jewellery designers, photographers, furniture makers, textile artists and
sculptors who take turns at stewarding the exhibitions and are
always happy to talk to visitors about the work on sale. For
information about exhibitions and to view a selection of each
member's work please visit our website.

SUSAN MEGSON GLASS

Susan Megson has recently relocated from Stow on the Wold to join
Campden's rich arts and crafts heritage. Susan represents British and
International glass blowers showcasing unique hand-blown glass art
pieces crafted by renowned artists within The Gallery @ The Guild.
Recent exhibitors include Ian Bamforth, Vic Bamforth, Yves Lohe and
Graham Muir.

CAROLINE RICHARDSON JEWELLERY

Tel.01386 841167 website: www.carolinejewellery.co.uk

Caroline is quickly establishing a reputation for creating desirable
contemporary jewellery. Her award winning work has a simple
understated elegance and is entirely bespoke. Items are available to
purchase and Caroline also designs and makes jewellery to
commission.

HART GOLD AND SILVERSMITHS (EST. 1888)

Tel. 01386 841100 website: www.hartsilversmiths.co.uk

This team of master craftsmen specialise in the best traditions of
handmade silver designing and making a wide range of domestic, civic and
ecclesiastical silverware. The workshop is the last operating remnant of C.
R. Ashbee's Guild of Handicraft. For more information please visit
www.hartsilversmiths.co.uk.

NEW ENGLAND COFFEE HOUSE

Tel. 01386 849251

Roasting its own beans and creating its own delicious blends, **New
England Coffee House** is fast becoming one of Campden's most
popular haunts. New England Coffee House also has a juice bar and
serves delicious organic ice cream and locally sourced paninis.
Come and join us for the best coffee in The Cotswolds! Open 7 days
a week 9am to 5pm.

HOLLY HOUSE B&B

Ebrington, Chipping Campden, Gloucestershire GL55 6NL
Tel: 01386 593213
e-mail: hutsbybandb@aol.com
website: www.hollyhousebandb.co.uk

Holly House B&B is quietly situated in the centre of the picturesque Cotswold village of Ebrington, with its quaint thatched cottages and the Norman church of St. Eadburgha. It is ideally situated for touring Shakespeare's Stratford-upon-Avon 12 miles away and the Cotswolds. Bedrooms are located in converted outbuildings and are all set around the attractive flower filled courtyard, each with its own private entrance. Breakfast is taken in the Garden Room, which forms part of the courtyard and provides an ideal place to plan the day ahead.

museum. In 1990 a group of local people formed the Guild of Handicraft Trust and in 1998 it was offered the chance to take over **Court Barn** and to turn it into a museum of local craftsmanship and design from the Arts and Crafts Movement onward. The centre opened in the summer of 2007.

Dover's Hill, a natural amphitheatre above the town, is the scene of the **Cotswold Olimpicks**, founded in the 17th century by Captain Robert Dover who lived at Stanway House. The Games followed the traditions of ancient Greece and added some more down-to-earth activities such as shin-kicking and bare-knuckle boxing. The lawlessness and hooliganism that accompanied the games led to their being closed down in 1852, but they were revived in a modern form in 1951 and are still a popular annual attraction on the Friday following the Spring Bank Holiday.

BROADWAY
10 miles NW of Stow on the A44

🍴 Broadway Tower 🌱 Snowshill Manor Garden

Just over the border into Worcestershire, where the Cotswolds join the Vale of Evesham, Broadway is one of the glories of the Cotswolds, a showpiece village with an abundance of scenic and historic

attractions. The renowned Lygon Arms entertained both King Charles and Oliver Cromwell, and **Broadway Tower** at the top of Fish Hill affords spectacular views over the Severn Vale.

A couple of miles southwest of Broadway, **Snowshill Manor Garden** (National Trust) is an Arts and Crafts garden designed to complement a handsome Cotswold manor house. Laid out by Charles Paget Wade as a series of outdoor rooms with terraces and ponds, the garden is now run on organic principles.

HIDCOTE BARTRIM
3 miles NE of Chipping Campden off the B4632

🌱 Hidcote Manor Garden

Hidcote Manor Garden is one of the most famous in the country, a masterpiece created in the first years of the 20th century by the eminent horticulturist Major Lawrence Johnston. A series of small gardens, each with a different character and appeal, Hidcote is renowned for its rare shrubs and trees, herbaceous borders and unusual plant species from all parts of the globe. Visitors can refresh themselves in the tea bar or licensed restaurant.

🎬 stories and anecdotes 🐦 famous people 🎨 art and craft 🎭 entertainment and sport 🚶 walks

SHAW FINE FOODS

Moore Road, Bourton-on-the-Water,
Gloucestershire, GL54 2AZ
Tel: 01451 820202
e-mail: tom_shawfinefoods@btconnect.com

A truly dynamite outfit, **Shaw Fine Foods** are purveyors of fine foodie ingredients from all over the UK. It is the perfect place to pick up a mouth-watering array of meats, cheeses, olives, homemade pies and other deli must-haves. Not to mention its extensive range of fine wines and local beers. The chic al fresco dining area is a convivial spot to enjoy a drink and a freshly prepared baguette, sandwich or salad with great filings at extremely affordable prices.

THE WATER GALLERY

Riverside, Bourton-on-the-Water, Cheltenham GL54 2DP
Tel: 01451 822255
e-mail: info@thewatergallery.co.uk
website: www.thewatergallery.co.uk

"Bourton-on-the-Water has been described as the 'Little Venice' of the Cotswolds and one of the most popular tourist spots in the region it is an entirely appropriate setting for **The Water Gallery**. The premises are as attractive as any in this lovely spot and Phil Moss has put every inch of space to the best possible use for displaying a wide collection of paintings, reproduction 18th-century maps, ceramics, glass, collectable items and a great range of small and inexpensive gifts. If you can't pay a visit to the store then log on to their website and peruse all these truly wonderful items that are also available to purchase online.

aviaries of parrots, falcons, pheasants, hornbills, toucans, touracos and many others, and tropical, temperate and desert houses are home to the more delicate species. Open all year, Birdland has a café and facilities for children, including a play area, pets' corner and penguin feeding time.

Cotswold Farm Park is the home of rare breed conservation with more than 50 breeding flocks and herds of farm animals. Voted Farm Park of the Year 2003, it is both interactive and educational, providing the opportunity to see unusual species of farm animals. Rabbit handling, bottle feeding of lambs and calves, and an adventure playground makes it ideal for children.

NORTHLEACH
10 miles S of Stow on the A429

🏛 Church of St Peter & St Paul

🏛 Chedworth Roman Villa

🏛 Keith Harding's World of Mechanical Music

A traditional market town with some truly magnificent buildings. It was once a major wool-trading centre that rivalled Cirencester in importance and as a consequence, possesses what now seems a disproportionately large church. The **Church of St Peter and St Paul**, known as the Cathedral of the Cotswolds, is a fine example of Cotswold Perpendicular, built in the 15th century with pinnacled buttresses, high windows and a massive square castellated tower. Treasures inside include an ornately carved font and some rare monumental brasses of which rubbings can be made (permits obtainable from the Post Office).

The town's most popular attraction is **Keith Harding's World of Mechanical Music**, which occupies a handsome period house in the main street. Keith's love of mechanical music goes back some 40 years and he has accumulated the finest collection of automata, both antique and modern, to be found anywhere. The exhibits range from a tiny singing bird concealed in a snuff box, to a mighty Welte Steinway reproducing piano of 1907. The instruments are introduced and played by the guides in the form of a live musical entertainment show and the tours include demonstrations of restored barrel organs, barrel pianos, musical boxes, polyphons, gramophones and antique clocks. Many of the clocks, musical boxes and automata on show are for sale.

Close to the pretty village of **Chedworth**, a couple of miles west of Northleach, is what must be the region's oldest stately home, the National Trust's **Chedworth Roman Villa** (see panel below), a large, well-preserved Romano-British villa discovered by chance in 1864 and subsequently excavated to reveal more than 30 rooms and buildings, including a bath house and hypocaust. Some wonderful mosaics are on display, one depicting the four seasons, another showing nymphs and satyrs. The villa lies in a beautiful wooded combe overlooking the valley of the Colne. A natural

Chedworth Roman Villa

Yanworth, nr Cheltenham, Gloucestershire GL54 3LJ
Telephone: 01242 890256
website: www.nationaltrust.org.uk

Chedworth Roman Villa is one of the best exposed Romano-British villa sites in Britain. It was discovered and excavated in 1864, and has been on display to the public since that time. The villa came to the National Trust in 1924. The site lies in a beautiful wooded combe overlooking the valley of the river Coln. A natural spring rises at the head of the combe, and the presence of a source of pure fresh water was probably the main reason why the villa was built in this spot.

The house itself was created about 120 AD, starting life as three separate buildings. Over the course of nearly three centuries, the villa evolved into the grand 4th century mansion whose ruins can be seen today. It was built along three sides of a rectangle, the two long wings running east to west. In its heyday there were two bath-houses, two large dining rooms, two kitchens, a small temple or shrine around the spring-head, a latrine and numerous other features, including many beautiful mosaics. It must have been a very grand house indeed.

Today you can see the ruins of the 1700 year old "stately home", and imagine yourself back in the 4th century. As you look at the surviving mosaics, the hypocausts (Roman underfloor central heating), bath-houses, latrine, water-shrine, and of course the many objects in the site museum, you get a flavour of life when Britain was part of the Roman Empire.

Cirencester

🏛 Corinium Museum   🏛 Church of St John Baptist

🍺 Brewery Arts House   🏊 Open Air Swimming Pool

The Capital of the Cotswolds, a lively market town with a long and fascinating history. As Corinium Dobonnorum it was the second largest Roman town in Britain (Londinium was the largest). Few signs remain of the Roman occupation, but the award-winning **Corinium Museum** features one of the finest collections of antiquities from Roman Britain, and reconstructions of a Roman dining room and garden give a fascinating and instructive insight into life in Cirencester of almost 2,000 years ago.

The main legacy of the town's medieval wealth is the magnificent **Church of St John Baptist**, perhaps the grandest of all the Cotswold wool churches, its 120ft tower dominating the town. Its greatest treasure is the Anne Boleyn Cup, a silver and gilt cup made for Henry VIII's second wife in 1535, the year before she was executed for adultery. Her personal insignia - a rose tree and a falcon holding a sceptre - is on the lid of the cup, which was given to the church by Richard Master, physician to Queen Elizabeth I. The church has a unique three-storey porch, which was used as the Town Hall until 1897.

Cirencester today has a thriving crafts scene, with workshops in the **Brewery Arts and Craft Centre**, a converted Victorian brewery that re-opened in 2008 after a £2.7 million refurbishment. The 12 resident craftworkers include a basket maker, jeweller, textile weaver, ceramicist and stained glass artist. A shop in the centre sells the best in British work, and there are galleries, a coffee

---

CARRIAGES AT THREE LTD

3 The Wool Market, Cirencester,
Gloucestershire GL7 2PR
Tel: 01285 651760
e-mail: sales@carriagesatthree.co.uk
website: www.carriagesatthree.co.uk

In a courtyard setting, opposite The Polly Tearooms and close to the town centre and market square, with good parking at nearby Waterloo carpark, **Carriages at Three** specializes in women's evening wear. One of the leading fashion retailers in the Cotswolds, the shop has two spectacular window displays that provide a beguiling sample of the vast choice within. More than 1,000 ball gowns, cocktail dresses, prom dresses, cruise wear, wedding wear and formal evening wear come in a stunning variety, from a simple classic black dress to a head turning one-off creation guaranteeing a grand and glamorous entrance.

Designers featured include Consortium, Bernshaw, Mori Lee, Crystal Breeze, John Charles, Joseph Ribkoff and Attire. Owners Suzi and Colin Black are always introducing ranges from new and up and coming labels such as Jaego, Tortoise and Arruba. Dresses come in a wide range of sizes, from 6 - 30 and there is an in house bespoke alteration service.

A full range of accessories, from shoes, bags and shawls to costume jewellery, is available to complete the ensemble. The staff at this unique place are among the best in the business and a chat with the customer will enable them to make sound suggestions on what will be most suitable for each individual. Carriages at Three is a place for the special occasion, and one that fully deserves the boast that this is 'where the best evenings begin'.

🏛 historic building   🏛 museum and heritage   🏚 historic site   🏞 scenic attraction   🌱 flora and fauna

WETPAINT GALLERY

The Old Chapel, 14 London Road, Cirencester,
Gloucestershire GL7 1AE
Tel: 01285 644990   Fax 01285 644992
email: cah@contemporary-art-holdings.co.uk
website: www.wetpaintgallery.co.uk

Established in 2002, Wetpaint Gallery is fast becoming one of the leading galleries in the area. Specialising in contemporary art and Modern Masters, Wetpaint Gallery promotes a range of established and emerging artists from across the country. Prints, paintings and ceramics are beautifully displayed in an old converted chapel where the atmosphere is friendly and

relaxed. The gallery operates a regular programme of exhibitions including artists such as Sir Terry Frost, David Hockney, John Piper, Graham Sutherland, Sir Peter Blake and Mary Fedden.

The gallery also operates a bespoke framing service using conservation materials and a free home consultancy service.

Wetpaint Gallery is a division of Contemporary Art Holdings Limited, an art consultancy with 18 years experience in the corporate sector, specialising in commercial environments such as conference centres, hotels and exhibition spaces. Contemporary Art Holdings also operates an_art rental service offering clients greater flexibility and creativity in their choice of artwork. For further information please visit www.contemporary-art-holdings.co.uk.

'Bowstring Bridge 2' by Andrea Murphy

house, arts and crafts classes and workshops.

Cirencester Open Air Swimming Pool, next to the park, was built in 1869 and is one of the oldest in the country. Both the main pool and the paddling pool use water from a private well. Other sites of interest include St Thomas' Hospital – 15th-century almshouses for destitute weavers – the Barracks of 1857, and a Yew Hedge that was planted in 1720. It now stands 40 feet high and is reputed to be the loftiest in Europe. It can be found in Cirencester Park, a 3,000-acre expanse, which was designed by the poet Alexander Pope.

Cirencester certainly lives up to its reputation as a market town with street markets on Monday and Friday; a craft market in the Corn Hall on Saturdays, and regular antiques markets on Fridays.

Spital Gate, Cirencester

[i] stories and anecdotes famous people art and craft entertainment and sport walks

Lechlade is the highest navigable point on the Thames and head of the Thames towpath walk. In and around the town visitors can hire rowing boats, go sailing or wind-surfing, and enjoy lake and river fishing.

A statue of Old Father Thames, originally created for the Great Exhibition of 1851,

---

THE CROWN INN

High Street, Lechlade, Gloucestershire GL7 3AE
Tel: 01367 252198
website: www.crownlechlade.co.uk

The Crown Inn is an original public house with a great atmosphere, friendly staff and clientele with excellent beers, wines and ciders. It has an attractive beer garden which compliments this idyllic Cotswold retreat, regular entertainment and a pool room and is ideally placed in the centre of Lechlade, a pretty market town on the River Thames and on the edge of the Cotswolds. Spend a lazy weekend break at the Crown Inn and enjoy the new en-suite bed and breakfast accommodation. Three recently built rooms enjoy a peaceful spot away from the pub, with views of the garden. A full English or Continental breakfast is included.

COTSWOLD WORKSHOP

High Street, Lechlade, Gloucestershire GL7 3AE
Tel: 01367 250115
e-mail: cotswoldworkshop@btconnect.com
website: www.cotswoldworkshop.co.uk

Here is a Mecca for those of us who love to furnish our homes with solid oak & pine furniture and quality accessories.

The freestanding furniture has been designed to be a perfect match for those with a taste for the traditional. If you appreciate elegance and attention to detail, then the **Cotswold Workshop** can offer an unrivalled choice from their range of solid oak and pine furniture for every room of the home.

The real beauty of this simple, timeless yet modern furniture is that it provides you with a stylish room that will never date. All furniture is displayed over two floors and it feels as though you are entering someone's home, mainly because manager Emma adds her feminine touch to the displays with lamps and cushions all beautifully arranged.

It doesn't end with furniture, at the Cotswold Workshop you can encounter wooden toys and gifts for children; soft furnishings; gifts for the home; plants & garden furniture and gifts for gardeners. Rangemaster cookers and appliances, and wood, laminate and tile flooring can also be supplied and installed - you never know what gems you might stumble upon. The showroom in Lechlade is open 10am-4pm, seven days a week.

---

overlooks St John's Lock, where barges loaded with building stone bound for Oxford and London have given way to pleasure craft. This bustling market town, surrounded by green meadows, boasts a fine 15th-century church with a slender spire and a structure that has remained unaltered since the early 1500s. In its lovely churchyard, in 1815, the poet Shelley was inspired to write his *Stanzas in a Summer Evening Churchyard*. The verses are inscribed on a stone at the churchyard entrance.

Another interesting building is the **Halfpenny Bridge**, built in 1792, which crosses the Thames in the town centre and has a tollhouse at its eastern end. The toll was last charged for pedestrians in 1839, and for cattle in 1885.

INGLESHAM
1 mile S of Lechlade off the A361

🏛 Church of St John the Baptist

The splendidly unspoilt **Church of St John the Baptist** dates mainly from the 13th century, with some notable later additions. The chief features are important wall paintings, 15th-century screens, 17th- and 18th-century pulpit and box pews and, perhaps its greatest treasure, a Saxon carving of the Virgin and Child blessed by the Hand of God. This is one of many churches in the care of the Churches Conservation Trust, formerly known as the Redundant Churches Fund. The trust was established to preserve churches, which though no longer needed for regular worship, are of historic or architectural importance.

turn of the 19th/20th centuries and revealed some remarkable treasures, most of which are now on display at Reading Museum. The dig also revealed the most complete plan of any Roman town in the country but, rather oddly, the site was 're-buried' and now only the 1.5 mile city wall is visible – the best-preserved Roman town wall in Britain. Also impressive is the recently restored 1st-century amphitheatre which lay just beyond the town walls.

Pamber Forest

Tucked in next to part of the Roman wall is the pretty **Church of St Mary**, which dates from the 1100s. It boasts a superb 16th-century screen with a frieze of angels and some unusual bench-ends from 1909 executed in Art Nouveau style.

PAMBER HEATH

7 miles N of Basingstoke, on minor road off the A340

🏛 Priory Church

There are three Pambers set in the countryside along the A340. At Pamber End stand the picturesque ruins of a once-magnificent 12th/13th-century **Priory Church**, idyllically sited in sylvan surroundings. Set apart from the village, they invite repose and meditation. Pamber Green, as you might expect, is a leafy enclave; but for anyone in search of a good country pub, the Pamber to make for is Pamber Heath. Lots of pubs have a few pots scattered around, but the collection at The Pelican in Pamber Heath is something else. There are hundreds of them hanging from the ceiling beams, in every imaginable shape and colour, some pewter and some ceramic.

HARTLEY WINTNEY

9 miles NE of Basingstoke, on the A30

🏛 West Green House 🏛 Old Church

🌿 Mildmay Oaks

Riding through Hartley Wintney in 1821, William Cobbett, the author of *Rural Rides* and a conservationist long before anyone had thought of such a creature, was delighted to see young oaks being planted on the large village green. They were the gift of Hartley Wintney's Lady of the Manor, Lady Mildmay, and were originally intended to provide timber for shipbuilding. Fortunately, by the time they matured they were no longer needed for that purpose and today the **Mildmay Oaks** provide the village centre with a uniquely beautiful setting of majestic oak trees.

Anyone with an interest in horticulture should also visit the magnificent gardens of **West Green House**, about a mile to the west of Hartley Wintney. Owned by the National Trust, this pretty early 18th-century house is surrounded by lovely gardens planted with a dazzling variety of trees, shrubs and plants. One of its interesting features is a stone column surmounted by an elaborate finial, which was erected in 1976. It bears a Latin inscription that declares that a large sum of money was needed to put the column in place, money "which would otherwise have fallen, sooner or later, into the hands of the Inland Revenue".

While you are in Hartley Wintney, a visit to the **Old Church**, south of the village, is well worth while. Parts of the building date back to medieval times, but the fascination of old St Mary's lies in the fact that, after being completely renovated in 1834, it has remained almost totally unaltered ever since. High-sided box pews line the main aisle, there are elegant galleries for choir and congregation spanning the nave and both transepts, and colourful funeral hatchments add to St Mary's time-warp atmosphere.

EVERSLEY
10 miles NE of Basingstoke, on the A327

🏛 Stratfield Saye House

🏕 Wellington Country Park

Charles Kingsley, author of such immensely popular Victorian novels as *The Water Babies* and *Westward Ho!*, was Rector of the village for 33 years from 1842 until his death in 1875, and is buried in the churchyard here. The gates of the village school, erected in 1951 for the Festival of Britain, include a figure of a boy chimney-sweep, the main character of *The Water Babies*. Kingsley was an attractive character with a burning passion for social justice, but modern readers don't seem to share the Victorian enthusiasm for his works. It's a sad fate for a prolific man of letters, although perhaps not quite so dispiriting as that met by one of Kingsley's predecessors as preacher at Eversley. He was hanged as a highwayman.

About four miles west of Eversley, **Stratfield Saye House** was just one of many

rewards a grateful nation showered on the Duke of Wellington after his decisive defeat of Napoleon at Waterloo. The Duke himself doesn't seem to have been reciprocally grateful: only lack of funds frustrated his plans to demolish the gracious 17th-century house and replace it with an even more impressive mansion, which he intended to call Waterloo Palace. Quite modest in scale, Stratfield Saye fascinates visitors with its collection of the Duke's own furniture and personal items such as his spectacles, handkerchiefs and carpet slippers. More questionable are the priceless books in the library, many of them looted from Napoleon's own bibliotheque. A good number of the fine Spanish and Portuguese paintings on display share an equally dubious provenance, 'relieved' during the Duke's campaign in those countries as 'spoils of

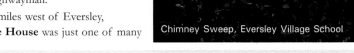

Chimney Sweep, Eversley Village School

🎬 stories and anecdotes 🦜 famous people 🎨 art and craft 🎭 entertainment and sport 🏕 walks

old girl in the town who was hacked into pieces by her assassin. With macabre humour, sailors used the same phrase to describe the recently-introduced tinned mutton for which they had a certain mistrust. Over the years, the saying became accepted as a contemptuous description for anything considered valueless: a poor way to remember an innocent girl.

There's a different sort of monument in Amery Street, a narrow lane leading off the market place. On a small brick house is a plaque commemorating the Elizabethan poet Edmund Spenser, who came to Alton around 1590 to enjoy its "sweet delicate air".

Well worth a visit while you are in Alton is the **Allen Gallery** in Church Street, home to an outstanding collection of English, Continental and Far Eastern pottery, porcelain and tiles. Housed in a group of attractive 16th- and 18th-century buildings, the gallery's other attractions include the unique Elizabethan Tichborne Spoons, delightful watercolours and oil paintings by local artist William Herbert Allen, and a comfortable coffee lounge. During the summer months, the charming walled garden at the rear of the gallery provides a lovely setting for sculpture exhibitions. More sculpture can be seen if you follow the **Alton Sculpture Trail**, although the word 'sculpture' is broadly defined to include a rare Edward VIII postbox and an early 19th-century mile plate.

Across the road from the Allen Gallery, the **Curtis Museum** concentrates on exploring 100 million years of local history with displays devoted to the "shocking tale of Sweet Fanny

---

LANTERN FOODS

23 Normandy Street, Alton, Hampshire, GU34 1DD
Tel: 01420 544522
e-mail: sales@lanternfoods.co.uk
website: www.lanternfoods.co.uk

Lantern Foods is situated in the appealing market town of Alton, surrounded by some of Hampshire's loveliest countryside. The shop is easily found adjacent to the Magistrates' Court and two minutes from both Rogers Court and Victoria Road car parks. John and Mary-Anne Barber began this enterprise after realising the lack of natural food outlets in the area. Determined to improve the situation, they aspire to support FairTrade stock organic and/or local products, while being environmentally sensitive in their operation.

A 'much loved' community shop, Lantern Foods offers an extensive selection of general groceries; fruit and vegetables many grown in county by Sunnyfields; dietary food products; eco-friendly household and toiletry products; as well as natural remedies and supplements. Many of the food items satisfy the needs of the 'free from' market, including 'dairy free', 'lactose free' and vegan. The ambience is relaxed; you can enjoy shopping in a light, clean and child-friendly setting.

The website provides excellent insight into the enthusiasm of the owners: it is extremely informative, providing the visitor with great recipe ideas, such as, Quinoa tabbouleh and' gluten free' batter mix for delicious fish and chips!

Open six days a week 9.30am – 5.30pm, closing at 4.30pm on Mondays and Saturdays.

🏛 historic building 🏛 museum and heritage 🏛 historic site 🝉 scenic attraction 🌱 flora and fauna

HEALEY AND JAMES

Hartley Park Farm, Selborne Road, Alton, Hampshire GU34 3HS
Tel: 01420 511761 Mobile: 07990 666585

Healey and James occupies an oak-framed barn on the Selborne Lavender Farm, a conspicuous landmark on the Alton to Selborne road. Rachel Healey is an established painter and works on the premises. The shop trades exclusively in the best available textiles, jewellery, accessories and other artefacts - old and new - from the Indian subcontinent.

Their shop is well known for its modern silk scarves and shawls - unsurpassed in the South of England for quality, range and value. However, all visitors to the barn are struck by the astonishingly vibrant and colourful displays of traditional hand-woven and embroidered textiles from Gujarat, Rajasthan, the Punjab and the Himalayas. Most of these items are no longer being made and are now seldom available in the subcontinent itself; they have been collected over many years. Healey and James are dedicated to promoting the appreciation of them as works of art and their use as single decorative pieces or as furnishings for the contemporary home.

Adams", other local celebrities such as Jane Austen, Lord Baden Powell, Montgomery of Alamein; and a colourful Gallery of Childhood with exhibits thoughtfully displayed in miniature cases at a suitable height for children.

On the western edge of the town lies The Butts, a pleasant open area of grassland that was once used for archery practice. Today, it is the setting for events such as the annual Victorian Cricket Match.

A good time to visit the town is mid-July when the Alton Show takes place. Established in 1840, this is one of southern England's most important agricultural gatherings with a wide range of events featuring such attractions as heavy horses, llamas, beagles, gun dogs and birds of prey.

Around Alton

SELBORNE
4 miles SE of Alton on the B3006

🐦 The Wakes and Oates Museum

🏛 Church of St Mary 🎨 Selborne Pottery

Like the neighbouring village of Chawton, Selborne also produced a great literary figure. **The Wakes** was the home of Gilbert White, a humble curate of the parish from 1784 until his death in 1793. He spent his spare hours meticulously recording observations on the weather, wildlife and geology of the area. A percipient publisher to whom Gilbert submitted his notes recognised the appeal of his humdrum, day-to-day accounts of life in what was then a remote corner of England. *The Natural History and Antiquities of Selborne* was

DURLEIGHMARSH FARM SHOP

Rogate Road, Durleighmarsh, nr Petersfield,
Hampshire, GU31 5AX
Tel: 01730 821626

Durleighmarsh Farm has a good selection of pick-your-own and ready-picked fruit and vegetables. This scenic pick-your-own site and farm shop is the best way to get the freshest and most delicious foods from field to fork. The only food miles are the ones that you take home with you!

Durleighmarsh Farm Shop offers a one-stop shop, if the produce hasn't been hand picked from the farm then it is locally sourced, such as Hill Farm apple juice, RotherValley organic meat and Weald Smokery smoked fish, cheese and plenty of cakes and pies baked by local ladies, as well as their chutneys and jams. The light fresh raspberry jam sharpened with a touch of lemon juice is well worth seeking out.

of the town. Set in an ancient walled plot, the garden has been planted in a style and with plants that would have been familiar to the distinguished 17th-century botanist, John Goodyer, who lived in Petersfield.

Other attractions include the Dragon Gallery, providing a showcase for contemporary artists; and the Petersfield Museum, housed in the former Courthouse.

Just a short walk from the town centre is **Petersfield Heath**, an extensive recreational area with a cricket ground and a pond for boating and fishing. The town's annual Taro Fair is held here in October and the heath is also notable as the site of one of the most important groups of Bronze Age barrows, or burial mounds, in the country.

Around Petersfield

STEEP
1 mile N of Petersfield, off the A3

Appropriately, the village is reached by way of a steep hill. The village is famous as the home of the writer and nature poet Edward Thomas who moved here with his family in 1907. It was while living at 2 Yew Tree Cottages that

he wrote most of his poems. In 1909 he and his wife Helen moved to the Red House (private) where his daughter Myfanwy was born in 1913. Many years later, in 1985, she unveiled a plaque on the house. Her former home featured in two of her father's poems, *The New House* and *Wind and Mist*. Thomas was killed in action during the First World War. His death is commemorated by two engraved lancet windows installed in 1978 in All Saints Church, and by a memorial stone on Shoulder of Mutton Hill above the village.

It was at Steep in 1898 that the educational pioneer John Badley established Bedales, the first boarding school for both sexes in the country. His "preposterous experiment" proved highly successful. Members of staff and pupils at Bedales call each other by their first names and there is no formal school uniform. There is an absence of petty rules and, says the school brochure, "because the pupils are listened to, they learn to listen to each other".

BURITON
2 miles S of Petersfield, on minor road off the A3

🏛 Uppark

An old church surrounded by trees and

🏛 historic building 🏛 museum and heritage 🏛 historic site 🌳 scenic attraction 🌿 flora and fauna

overlooking a tree-lined duck pond is flanked by an appealing early 18th-century Manor House (private) built by the father of Edward Gibbon, the celebrated historian. The younger Gibbon wrote much of his magnum opus *Decline and Fall of the Roman Empire* in his study here. He was critical of the house's position "at the end of the village and the bottom of the hill", but was highly appreciative of the view over the Downs: "the long hanging woods in sight of the house could not perhaps have been improved by art or expense".

Buriton Village

About five miles southeast of Buriton, **Uppark** (National Trust), is a handsome Wren-style mansion built around 1690 and most notable for its interior. Uppark was completely redecorated and refurnished in the 1750s by the Fetherstonhaugh family and that work has remained almost entirely unchanged – not only the furniture but even some of the fabrics and wallpapers remain in excellent condition. The servants' rooms are as they were in 1874 when the mother of HG Wells was housekeeper here – the writer's recollections of life at Uppark with his mother are fondly recorded in his autobiography.

CHALTON
5 miles S of Petersfield off the A3

🏛 Butser Ancient Farm

Situated on a slope of chalk down, Chalton is home to **Butser Ancient Farm,** a reconstruction of an Iron Age farm that has received worldwide acclaim for its research

methodology and results. There's a magnificent great roundhouse, prehistoric and Roman crops are grown, ancient breeds of cattle roam the hillside, and metal is worked according to ancient techniques. The latest project here is the construction of a replica Roman villa, complete with hypocaust, using the same methods as the Romans. A wonderful living laboratory, the farm is open one weekend each month when there are themed events. Courses providing hands-on experience in ancient crafts and archaeological techniques are available. All necessary tools are provided and course prices include materials.

HAMBLEDON
8 miles SW of Petersfield, off the B2150

A village of red brick Georgian houses and well-known for its vineyard, Hambledon is most famous for its cricketing connections (see walk on page 182). It was at the

Hambledon

Distance: *6.8 miles (11.0 kilometres)*
Typical time: *150 mins*
Height gain: *189 metres*
Map: *Explorer 119*
Walk: *www.walkingworld.com ID:2139*
Contributor: *Sylvia Saunders*

ACCESS INFORMATION:

Hambledon is to be found nine miles southwest of Petersfield and 10 miles north of Portsmouth. From the Petersfield to Portsmouth A3(T)/A3M take the turn off signposted to Clanfield, Chalton and Hambledon. Hambledon is well signposted from here, but be careful not to miss the turn off to the right when leaving Clanfield. Park in the main road near to The Vine. There is a No 45 bus service from Portsmouth city centre to Hambledon run by First. Check out their website www.firstgroup.com for more information.

DESCRIPTION:

This circular walk is a must for those who are interested in cricket, lovers of good food and beer in idyllic country pubs, or those who just like a cracking good walk in the beautiful, gentle Hampshire countryside. The walk starts from The Vine in Hambledon. The route takes you along Windmill Down with far-reaching views over Hampshire countryside and then past the current cricket ground at Ridge-Meadow. Walking through a mixture of woodland and fields you arrive at The Bat and Ball Inn, which is known as the first headquarters of English cricket. The original Hambledon cricket ground is on Broadhalfpenny Down and opposite the pub.

The return route takes you along well defined tracks and through farmland with some super views as far as the Isle of Wight on a clear day. There is a steep descent down a quiet lane back to Hambledon's West Street and The Vine. Dog owners may find it useful to know that my dog, a slim, fit Labrador who cannot jump, managed to get through all the stiles and fences.

FEATURES:

Hills or Fells, Pub, Wildlife, Birds, Flowers, Great Views, Butterflies, Public Transport, Restaurant, Teashop, Woodland.

WALK DIRECTIONS:

1 | With The Vine on your left-hand side, walk along West Street until you reach a lane on the left marked Unsuitable for HGVs. Turn left and walk up this lane. When the lane turns into a driveway, walk straight on and go over the stile into the field.

2 | Walk straight ahead with the flint wall on your right-hand side. At the end of the wall you will find a metal kissing-gate. Pass through this gate and again walk with the wall on your right with a field fence on your left. This path brings you out at the churchyard. Walk straight ahead through the churchyard and you will shortly emerge out onto a lane. Turn left on this lane for a few metres and you will see the school entrance on your right hand side.

3 | Turn right here and walk through the school entrance. When you reach the end of the buildings you are met with a choice of two footpaths. Turn left here and walk uphill past the back of the school building where you will see the entrance to a field on your right. Fork right across the field along the footpath. At the field corner, walk straight across into the next field and continue uphill with the hedge on your right-hand side. Enjoy the panoramic view as you descend until you reach a lane.

4 | Turn right onto the lane. Ignore the left-hand turn to Chidden, shortly after which you will pass Ridge-Meadow, the current home of Hambledon cricket club where they have played since 1782. Carry on along the road until you reach the crossroads.

5 | Turn left here. After you have passed the big house on this corner (Park House) you will see a track marked with a fingerpost. Turn left onto this track. After a short distance you will see a metal gate ahead. Pass through the gap on the right-hand side of this gate and walk along the track on the right-hand side of the field. Follow the track as it leaves the field and enters woodland. You will arrive at a sign that says Wildlife Conservation Area, do not enter. Turn left here along the footpath and follow it into the field. Here you will see two footpaths, both crossing the field.

6 | Take the right-hand path and walk diagonally across the field to the hedge and footpath post. If the path is unclear, head for the gap in the trees and as you get nearer to it you will spot a yellow marker.

7 | Turn right here and walk along the field edge with the hedge on your left-hand side. Follow this route until you see a wooden post directing the footpath

into woodland. This post is about halfway between the previous post and the field corner. Turn left here into the woodland. Walk the narrow, winding path. There are a few animal routes going off it which may confuse you. If in doubt, take a route to the left rather than to the right. The woodland doesn't last for long - you soon emerge into a field. Turn right here walking along the field edge with the hedge/trees on your right hand side. Follow the footpath out to the road.

8 | Cross straight over to the metal gate opposite. There isn't a stile but you can open the gate by way of a chain on the right-hand side. Follow the field edge on the left-hand side to the stile ahead.

9 | Cross over the stile and turn right, walking with the fence on your right-hand side. Continue in the same direction crossing several stiles until you reach the road.

10 | Cross the stile and turn right along the road. You will soon arrive at The Bat and Ball Inn with the original Broadhalfpenny cricket ground opposite. Here you will see the monument marking the birthplace of cricket. Pass the pub and arrive at the crossroads.

11 | Turn right here along the road signposted to Hambledon, Fareham. Walk along the road until you see a road turning off to the right. Opposite this you will see a footpath and stile off to your left.

12 | Climb this stile and you will be met with a choice of two routes, neither of which is defined. Head for the stile that you can see up the hill and slightly to the right - at the end of the hedge line. Go over the stile and turn right along the track, but before you set off, pause to drink in the view. Continue along the track until you reach Scotland Cottage. Just past the cottage you will see a footpath off to the left. (The fingerpost here seems to get broken down quite frequently, so don't necessarily expect to see it. The footpath is between the large stone and the wooden pole. Don't be confused by the green arrow on the pole – this marks the metalled track that you are about to leave.)

13 | Turn left along this footpath and walk until you emerge out onto a track.

14 | Turn right along this track. In a short distance you will see a large tree ahead and a huge pile of manure! This manure heap has been here for years and I have every faith that it will have been renewed. Turn left here and you will soon arrive at a junction of tracks.

15 | Turn right here and continue walking until you reach a rather smelly pond and some farm buildings.

16 | Turn left here along the track just past the pond but before the buildings. When you reach the metal gate cross over the stile next to it. Follow the track up to another metal gate and stile, passing a barn on your left-hand side. Go over this stile and continue walking straight ahead with the trees on your right-hand side and you will arrive at another stile. Cross over and then follow the line of the telegraph poles until you reach another stile. Cross over this stile. Just follow the line of telegraph poles and you cannot go wrong. You will arrive at a stile. Go over this stile and cross straight over the track into the field.

17 | Again, follow the line of the telegraph poles across this field and you will arrive at a stile. Cross over this stile into the narrow field still following the telegraph poles. Ignore the footpath off to the left as the field narrows further. Continue along in the same direction, finally losing the telegraph poles, and you will arrive at a stile next to a metal gate.

18 | Cross this stile and walk straight ahead between the horseboxes. In a few metres you will arrive at a driveway. Turn left along this driveway and you will soon arrive at several metal gates. Turn right along the footpath between the two metal gates on your right. This will bring you out upon a private driveway next to a house. Walk down the driveway and you will see two roads off to your right.

19 | Take the second right turn along the road walking down Speltham Hill until you arrive at the junction with West and East Street.

20 | Turn left here and walk back to The Vine.

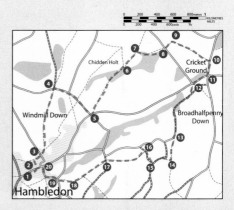

Hambledon Cricket Club that the rules of the game were first formulated in 1774. The club's finest hour came in 1777 when the team, led by the landlord of the Bat and Ball Inn, beat an All England team by an innings and 168 runs! A granite monument stands on Broadhalfpenny Down where the early games were played.

The village itself featured in the Domesday Book and, in the 13th century, was granted a licence to hold a market. About this time, the church was extensively rebuilt around the original Saxon church. Many of the village houses have their 16th-century origins concealed by the striking Georgian facades.

EAST MEON
5 miles W of Petersfield, on minor road off the A3 or A272

🏛 Tournai Font

Tucked away in the lovely valley of the River Meon and surrounded by high downs, East Meon has been described as "the most unspoilt of Hampshire villages and the nicest". As if that weren't enough, the village also boasts one of the finest and most venerable churches in the county. The central tower, with walls four feet thick, dates back to the 12th century and is a stunning example of Norman architecture at its best. Inside, the church's greatest treasure is its remarkable 12th-century **Tournai Font** of black marble, exquisitely carved with scenes depicting the Creation and the fall of Adam and Eve. Only seven of these wonderful fonts are known

to exist in England (four of them in Hampshire) and East Meon's is generally regarded as the most magnificent of them.

In the churchyard are buried Thomas Lord, founder of the cricket ground in London, and the mother of the spy Guy Burgess. Her son's ashes were sprinkled on her grave in a suitably clandestine night-time ceremony.

Just across the road is the 15th-century Courthouse, which also has walls four feet thick. It's a lovely medieval manor house where for generations the Bishops of Winchester, as Lords of the Manor, held their courts. It would have been a familiar sight to the "compleat angler" Izaac Walton, who spent many happy hours fishing in the River Meon nearby.

Northwest Hampshire

Some of Hampshire's grandest scenery lies in this part of the county as the North Downs roll westwards towards Salisbury Plain. There's just one sizeable town, Andover, and one major city, Winchester: the rest of the region is quite sparsely populated (for southern England) with scattered villages bearing evocative names such as Hurstbourne

East Meon Courthouse

Tarrant and Nether Wallop. Winchester is of course in a class of its own with its dazzling Cathedral, but there are many other attractions in this area, ranging in time from the Iron Age Danebury Hill Fort, through the Victorian extravaganza of Highclere Castle, to Stanley Spencer's extraordinary murals in the Sandham Memorial Chapel at Burghclere.

Andover

St Mary's Church   Museum

Heritage Trail   Museum of the Iron Age

Finkley Down Farm Park

Andover has expanded greatly since the 1960s when it was selected as a 'spillover' town to relieve the pressure on London's crowded population. But the core of this ancient town, which was already important in Saxon times, retains much of interest. One outstanding landmark is **St Mary's Church**, completely rebuilt in the 1840s at the expense of a former headmaster of Winchester College. The interior is said to have been modelled on Salisbury Cathedral, and if it doesn't quite match up to that sublime building, St Mary's is still well worth a visit.

Equally striking is the Guildhall of 1825, built in classical style, which stands alone in the Market Place where markets are still held every Tuesday and Saturday. Andover has also managed to retain half a dozen of the 16 coaching inns that serviced 18th-century travellers at a time when the fastest stagecoaches took a mere nine hours to travel here from London. As many as 50 coaches a day stopped at these inns to change horses and allow the passengers to take refreshments.

For a fascinating insight into the town's long history, do pay a visit to the **Andover Museum** in Church Close. There are actually two museums here, both of them housed in buildings that began life as elegant Georgian town houses in 1750 and were later extended to serve as Andover's Grammar School from the 1840s to 1925. The Andover Museum traces the story of the town from Saxon times to the present day, with a range of colourful exhibits that include a 19th-century Period Room. There's also a fascinating display evoking Victorian Andover and a workhouse

Finkley Down Farm Park

Andover, Hampshire SP11 6NF
Tel: enquiries/Bookings: 01264 324141
Tel: (24 Hour Information): 01264 352195
websitewww.finkleydownfarm.co.uk

Finkley Down Farm Park is a family run children's farm with all the character of a traditional farm but in a safe, friendly environment. It's an exciting day out that the whole family will love. Generations of children have enjoyed feeding the lambs and grooming the ponies during the activities, which take place throughout the day, or you can wander around and pet the animals at your leisure. A happy combination of education and fun, Finkley boasts a large adventure playground with a good old fashioned tree house and trampolines. A tea room serves a selection of snacks and drinks and the gift shop has a large array of toys and gifts.

stories and anecdotes   famous people   art and craft   entertainment and sport   walks

FAIRGROUND CRAFT

Weyhill, Andover, Hampshire SP11 0QN
Tel: 01264 773438
e-mail: info@fairgroundcraft.co.uk
website: www.fairgroundcraft.co.uk

Variety is the spice of life, and that is precisely what you find at the **Fairground Craft and Design Centre**. The eleven very different studios, workshops, the gallery and the splendid licensed café all mean there is a great deal going on to enthral and enjoy within this exhilarating and creative enclave.

- **The French Collection Gallery & Studio - Soraya French**
  Soraya is a professional artist, tutor and author. She works in all painting mediums. The studio is her main workspace where she also runs occasional workshops and has a selection of her paintings, prints and books for sale.

- **Busy Hands** - Pauline Foster's Busy Hands does just what the name says and keeps your hands artistically busy. Pauline is master of the art of papercraft, designing and making beautiful cards and other intricate work, which she sells, demonstrates and teaches in her studio.

- **Cove Contemporary Jewellery** - Marc Johnson handcrafts fine contemporary jewellery, stock designs, and re-modelling. He uses sourced or the customers own stones, creating bespoke one-off pieces.

- **Stained Glass Studio** - In Heather McNeilly's well established studio, as well as designing and creating larger pieces such as windows and door panels, Heather also makes a range of striking stained glass giftware, including mirrors and light catchers, her love of nature frequently being reflected in her work.

- **Plane Wood** - Robin Geard of Plane Wood is a highly skilled and qualified cabinet maker. Specialising in antique repair and restoration he also undertakes commissions and makes unique gift items.

- **Fair's Fayre** - Helen Carter has a passion for Fairtrade that gives overseas producers a fair wage, good working conditions and dignity. Helen's workshop, aptly named Fair's Fayre, offers an attractive diversity of selected and imported giftware.

- **Acorn Crafts** - Ron Caddy is a specialist penmaker and woodturner producing unique hand-crafted pens using woods from around the world and New Forest antler. Each being from natural and sustainable materials.

- **Rare Metal Design** - Maggie's work is informed both by craft tradition and contemporary design theory. Original and elegant, Maggie's jewellery can be bought direct from the workshop or online.

- **Parker's Handmade Cakes and Chocolates** - Superb handmade chocolates, chocolate wedding and celebration cakes, chocolate figures, fun chocolate and elegant chocolate all vie for your attention!

- **Metal Storm** - Marek Woznica has been crafting fine items of metalwork and jewellery since 1990. He hand carves his original designs in pewter, producing a range of brooches, pendants and buckles.

- **Fabricraft** - Lianne Hill specialises in high quality hand-crafted Christmas stockings, many of which can be personalised. Also hundreds of fabric designs in pre-tied and self-tie bow ties, personalised shoe bags together with fabrics for sale.

Also sitting within this vibrant community of craft studios, next to the Gallery, which has an eclectic range of exhibitions, is our own gourmet delight, the **Ewe and I Café**. A family run business with fresh wholesome and locally produced food.

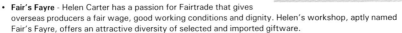
🏠 historic building 🏛 museum and heritage 🏛 historic site 🞕 scenic attraction 🌿 flora and fauna

Hardy's *Mayor of Casterbridge* it appears as the Weydon Priors Market where the future mayor sells his wife and child.

A good family day out can be enjoyed at the **Hawk Conservancy Trust** (see panel on page 187) where there are more than 250 birds of prey to see in 22 acres of grounds. The Hawk Conservancy is one of the largest collections of raptors in the world. Flying demonstrations take place three times daily and include species such as owls, eagles, vultures and condors, falcons, kites, hawks and secretary birds. The grounds here are also home to Shire horses, Sika deer, Hampshire Down sheep and red squirrels that have been given their own aerial runway.

THRUXTON
4 miles W of Andover off the A303

   🏍 Motor Racing Circuit

This large village with many thatched cottages is well known for its **Motor Racing Circuit**, which is built on a Second World War airfield. Its annual calendar of events takes in many aspects of sport, including Formula Three, Touring Cars, British Super Bikes, Trucks and Karts.

NETHER WALLOP
8 miles SW of Andover, on minor road off the A343

   🏛 St Andrew's Church

The names of the three Wallops (Over, Middle and Nether), have provided a good deal of amusement to visitors over the centuries, so it's slightly disappointing to discover that Wallop is just a corruption of the Old English word *waell-hop*, meaning a valley with a stream. At Nether Wallop the stream is picturesquely lined with willow trees, while the village itself is equally attractive with many thatched or timbered houses. The most notable building in Nether Wallop is **St Andrew's Church**, partly because of its Norman features and handsome West Tower of 1704, but also because of its striking medieval wall paintings, which provide an interesting contrast with Stanley Spencer's at Burghclere. Some 500 years old, these lay hidden for generations under layers of plaster and were only rediscovered in the 1950s. The most impressive of them shows St George slaying the dragon. Outside St Andrew's stands an item that ranks high on the list of churchyard oddities. It's a dark grey stone pyramid, 15ft high, with red stone flames rising from its tip. This daunting monument was erected at his own expense, and in memory of himself, by Francis Douce, 'Doctor of Physick', who died in 1760. Dr Douce also left an endowment to build a village school on condition that the parishioners would properly maintain the pyramid.

MIDDLE WALLOP
7 miles SW of Andover on the A343

   🏛 Museum of Army Flying 🏛 Danebury Ring
   🍇 Danebury Vineyards

The village of Middle Wallop became famous during the Battle of Britain when the nearby airfield was the base for squadrons of Spitfires and Hurricanes. Many of the old buildings have been incorporated into the **Museum of Army Flying**, which traces the development of Army Flying from the balloons and kites of pre-First World War years, through various imaginative dioramas, to a helicopter flight simulator in which visitors can test their own skills of 'hand and eye' coordination. The Museum has more than 35 fixed-wing and rotary aircraft on display, and other attractions include a museum shop, licensed café and restaurant, and a grassed picnic area.

JOHN DAVIS WOODTURNING & WEAVERS LOFT

The Old Stables, Chilbolton Down Farm,
Stockbridge, SO20 6BU
Tel: 01264 811418 Weavers Loft
Tel: 01264 811070 John Davis Woodturner
e-mail: oldstablesgallery@tiscali.co.uk
webiste: www.theoldstablesgallery.co.uk

The Old Stables Gallery is on a sheep farm just west of Stockbirdge on the A30 London road. It is now home to two independent businesses, **John Davis Woodturning** downstairs and Julia Ross in the **Weavers Loft**, on the first floor. Julia weaves with cashmere, linen, silk and wool producing a unique range of shawls and scarves. Also on sale is a selection of hand spun, hand painted yarns, beads and beaded jewellery.

John is a registered Professional Woodturner producing a full range of beautiful hand turned pieces both functional and sculptural, using native and exotic woods. He specializes in the use of Australian Burrs, which he imports and sells along with tools, wood and lathes. Both studios run a range of courses and taster sessions for beginners. For beginners details please contact us.

costume exhibition and enjoy the riverside garden. There's also a tearoom and gift shop.

To the east of Whitchurch is Bere Mill, a weather-boarded construction where a Frenchman, Henri Portal, set up a paper-making business in the early 18th century. By 1742, Portal's mill had won the contract to supply bank-note paper to the Bank of England and he moved his operation upstream to Laverstoke. Now in Overton, the business continues to make paper for bank notes and supplies it to more than 100 countries.

LONGPARISH

6 miles E of Andover, on the B3048

Living up to its name, Longparish village straggles alongside the River Test for more than two miles. This stretch of the river is famously full of trout, but no one has yet

beaten the record catch of Colonel Peter Hawker who lived at Longparish House in the early 1800s. According to his diary for 1818, in that year this dedicated angler relieved the river of no less than one ton's weight of the succulent fish. A previous owner of the colonel's house had actually captured double that haul in one year, but the bounder had cheated by dragging the river.

Longparish Upper Mill, in a lovely location on the river, is a large flour mill with a working waterwheel. Visitors can see the restoration work in progress.

BURGHCLERE

11 miles NE of Andover, off the A34

[ft] Sandham Memorial Chapel

A couple of miles northeast of Highclere Castle, at Burghclere, the **Sandham**

Memorial Chapel (National Trust) is, from the outside, a rather unappealing construction, erected in 1926 by Mr and Mrs JL Behrend in memory of a relation, Lieutenant Sandham, who died in World War I. Their building may be uninspired but the Behrends can't be faulted on their choice of artist to cover the walls with a series of 19 murals. Stanley Spencer had served during the war as a hospital orderly and 18 of his murals represent the day-to-day life of a British Tommy in wartime. The 19th, covering the east wall of the Chapel, depicts the Day of Resurrection with the fallen men and their horses rising up. The foreground is dominated by a pile of white wooden crosses the soldiers have cast aside. The whole series is enormously moving, undoubtedly one of the masterpieces of 20th century British art.

FACCOMBE
12 miles N of Andover, on minor road off the A343

🏛 Highclere Castle

This appealing little village, which is owned by the Faccombe Estate, is tucked away in the Hampshire countryside close to the Berkshire border. It is set on chalk downs some 750 feet above sea level with the highest points of the North Downs, Pilot Hill and Inkpen Beacon, both nearby. An extra attraction for walkers is the Test Way, a long-distance footpath that runs from Inkpen Beacon to the south coast following the track of the disused 'Sprat & Winkle' railway.

About five miles west of Faccombe, **Highclere Castle** is a wondrous example of Victorian neo-Gothic architecture at its most exuberant. If the central tower reminds you of another well-known building, that may be because the castle was designed by Sir Charles Barry, architect of the Houses of Parliament. It stands on the site of a former palace of the Bishops of Winchester, overlooking an incomparably lovely park, one of Capability Brown's greatest creations. Highclere is the family home of the 8th Earl and Countess of Carnavon. It was the 5th Earl who was with Howard Carter in 1922 at the opening of Tutankhamun's tomb. A small museum in the basement of the castle recalls that breathtaking moment. Another display reflects the family's love of, and success in, the racing and breeding of horses. In addition to the superb parkland, there's also a walled garden planted entirely with white blooms, a gift shop, restaurant and tearooms.

Winchester

🏛 Cathedral 🏛 College 🏛 The Great Hall

🏛 Wolvesey Castle 🐦 Jane Austen's House

🏛 The Brooks Experience 🏛 Hospital of St Cross

🐦 Marwell Zoological Park 🐦 Keats' Walk

🐦 Hyde Abbey Garden

One of the country's most historic cities, Winchester was adopted by King Alfred as the capital of his kingdom of Wessex, a realm which then included most of southern England. There has been a settlement here since the Iron Age, and in Roman times, as Venta Belgarum, it became an important military base. **The Brooks Experience**, located within the modern Brooks Shopping Centre, has displays based on excavated Roman remains with its star exhibit a reconstructed room from an early 4th-century town house.

When the Imperial Legions returned to Rome, the town declined until it was

Just south of the cathedral, on College Street, are two other buildings of outstanding interest. 8 College Street, a rather austere Georgian house with a first-floor bay window, is **Jane Austen's House** in which she spent the last six weeks of her life in 1817. The house is private, but a slate plaque above the front door records her residence here. Right next door stands **Winchester College**, the oldest school in England, founded in 1382 by Bishop William of Wykeham to provide education for 70 'poor and needy scholars'. Substantial parts of the 14th-century buildings still stand, including the beautiful Chapel. The Chapel is always open to visitors and there are guided tours around the other parts of the college from April to September. If you can time your visit during the school holidays, more of the college is available to view.

Two years after Jane Austen was buried in the cathedral, the poet John Keats stayed in Winchester and it was here that he wrote his timeless *Ode to Autumn – Season of mists and mellow fruitfulness*. His inspiration was a daily walk past the cathedral and college and through the Water Meadows beside the River Itchen. A detailed step-by-step guide to **Keats' Walk** is available from the Tourist Information Centre.

The city's other attractions are so numerous one can only mention a few of the most important. **The Great Hall**, off the High Street, is the only surviving part of the medieval castle rebuilt by Henry III between 1222 and 1236. Nikolaus Pevsner considered it "the finest medieval hall in England after Westminster Hall". A striking feature here is the legendary Round Table of Arthurian legend, which was made on the orders of Edward I some 700 years ago. Originally, the

THE BRIDGE PATISSERIE

20 Bridge Street, Winchester,
Hampshire SO23 9BH
Tel: 01962 890767
website: www.thebridgepatisserie.co.uk

The Bridge Patisserie has grown up! Along with the creation of splendid, informative website and a recently completed an extension, this delightful patisserie now gives you more space and seats so that you can enjoy your coffee and cakes in comfort. The food is equally enjoyable either eaten in or out. The shop's sumptuous new coffee lounge and lovely décor make it the perfect place to meet friends, escape the office and unwind.

As soon as you enter you are faced with a mouth-watering display of home made goodies. Choose from a fine selection of coffees, cakes, savoury items and quality chocolates. Their savoury items are the perfect choice for a great lunch at a great price. With so much on offer, all equally tempting the choice is difficult but the very friendly staff are more than willing to offer advice. Chocolates are their speciality, they are handmade locally and once you try one of these delicious treats, a high street brand will never compare. Visit their website and make sure you stay well informed!

🏛 historic building 🏚 museum and heritage 🏛 historic site 🏞 scenic attraction 🦋 flora and fauna

huge table was unpainted, but Henry VIII had it painted to depict himself as Arthur's descendant.

Located within the castle grounds are no fewer than six military museums, including the Gurkha Museum, the King's Royal Hussars Museum, whose displays include an exhibit on the famous Charge of the Light Brigade, and the Royal Green Jackets Museum, which contains a superb diorama of the Battle of Waterloo.

Other buildings of interest include the early 14th-century Pilgrim Hall, part of the Pilgrim School, and originally used as lodgings for pilgrims to the shrine of St Swithun, and **Wolvesey Castle** (English Heritage), the residence of the Bishops of Winchester since 963AD. The present palace is a gracious, classical building erected in the 1680s, flanked by the imposing ruins of its 14th-century predecessor, which was one of the grandest buildings in medieval England. It was here, in 1554, that Queen Mary first met Philip of Spain and where the wedding banquet was held the next day. Also well worth a visit is the 15th-century **Hospital of St Cross,** England's oldest

Hospital of St Cross, Winchester

THE CLOCK-WORK-SHOP

6a Parchment Street, Winchester,
Hampshire SO23 8AT
Tel: 01962 842331 Mobile: 07885 954302
website: www.clock-work-shop.co.uk

Everyone visiting the historic city of Winchester should take time to look in at the **Clock-Work-Shop**, which occupies two floors of an old building in a side street just off the main street. Owned by Peter Ponsford-Jones and run by him and his partners Kevin Hurd and Richard Scorey, the shop specialises in the sale, purchase, repair, restoration, after care and valuation of antique clocks, mostly English and mostly from the period from the 17th century to the First World War. Around 100 clocks are usually on display, including carriage clocks, wall clocks, mantel clocks and long case clocks, and the shop also deals in fine antique barometers and has a small stock of pocket watches.

The shop hours are 9am to 5pm Monday to Saturday, when all the clocks are available to view, but customers can 'visit' the shop at any time of the day or night by accessing the splendid website, which includes comprehensive details, including photographs and prices, of the full stock. A typical entry from the long case clock catalogue: 'A very handsome 8 day longcase of super quality. The silvered dial is particularly beautiful - a real work of the engraver's art! The oak case has excellent colour, finish and proportions. A most original clock. Circa 1780. Local delivery and set-up.' With notes as interesting and tempting as these, a browse through the website could easily result in a real-life visit to the shop. All sales and repairs carry a three-year guarantee.

ROMSEY

10 miles SW of Winchester, on the A27/ A3090

🏛 Abbey 🏛 Broadlands 🏛 King John's House

🏛 Moody Museum 🏛 Romsey Signal Box

'Music in stone', and 'the second finest Norman building in England' are just two responses to **Romsey Abbey**, a majestic building containing some of the best 12th and 13th century architecture to have survived. Built between 1120 and 1230, the Abbey is remarkably complete. Unlike so many monastic buildings which were destroyed or fell into ruin after the Dissolution, the abbey was fortunate in being bought by the town in 1544 for £100 – the bill of sale, signed and sealed by Henry VIII, is displayed in the south

Romsey Abbey

RANVILLES FARM HOUSE

Owners: Bill and Anthea Hughes

Pauncefoot Hill, Romsey, Hampshire SO51 6AA
Tel: 023 80 814481
e-mail: info@ranvilles.com website: www.ranvilles.com

Secluded, self-contained "love nest" or family retreat, **Ranvilles Farm House** caters for all even your pet! Whether you are simply looking for somewhere to relax and unwind or need a touring base from which to explore Hampshire's numerous attractions, including the cathedral cities of Winchester and Salisbury or The New Forest, Ranvilles House couldn't be better placed.

Nestled within five acres of attractive gardens and paddock, this lovely house comprises a spacious and charming Grade II* listed property of considerable character, with five en-suite bedrooms all wonderfully furnished with antiques.

Alternatively seek out serenity in the self-contained, beautiful and recently converted barn suite with its own garden. Guests can find a delicious food basket full of wonderful treats in the fully equipped kitchen. Other luxurious furnishings include a super king-size bed, 32" flat screen TV with Sky and the 'wow' factor bathroom. Recognised as a five star accommodation by Enjoy England you can expect truly exceptional facilities with a wealth of luxury.

Steeped in history, Ranvilles Farm dates from the 14th Century when Richard de Ranville came from Normandy and settled here with his family. Visit the website and take a virtual tour which gives an informative insight into the farmhouse. The tour is designed to give guests a chance to view, both the inside of the house, including all the bedrooms and the exterior of the house.

🏛 historic building 🏛 museum and heritage 🏛 historic site 🗺 scenic attraction 🌿 flora and fauna

AVALON CRYSTALS

6 Dukes Mill, Broadwater Road, Romsey,
Hampshire, SO51 8PJ
Tel: 01794 516644
website: www.avaloncrystals.co.uk

Avalon Crystals is a positive treasure trove of natural crystals and crystal goods; situated in a pedestrianised area it is very user friendly and quiet. This shop will greet you with sparkling windows of superb crystals.

Step inside this Aladdin's cave to discover a huge range of intriguing products, from gifts to specialist services - much more than just crystals can be found here: gemstones, incense, Mind Body & Spirit literature, mood music, wind chimes, T-shirts, aromatherapy products and a stunning selection of silver jewellery.

Under the determined hand of a powerful team who love crystals and gemstones, Avalon Crystals has become a port of call for anyone looking for that special 'something'. Established in 1999, owner Gary Onslow has a wealth of experience in fulfilling his customer's requirements, whether you are a serious collector or just someone who loves beautiful things, you will find a welcome here. Gary is also a fully qualified ear and body piercer, so if you want your first or a new piercing look no further.

Filled to the brim with gorgeous affordable high quality crystals and much more; it is well worth a detour if you are an enthusiast. Do go and visit.

---

choir aisle. Subsequent generations of townspeople have carefully maintained their bargain purchase. The abbey's most spectacular feature is the soaring nave, which rises more than 70ft and extends for more than 76ft. Amongst the abbey's many treasures is the 16th-century Romsey Rood, which shows Christ on the cross with the hand of God descending from the clouds.

Just across from the Abbey, in Church Court, stands the town's oldest dwelling, **King John's House**, built around 1240 for a merchant. It has served as a royal residence but not, curiously, for King John who died some 14 years before it was built. He may though have had a hunting lodge on the site. The house is now a museum and centre for cultural activities; the garden has been renovated and replanted with pre 18th-century plants.

The **Moody Museum** occupies the Victorian home of the Moody family who were cutlers in Romsey from the 18th century up until the 1970s. Visitors are greeted by (models of) William Moody and his sister Mary in a reconstruction of the family parlour, and the exhibits include fixtures and fittings from the family's gun shop.

Train enthusiasts will want to seek out the curious exhibit located behind the infants' school in Winchester Road. **Romsey Signal Box** is a preserved vintage signal box in working order, complete with signals, track and other artefacts.

Romsey's most famous son was undoubtedly the flamboyant politician Lord Palmerston, three times Prime Minister during the 1850s and 1860s. Palmerston lived at Broadlands, just south of the town, and is commemorated by a bronze statue in the

---

🎭 stories and anecdotes 🐦 famous people 🎨 art and craft 🖌 entertainment and sport 🚶 walks

heritage. Visiting heritage, art, craft and photography exhibitions are also held here. The **Point Dance and Arts Centre** stages a full programme of theatre, dance, cinema and music events, while the **Beatrice Royal Contemporary Art and Craft Gallery** offers exhibitions of art, sculpture, ceramics, jewellery and textiles.

Bishops Waltham Palace Ruins

Just outside the town is the **Lakeside Country Park**, home to a variety of wildlife and also a place for model boating, windsurfing and fishing. Here, too, is the Eastleigh Lakeside Railway, a miniature steam railway that provides trips around the park.

To the south of Eastleigh lies Southampton International Airport, the home of Carill Aviation where you can take off for a scenic flight over the Solent, or sign up for a trial flying lesson.

BISHOP'S WALTHAM

10 miles NE of Southampton, on the B2177/ B3035

🏛 Palace 🏛 Jhansi Farm Rare Breeds Centre

Bishop's Waltham is a charming and historic small town. It was the country residence of the Bishops of Winchester for centuries, and through the portals of their sumptuous **Palace** have passed at least 12 reigning monarchs. Amongst them were Richard the Lionheart returning from the Crusades, Henry V mustering his army before setting off for Agincourt, and Henry VIII entertaining Charles V of Spain (then the most powerful monarch in Europe) to a lavish banquet. The palace's days of glory came to a violent end during the Civil War when Cromwell's troops battered most of it to the ground. The last resident bishop was forced to flee, concealing himself beneath a load of manure.

Set within beautiful moated grounds, the ruins remain impressive, especially the Great Hall with its three-storey tower and soaring windows. Also here are the remains of the bakehouse, kitchen, chapel and lodgings for visitors. The Palace is now in the care of English Heritage and entrance is free.

The town itself offers visitors a good choice of traditional and specialist shops, amongst them a renowned fishmonger, butcher, baker – even a candlemaker. And just north of the town you can visit one of the country's leading vineyards. Visitors to **Northbrook Springs Vineyard** are offered a tour of the vineyard, which explains the complex, labour-intensive process of planting, growing, pruning and harvesting the vines, and a free tasting in the Vineyard Shop (open Tuesday to Sunday) of a selection of crisp, clear, flavourful wines.

BOTLEY

7 miles E of Southampton on the A334

Set beside the River Hamble, Botley is an attractive village of red brick houses, which remains as pleasant now as when William Cobbett, the 19th-century writer and political commentator, described it as "the most delightful village in the world….it has everything in a village I love and none of the things I hate". The latter included a workhouse, attorneys, justices of the peace – and barbers. The author of *Rural Rides* lived a very comfortable life in Botley between 1804 and 1817, and he is honoured by a memorial in the Market Square.

NETLEY

5 miles SE of Southampton, off the A3025

🏛 Netley Abbey   🏛 Netley Hospital

🚶 Royal Victoria Country Park

A Victorian town on the shores of the Solent, Netley was brought into prominence when a vast military hospital was built here after the Crimean War. The foundation stone of **Netley Hospital** was laid by Queen Victoria in 1856 and the hospital remained in use until after the Second World War. A disastrous fire in the 1960s caused most of the buildings to be demolished, but the hospital's Chapel, with its distinctive 100ft tower, did survive and now houses an exhibition about the hospital from the time of Florence Nightingale. The rest of the site has been developed as the **Royal Victoria Country Park** offering

LAKESIDE B&B

48 Stag Drive, Batleigh, Lakeside,
Hedge End, Hampshire SO30 2QN
Tel: 01489 780618
Fax: 01489 797192
e-mail: enquiries@lakesidebandb.co.uk
website: www.lakesidebandb.co.uk

Located in a rural position in the village of Hedge End and overlooking the grounds of Botleigh Grange Hotel, **Lakeside B&B** is a stylish modern building constructed in 2005 and beautifully decorated by owners Suzie and Jim Oakley. The house has a garden seating area and, inside, offers a choice of single, double or king-size rooms. They are all well-equipped with the usual facilities of TV, DVD, en suite bathrooms, hairdryers and tea and coffee making facilities.

Not only do Suzie and Jim provide you with a breakfast choice of a Full English or kippers but they also offer a packed lunch and evening meal of the day for an additional cost. They will also pick you up from Southampton Airport or Parkway railway station for a small fee if you wish. There are plenty of local attractions including The Rose Bowl cricket ground, pubs and restaurants, retail shopping, a spa, fishing, bowling green, tennis courts - and some lovely walks. The Oakleys have an arrangement with the Botleigh Grange Hotel permitting guests to use their Spa and fishing facilities for a small fee. Lakeside accepts payment by credit card.

Lyndhurst and the surrounding forest. At the other end of the town, Swan Green, surrounded by picturesque thatched cottages, provides a much-photographed setting where cricket matches are held in summer.

Around Lyndhurst

MINSTEAD

2 miles NW of Lyndhurst off the A337

Church of All Saints · Furzey Gardens · Rufus Stone

The village of Minstead offers two interesting attractions, one of which is the **Church of All Saints**. During the 18th century, the gentry and squirearchy of Minstead seem to have regarded church attendance as a necessary duty, which, nevertheless, should be made as agreeable as possible. Three of the village's most affluent residents paid to have the church fabric altered so that they could each have their own entrance door leading to a private 'parlour', complete with open fireplace and comfortable chairs. The squire of Minstead even installed a sofa on which he could doze during the sermon. It's easy to understand his concern since these sermons were normally expected to last for at least an hour; star preachers seem to have thought they were short-changing their flock if they didn't prate for at least twice that long. It was around this time that churches began introducing benches for the congregation. The church also has a three-decker pulpit and a two-tiered gallery; the lower tier for musicians; the upper for children from the Poor School.

Admirers of the creator of Sherlock Holmes, Sir Arthur Conan Doyle, will want to pay their respects at his grave in the churchyard here. A puzzle worthy of Sir Arthur's great detective is the idiosyncratic sign outside the Trusty Servant pub in the village. Instead of showing, as one might expect, a portrait of a dutiful domestic, the sign actually depicts a liveried figure with the feet of a stag and the face of a pig, its snout clamped by a padlock. A 10-line poem underneath this peculiar sign explains that the snout means the servant will eat any old scraps, the padlock that he will tell no tales about his master, and the stag's feet that he will be swift in carrying his master's messages.

Minstead's other main attraction is **Furzey Gardens**, eight acres of delightful, informal woodland gardens designed by Hew Dalrymple in the 1920s, and enjoying extensive views over the New Forest towards the Isle of Wight. Beautiful banks of azaleas and rhododendrons, heathers and ferns surround an attractive water garden, and amongst the notable species growing here are incandescent Chilean Fire

Furzey Gardens, Minstead

Rufus Stone, Minstead

Trees and the strange Bottle Brush Tree. Also within the gardens are a 16th-century thatched cottage, a craft gallery and a tearoom.

To the northwest of Minstead stands the **Rufus Stone** that is said to mark the spot where William Rufus (William II) was killed by an arrow while out hunting. William's body was carried on the cart of Purkis the charcoal burner to Winchester where William's brother had already arrived to proclaim himself King. William had not been a popular monarch and his funeral in the cathedral at Winchester was conducted with little ceremony and even less mourning.

ASHURST
2 miles NE of Lyndhurst on the A35

- Otter, Owl & Wildlife Conservation Park
- Longdown Activity Farm

Just to the east of the village, in acres of ancient woodland, is the **New Forest Otter, Owl and Wildlife Conservation Park**. Conservation is the key word here. The park has an ongoing breeding programme for otters and barn owls, both of which are endangered species. Visitors can meander along woodland trails and encounter the otters and owls in their enclosures along with other native mammals such as deer, foxes and badgers.

There are more animals to be seen at close quarters at **Longdown Activity Farm** where

visitors can handle small animals, bottle-feed goat kids and calves, and meet pigs, ponies, alpacas, ducks and more. There's a large picnic area, extensive indoor and outdoor play areas, a gift shop and a tearoom.

TOTTON
6 miles NE of Lyndhurst on the A36

- Eling Tide Mill

Set beside Eling Creek, **Eling Tide Mill** has been harnessing tidal power to mill flour for a thousand years. Wholemeal flour is produced from wheat grown in the New Forest and is on sale in the Mill shop along with a selection of gifts. There's also a Heritage Centre and a café.

MARCHWOOD
5 miles E of Lyndhurst off the A326

- British Military Powerboat Trust

The military port at Marchwood was built in 1943 for the construction of the Mulberry harbours deployed in Normandy after the D-Day landings. Today, the port provides a base for ships of the Royal Fleet auxiliary. Close by, at Cracknore Head, is the **British Military Powerboat Trust** where a number of historic military craft are on display. Visitors can wander around the craft in the static exhibition area, and take boat trips on certain days.

HYTHE
8 miles SE of Lyndhurst off the A326

This is one of the very best places to watch the comings and goings of the big ships on Southampton Water, and no visit here is complete without taking a ride up the pier on the quaint little electric train, the oldest electric pier train in the world. From the end of the pier a ferry plies the short route across

Stevenage

🏛 Museum �󠀢 Six Mills

The town grew up along the Great North Road, and as traffic increased from the 13th century it developed round its parish church, the main road becoming its High Street. Stevenage was designated the first of Britain's New Towns in 1946. The idea of New Towns grew from the severe shortage of housing following the Second World War air raids on London. The first new houses in Stevenage were occupied in 1951; the new town centre was completed in 1957. Within the new town area, by a roundabout near the railway station, rise **Six Hills**, reputed to be Roman burial mounds. The history of the town, from the earliest days to the development of the New

Town and the present day, is told in the **Stevenage Museum** in the undercroft of St George's Church.

Stevenage became Hilton in the classic novel *Howards End* by EM Forster, who spent much of his childhood at Rooks Nest on the outskirts of town.

Around Stevenage

KNEBWORTH
3 miles S of Stevenage off A602

🏠 Knebworth House

🏠 Church of St Mary & St Thomas

Knebworth House has been the home of the Lytton family since 1490. The present magnificent High Gothic mansion house was

---

BROOKFIELD FARM

Aston End Road, Aston, Stevenage, Hertfordshire SG2 7EU
Tel: 01438 880228 Fax: 01438 880790
e-mail: info@brookfield-farm.co.uk
website: www.brookfield-farm.co.uk

When it comes to freshly cut meat there's nothing better than heading down to **Brookfield Farm** and choosing from a range of carefully cut beef, pork, bacon, sausages and mince. Brookfield Farm is a friendly, family run farm shop specialising in providing good service and high quality meats from the farm and selected local suppliers. They have their own herd of prize winning, pedigree Aberdeen Angus cattle and supply shorthorn beef, lamb, pork and chicken from carefully selected local sources.

The butchery also has a game licence so you can buy pheasant, venison and rabbit. However, it is still the pedigree Aberdeen Angus herd of cattle that provide the shop with such top class beef. Using only traditional native beef breeds ensures all their beef is consistently flavoursome and succulent.

If you are a sausage connoisseur you'll be pleased to know that there is an extensive range to choose from. All sausages are hand made in the farm shop using only the finest ingredients, the best seller is a delicious peppery sausage labelled 'Aston'.

You can also visit the online shop where you can order and pay for products from the extensive range to collect at a time convenient for you. They hope to develop this service and will be offering delivery for a small charge in the near future.

🏠 historic building   🏛 museum and heritage   ⓘ historic site   🗘 scenic attraction   🌱 flora and fauna

built in 1843 to the design of the Victorian statesman and novelist, Edward Bulwer-Lytton, who wrote *The Last Days of Pompeii*. However, fragments of the original Tudor house remain, including parts of the Great Hall, and there is also some superb 17th-century panelling. Other members of the Lytton family of note include Constance, a leading figure in the suffragette movement, and Robert, Viceroy of India. The Raj Exhibition at the house brings to life the story of Lord Lytton's viceroyship and the Great Delhi Durbar of 1877. The house has also played host to such notable visitors as Elizabeth I, Benjamin Disraeli, Sir Winston Churchill and Charles Dickens, who took part in amateur theatrical performances here. Dickens christened his 10th child Edward Bulwer Lytton Dickens in honour of their great friendship. The grounds of Knebworth House are also well worth visiting. As well as the beautiful formal gardens laid out by Lutyens, there is a wonderful herb garden established by Gertrude Jekyll, a lovely Victorian wilderness area, a maze that was replanted in 1995, and acres of grassland that are home to herds of red and sika deer. Children will enjoy the adventure playground, where they will find Fort Knebworth, a Dinosaur Trail, a monorail suspension slide and a bouncy castle among the amusements.

Also within the grounds is the **Church of St Mary and St Thomas**, which contains some spectacular 17th- and 18th-century monuments to members of the Lytton family. Especially striking is the memorial to Sir William Lytton who died in 1705. A well-

Knebworth House

fed figure with a marked double chin and dressed in the height of early 18th-century fashion, Sir William reclines gracefully atop his tomb, his expression one of impermeable self-satisfaction.

BENINGTON
4 miles E of Stevenage off the B1037

A very attractive village, Benington has a lovely green fringed by 16th-century timber-and-plaster cottages. The village church dates from the 13th century, and next to it, on the site of a largely disappeared castle, is a spacious Georgian house known as Benington Lordship. The house is private, but the superb grounds are open at restricted times. The hilltop gardens include lakes, a Norman keep and moat (the remains of the castle), a kitchen, rose and water gardens, a charming rockery, magnificent herbaceous

St Albans

🏛 Clock Tower 🏛 Verulamium Museum

🏛 Verulamium 🏛 Museum of St Albans 🏛 Abbey

🏛 Organ Museum 🏛 Kingsbury Watermill

🏛 Redbournbury Mill

This historic cathedral city, whose skyline is dominated by the magnificent Norman abbey, is a wonderful blend of the old and new. One of the major Roman cities in Britain, the remains of **Verulamium** were excavated only quite recently, but there was a settlement here before Julius Caesar's invasion in 54BC. Attacked and ruined by Boadicea (Boudiccea) in the 1st century, the city was rebuilt and today the remains of the walls, Britain's only Roman theatre (as distinct from an amphitheatre) and a hypocaust can still be seen in Verulamium Park. Also in the park is the **Verulamium Museum**, where the story of everyday life in a Roman city is told; among the displays are ceramics, mosaic floors, personal possessions and room re-creations.

Designated as a cathedral in 1877, **St Albans Abbey** was built on the site where Alban, the first British martyr, was beheaded in 303AD for sheltering a Christian priest. Dating from the 11th century and built from flint and bricks taken from the Roman remains, the Cathedral has been added to and altered in every century since. It was the premier Abbey of medieval England until its monastic life ended in 1539, when all but the Abbey Church and Gatehouse were destroyed. Among its many notable features, the

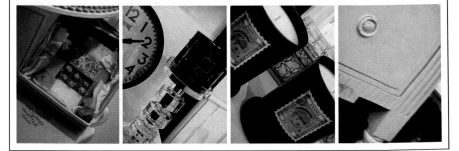

medieval paintings, said to be unique in Britain, are the most interesting. In the nearby Church of St Michael are the tomb and life-size monument of Lord Chancellor Francis Bacon (1561-1626), 1st Baron Verulam and Viscount St Albans, who lived in St Albans for the last five years of his life. The shrine of St Alban is a beautiful structure of carved Purbeck marble made in 1308. It was restored in 1993. In 2002, a bone believed to be of St Alban was given to the Cathedral by the Church of St Pantaleon in Cologne.

In the town's central market place stands the **Clock Tower**, the only medieval town belfry in England, built between 1403 and 1412. Originally constructed as a political statement by the town, it asserted the citizens'

freedom and wealth in the face of the powerful Abbey, as the town was allowed to sound its own hours and ring the curfew bell. The original 15th-century bell, Gabriel, is still in place.

Close to the peaceful and tranquil Verulamium Park, on the banks of the River Ver, is **Kingsbury Watermill**, a wonderful 16th-century mill that is built on the site of an earlier mill that was mentioned in the Domesday Book. Beautifully restored, the waterwheel is still turned by the river and visitors can not only enjoy this idyllic setting, but they can also see the working milling machinery and a collection of agricultural implements.

Two other museums in the town are well

BATTLERS GREEN FARM

Common Lane, Radlett, Hertfordshire WD7 8PH
e-mail: info@battlersgreenfarm.co.uk
website: www.battlersgreenfarm.co.uk

Battlers Green Farm Rural Shopping Village has grown incrementally over the past half-century. Starting with a single farm shop, it gradually expanded to achieve its present complement of a dozen or so highly distinctive stores. Quite apart from its ample free parking, the shopping village offers a unique experience.

Aga cookers & kitchenware

The Aga name has long been synonymous with good food and fine living. Our cookers are one of the world's most recognisable design icons and an Aga cooker is surprisingly easy to own!
Tel: 01923 289726   e-mail: radlett@aga-rayburn.co.uk

Andrew Brown furnishings

An eclectic mix of classic, period and contemporary pieces for the home. Centuries and styles mingle in what is quintessentially a modern space created in an old barn.
Tel: 01923 856343   e-mail: infor@andrebrownhome.com

The Antique Shop antiques

A veritable treasure trove of antiques, collectables and objects d'art. Re-opening in September 2007, after a period of refurbishment, the shop will offer something special for all and at very competitive market prices.
Tel: 01923 855384

Battlers Green Farm Shop food & wine

The Farm Shop remains the shopping village's anchor store, a genuine original that stocks everything you might expect, and more.
Tel: 01923 856551   e-mail: info@battlersgreenfarm.co.uk

Brimarks Butchers butchers

Our independent company maintains what we sincerely believe to be the highest standards of animal welfare while providing top quality meats.
Tel: 01923 853591

The Bull Pen tearooms

When visiting Battlers Green don't forget to take a break in these attractive tearooms with their spacious dining area and traditional décor.
Tel: 01923 857505   e-mail: thebullpen@btinternet.com

🏠 historic building 🏛 museum and heritage 🏚 historic site 🌀 scenic attraction 🌱 flora and fauna

Classic Framing picture framing
Professional picture framing at the highest quality offered in a variety of materials.
Tel: 01923 853902   e-mail: classicframing@tiscali.co.uk

Destiny holistics
Destiny boasts shelves full of happy, sparkly crystals from all over the planet and a selection of books and CDs as well as incense, oils and gifts.
Tel: 01923 852522   e-mail: destinyshop@tiscali.co.uk

Dynatique gift shop
Come and see our intriguing selection of imaginative gifts for all occasions.
Tel: 01923 853837   e-mail: dynateck1@btconnect.com

Fired Earth sanitaryware
A unique resource for people with a sense of individuality and authenticity who want to create beautiful homes in any style.
Tel: 01923 855382   e-mail: radlett@firedearth.com

The Flower Grove florists
We invite you to come and browse our beautiful displays or enquire about our bespoke floral services for your special event.
Tel: 01923 858377

Laline cosmetics & beauty products
A new range of bath, bodycare and home accessories, hand-made with natural oils and fragrances sourced in France.
Tel: 01923 857474   e-mail: info@laline.co.uk

The Loose Box pet store
Hertfordshire's premier pet store supplies a range of accessories and good quality food for all pets including many natural feedstuffs.
Tel: 01923 852616

Maine Sail fishmongers
Daily supplies of the finest and fresh fish direct from Billingsgate Markets.
Tel: 01923 853177   e-mail: info@mainesail.com

Realli-Ski ski simulator and lessons
Learn faster and ski better on 'Realli-Snow', the surface that lets you experience the sensation of skiing on real ski runs.
Tel: 0845 838 2811   e-mail: watford@realli-ski.com

Canal. One of these boats has been renovated and bears the name *Albert*.

WATFORD
5 miles S of Hemel Hempstead on the A411

🏛 Bedford Almshouses 🏛 Museum

🌿 Cheslyn House

Originally a country market town, Watford was transformed in the 19th century by the arrival of the railway, which brought new industry and new building. Among the few earlier buildings to survive the rapid development are the five-gabled **Bedford Almshouses**, which date back to 1580, and the early 18th-century Fuller and Chilcott school. On the high street stands the splendid Mansion House, once the offices of the Benskin Brewery and now home to **Watford Museum**, where visitors can learn about the industrial and social history of the town. The local brewing and printing industries feature prominently, along with a tribute to Watford Football Club.

In the north of the town, off the A411 Hemel Hempstead road, Watford Council manages the gardens at **Cheslyn House**. The 3½-acre garden has woodland, lawns, a bog garden, rock garden, splendid herbaceous borders and an aviary, and is open from dawn to dusk every day except Christmas.

Tring

🏛 St Mary's Church 🏛 Mansion House

🏛 Natural History Museum at Tring

🏛 Market House

Situated on the edge of the Chiltern Hills and on the banks of the Grand Union Canal, Tring is a bustling little market town whose character has been greatly influenced by the Rothschild family. However, the members of this rich and famous family are not the only people of note to be associated with the town. In **St Mary's Church** can be found the grave of the grandfather of the first US president, George Washington, while the 17th-century **Mansion House**, designed by Sir Christopher Wren, was reputedly used by Nell Gwynne.

The town's narrow winding High Street, off which lead little alleyways and courtyards, contains many late-Victorian buildings, all designed by local architect William Huckvale. Of particular note is the **Market House**, built by public subscription in 1900 to commemorate, albeit a little late, Queen Victoria's Diamond Jubilee. A fine example of the Arts and Crafts style, so popular at the turn of the century, the building was later converted into a fire station and today it serves as the town council chamber.

The old Silk Mill, first opened in 1824, once employed over 600 people, but towards the end of the 19th century the silk trade fell into decline and Lord Rothschild ran the mill at a loss to protect his employees rather than see them destitute. Unable to carry on in this fashion, the mill closed to the silk trade and, after losing some of its height, the building was converted into a generating station. From 1872 to the 1940s, the Rothschild family lived at Tring Park and from here they exercised their influence over the town. Perhaps their greatest gift to the town is the Walter Rothschild Zoological Museum, now the **Natural History Museum at Tring**, one of the finest collections of stuffed mammals, birds, reptiles and insects in the UK. It includes examples of several animals now extinct, and a model of a dodo. The collection was given to the nation by Walter Rothschild on his death in 1937. An eccentric man with a great interest in natural history, Walter collected more than 4,000 rare and extinct species of animals, birds and reptiles.

Tring's focal point is The Square, remodelled in 1991 and featuring an ingenious Pavement Maze in the form of a zebra's head - a tribute to Walter's work. The town's war memorial, unveiled in 1919, stands in The Square, as does the flint and Totternhoe stone Church of St Peter and St Paul. Dating chiefly from the 15th century, this parish church contains some fine medieval carvings as well as 18th-century memorials.

Extending south from close to the town centre, Tring Park provides 300 acres of excellent walking.

Around Tring

MARSWORTH
2 miles N of Tring off B489

ik Nature Reserve

Mentioned in the Domesday Book and situated on the banks of the Grand Union Canal, Marsworth was known as Mavvers to the canal people. The village is home to the

Tring Reservoirs

Wilstone, Hertfordshire HP23 4LN
website: www.tring.gov.uk/info/reserv.htm

When the Grand Junction Canal was built, between 1793 and the early 1800s, it opened up the first cost-effective trading route between the new Industrial towns of the Midlands and London's markets and ports. Products were being mass-produced for the first time in history and the canals provided the vital link between producers and customers. Black Country coal could be delivered cheaply to London, making it

affordable to poor families. Farmers could send their grain and livestock to the big cities, making farming a profitable business and reducing the fear of famine for city dwellers.

In the 1830s, new locks were dug alongside some of the existing locks to speed up boat traffic through busy sections of canal. Take a close look at the bridge at Startop's End and the dry dock at the Wendover Arm junction and you can see where these locks were located. To calculate how many locks full of water to supply to the canal each day, the Reservoir Attendant has to estimate the number of boats likely to cross the summit. This is based on the time of year and readings from automatic counters in the locks. The weather must also be checked· on a sunny day as much as 25 mm (1 inch) of water can evaporate from the summit pound.

The Reservoirs are connected to Tringford Pumping Station by a network of underground, brick-lined passageways. Water flows through these, by gravity, to deep wells beneath the station. When the pumps are switched on, water rises up the wells, into the Wendover Arm Canal and then flows to the summit. Water is usually taken from Wilstone Reservoir first with Startop's End as a back up. Tringford Reservoir is rarely used to avoid sudden drops in water level, which would disturb the wildlife and trout fishery.

🗐 stories and anecdotes 🐿 famous people 🎨 art and craft 🥾 entertainment and sport 𝆐 walks

PELHAM HOUSE GALLERY

9 Bath Road, Cowes,
Isle of Wight, PO31 7QN
Tel: 01983 247715
Best known as the world's premiere yachting centre, Cowes is the islands main port with a natural harbour at the mouth of the Medina River. It is here, housed in an 18th Century historic building that you will discover the delightful **Pelham House Gallery**.

Opened in June 2006, this light and airy gallery provides an enticing and intimate shopping experience with a large selection of contemporary fine arts and crafts. Joint owners Alison and Dawn who both hold a BA Hons in design crafts have worked as freelance artists since 2000. Their passion for fine craftsmanship is clearly apparent and the work on sale has been carefully selected, creating a varied exhibit reflecting a coastal lifestyle.

If you're looking for an individual and carefully crafted work of art and enjoy picturesque coastline, why not take a trip to Pelham House Gallery and indulge in both the love of art and the great outdoors.

Westland's factory doors were painted with a giant Union Jack to mark the Queen's Jubilee in 1977 – a piece of patriotic paintwork that has been retained by popular demand. Two museums in Cowes have a nautical theme. The **Sir Max Aitken Museum** in an old sailmaker's loft in West Cowes High Street houses Sir Max's remarkable collection of nautical paintings, instruments and artefacts, while the **Cowes Maritime Museum** (free) charts the island's sea-faring history and has a collection of racing yachts that includes the Uffa Fox pair *Avenger* and *Coweslip*. (Uffa Fox, perhaps the best known yachtsman of his day, is buried in the Church of St Mildred at Whippingham, a few miles south of Cowes.)

Across the River Medina, linked by a chain ferry, East Cowes is most famous for **Osborne House**, a clean-cut, Italianate mansion designed and built by Prince Albert

in 1846. Queen Victoria loved "dear beautiful Osborne" and so did her young children. They had their very own house in its grounds, a full-size Swiss Cottage, where they played at house-keeping, cooking meals for their parents, and tending its vegetable gardens using scaled-down gardening tools. In the main house itself, visitors can wander through both the State and private apartments, which are crammed with paintings, furniture, ornaments, statuary and the random bric-à-brac that provided such an essential element in the decor of any upper-class Victorian home. Osborne House possessed a special place in the Queen's affections. It had been built by the husband she adored with an almost adolescent infatuation: together they had spent many happy family days here. After Albert's premature death from typhoid in 1861, she often returned to Osborne. Her staff had instructions to lay out the Prince's clothes in his dressing-room each night, and the Queen herself retired to bed with his nightshirt clasped in her arms. In 1901 she returned to Osborne for the last time, dying here on January 22nd in her 83rd year, her death coincidentally signalling the beginning of the slow decline of the British Empire over which she had presided as Queen-Empress.

Osborne House and its grounds featured prominently in the film *Mrs Brown* (2001) starring Judi Dench and Billy Connolly, which explored the controversial relationship between the Queen and her Scottish ghillie, John Brown.

WHIPPINGHAM
3 miles S of Cowes on the A3021

🏛 Barton Manor

Queen Victoria also acquired **Barton Manor** (see panel below) at nearby Whippingham, a peaceful retreat whose grounds are occasionally open to the public. Prince Albert had a hand in the design of the gardens and of the ornate Church of St Mildred, where the contractor and co-designer was

AJ Humbert, who was also responsible for Sandringham. The royal family regularly worshipped at St Mildred's, which is predictably full of royal memorials, including a monument to Victoria's son-in-law Prince Henry of Battenberg, who succumbed to malaria in Africa at the age of 38. Alfred Gilbert's wonderful art nouveau screen in the chancel arcade is a unique work of art, and other notable pieces are a bronze angel and the font (both of them designed by Princess Louise, a daughter of the Queen), a memorial to Albert and a chair used by the Queen.

WOOTTON CREEK
3 miles W of Ryde, off the A3054

🦋 Butterfly World

Wootton Creek is notable for its ancient bridge and mill-pond, and as the western terminus of the Isle of Wight Steam Railway, with an old wooden booking office and signal box moved from elsewhere on the island. It is also the home of **Butterfly World & Fountain World**. This complex comprises a sub-tropical indoor garden with hundreds of exotic butterflies flying free; a colourful Italian garden with computer-controlled fountains; a

Barton Manor
Whippingham, East Cowes, Isle of Wight PO32 6LB
Tel: 01983 528989 Fax: 01983 528671

The estate of Barton is first mentioned in the Doomsday Book of 1086, and after a period as an Augustinian oratory was run as a farm until the 19th century. When Queen Victoria and Prince Albert bought Osborne House, **Barton Manor** became their home farm. In 1902, after the Queen's death, King Edward VII made a gift of Osborne to the nation and kept Barton Manor until 1922 when it was sold into private hands. The gardens are a real delight, with the rhododendron walk, the splendid rose maze, a water garden, a secret garden and the national collections of Watsonia and red hot pokers. The estate is open on special days in the year in aid of the local Earl Mountbatten Hospice.

📖 stories and anecdotes　🐦 famous people　🎨 art and craft　🎭 entertainment and sport　🚶 walks

ROOM4

30 Union Street, Ryde, Isle of Wight, PO33 2DT
Tel: 01983 611973
e-mail: mike.no@hotmail.com
website: www.room4cafe.com

Located in the heart of Ryde, **Room 4** provides the perfect place to enjoy a coffee, glass of wine or slice of cake with friends. With so much on offer from contemporary fare to traditional bites, and wines to espressos there is something to satisfy everyone.

Owner Michael Boyle and his team of friendly staff have made sure that this charming bistro is relaxed and comfortable whilst remaining sophisticated, making it a delightful place to take a break from shopping during the day. During the evening, the lighting is softened creating a warm and welcoming atmosphere and a new irresistible Pizzeria menu is available. Every effort has been made to ensure that the Italian gourmet pizzas are as fresh and tasty as possible, with only the best ingredients being used. The pizzas each have a thin base and are cooked at 375 degrees C on an authentic stone base, ventilated pan allowing the bases to be crisp & clean. Not only does the evening menu offer a tempting range of gourmet pizzas but it also provides a large selection of starters and Salads of Distinction to accompany your main course.

Room4 has proved extremely popular, with loyal customers returning time and time again to sample the wide selection of freshly made lunches. With such a wide variety of fillings to go with baguettes, wraps, sandwiches, toasties, jacket potatoes and salads you could discover a new favourite during every visit. Room4 is also renowned for its delicious Italian Coffees and its huge selection of teas with over 50 different varieties to choose from.

Having created such an enjoyable place to dine it comes as no surprise that Room4 was voted 'Best Family Dining Venue in Ryde 2007'. Despite it's chic and luxurious interior, Room4 is extremely good value for money making it a perfect venue for the whole family.

Enjoy the food, enjoy the ambience...love Room4

🏰 historic building 🏛 museum and heritage 🏚 historic site ⚜ scenic attraction 🌿 flora and fauna

JOELLE

5 Cross Street, Ryde, Isle of Wight PO33 2AA
Tel: 01983 615708
e-mail: valboynton@tiscali.co.uk

With a very art deco theme, Joelle is a unique boutique style shop, a 'world of glamour', where glamour meets tenderness filled with exciting ranges of fine French lingerie, ladies accessories, children's toys, bedroom furniture and much more. It is very much a ladies and children orientated shop and provides the perfect place to find that special gift or for a bit of self-pampering. Craft work is also a speciality here, where glass beaded jewellery is made, and can on request provide your favourite colours. Knitted hats are made by the owner herself, Val together with knitted broaches, mitts, scarves (both casual and dressy) and handbags are sold here. Walking stick and toiletries are available for gentlemen. There are many children toys imported from Germany and soon story books in different languages.

The bedroom furniture is French boudoir style, with attractive wallpapers, pictures, chest of drawers, dressing tables and quaint storages boxes. Other products include a variety of mirrors, French white washed furniture, oils, soap, linen , vintage clothing, decorative cushions, Lampe Berger (Fragranced lamps), and fabrics for making blinds, cushions and other home accessories.

Everything in the shop is unique and collectable.

BEAUTIFUL HAND-CRAFTED GIFTS

ORIGIN IOW is a small family run business on the Isle of Wight. 90% of the products are made on the island with a high percentage being hand made.

They include:

- Isle of Wight lavender
- 3 IOW Chocolatiers
- Naturally Wight skin care
- Beautiful Isle of Wight fine bone china
- Natural bath and body products
- A selection of soft furnishings inc personalised door stops, bags and cushions.
- Ericas fabulous sherry shallots and Jams, marmalades and chutneys all hand made on the island.

And their very own natural candles are made from soy wax and fragranced with essential oils. They range from; uplifting zesty lemon, comforting vanilla, relaxing lavender and bergamot, and restoring tuberose and hibiscus. Pure and natural they are all hand made on the island.

1A Union Street, Ryde, Isle of Wight PO33 2EA
Tel: 01983 616095

THE CRAB & LOBSTER INN

32 Forelands Field Road, Bembridge,
Isle of Wight PO35 5TR
Tel: 01983 872244
e-mail: crab.lobster@bluebottle.com
website: www.crabandlobsterinn.co.uk

The Crab & Lobster Inn enjoys a superb coastal location with un-equaled sea views over Bembridge Ledge on the Isle of Wight. This sought after hostelry has a proven track record of popularity with both locals and visitors alike. Situated by the coastal path at the most Eastern part of the island, visitors are provided with a good base in which to enjoy the Island and benefit from easy access to a range of coastal walks and views.

Renowned for it's fresh fish and lobster caught just off the shore, seafood can be enjoyed all year round. In addition to this, the Inn prides itself on sourcing delicious local produce wherever possible. Factors such as these have helped The Crab & Lobster Inn achieve the prestigious Dining Pub of The Year Award in 2006 and 4 AA stars.

The Inn boasts a large capacity, seating 150 people with additional room for 104 outside. Dining at The Crab & Lobster Inn is a mixture of attractive patio areas with sea views, or the traditional intimate beamed interior of the bar. With welcoming open fires burning from 1st September, it has all the ingredients for a relaxed and enjoyable experience.

Food is served from 12.00 - 2.30 pm every lunchtime, 6.00 – 9.00 pm Sunday to Thursday evenings and 6.00 - 9.30 pm Friday and Saturday evenings. As you would expect, the comprehensive menu has a heavy seafood influence, but also includes tasty traditional choices as well as vegetarian options, meaning that there really is something to satisfy all tastes. Perhaps try the delicious surf and turf: a half lobster with 6 oz steak, with tomatoes, mushrooms, lemon, garlic, Madeira sauce and fries. Daily specials are available on the board to offer additional choice. The Inn strives to ensure that all of its meals are GM free to the best of knowledge.

Bed & Breakfast is now offered at The Crab & Lobster Inn, with five new en-suite bedrooms available. 2 x twin/double, 1 x 4 poster, 1 x small double and 1 x family room for two adults and two children (sharing a bunk bed). All rooms are light and airy, with some boasting stunning sea views that help to make a location for the perfect escape. A television and tea and coffee making facilities are available in all of the rooms as standard.

de Condé and having made sure that his will was in order, contrived his murder. Although she was tried for the crime, political considerations led to the case being quietly dropped. Sophie returned to England with her ill-gotten gains, but in her last years she seems to have been stricken with remorse and gave lavishly to charity.

BEMBRIDGE
5 miles SE of Ryde, on the B3350

🏠 Windmill 🏛 Maritime Museum

🏛 Roy Baker Heritage Centre

The most easterly point of the island, this popular sailing centre was itself an island until the reclamation of the huge inland harbour of Brading Haven in the 1880s. The story of that major work is one of many aspects of the town's history that features in the **Shipwreck Centre & Maritime Museum**, which also displays ship models, artefacts from shipwrecks, and diving equipment, as well as action videos of underwater footage and lifeboat rescues. The Shipwreck Centre has moved to Arreton Barns (see under Arreton, page 291). A fascinating exhibition of life in Bembridge, past and present, is portrayed in photographs and artefacts at the **Bembridge Roy Baker Heritage Centre** in Church Road.

Also well worth a visit is the **Bembridge Windmill** (National Trust). Dating from around 1700, it is the only windmill to have survived on the island and much of its wooden machinery is still intact. There are spectacular views from the top floor.

BRADING
2 miles N of Sandown on the A3055

🏠 Nunwell House & Gardens 🏠 Morton Manor

🏛 Lilliput Museum 🏛 Roman Villa

🏠 Brading Experience

For what is little more than a large village, Brading is remarkably well-stocked with visitor attractions. Amongst them are a diminutive Town Hall with whipping post and stocks outside, and a fine church housing some striking tombs of the Oglander family. The most ancient of the village's sights is the **Brading Roman Villa**, which in the 3rd century was the centre of a rich and prosperous farming estate. Discovered in 1880, the villa covers some 300 square feet and has fine mosaic floors with a representation of that master-musician, Orpheus, charming wild animals with his lyre.

The oldest surviving house on the island is now home to the **Brading Experience**, an all-weather family attraction displaying scenes and characters from island history. Naturally,

Bembridge Windmill

THE BIKE SHED

Perreton Farm, East Lane, Merstone,
Isle of Wight, PO30 3DL
Tel: 01983 868786
e-mail: sales@the-bikeshed.co.uk
website: www.the-bikeshed.com

Merstone is a quaint little hamlet on the Isle of Wight and it is here, tucked away on a delightful rural farm, that you will find **The Bike Shed** housed in a classic barn. Established for 10 years, owner Jeffrey Smith has built up a wide and varied selection of bikes, scooters and accessories for sale and hire, as well as a range of electric bikes.

The list is endless ranging from Mountain, Comfort and Hybrid to Road, Performance and much more with well known brands like Giant and Trek (Altura and Avid). There are bicyles for both genders and all ages and you can try before you buy using the bike testing area facility to ensure that what looks good is also equally as nice to ride. For those who are keen cyclists and already have a bike of their own The Bike Shed also stocks a range of accessories such as lighting and helmets.

The Bike Shed has been approved by local Trading Standards Services and provides a reliable and customer friendly service. With everyone looking to promote a greener way of life, bicycles are becoming a lot more popular and enable you to keep fit whilst enjoying the ride at the same time. And there is no better place to enjoy a bike ride than the picturesque Isle of Wight.

THE GARLIC FARM

Newchurch, Isle of Wight PO36 0NR
Tel: 01983 865378 Fax: 01983 862294
e-mail: colin@thegarlicfarm.co.uk
website: www.thegarlicfarm.co.uk

The Garlic Farm is the UK's premier grower of garlic and source of all things connected with garlic. Colin Boswell has been the driving force behind the farm for more than 30 years, and his wife Jenny and their five children are all involved in various ways in the business. Intrigued by the ancient origins of garlic and its wide range of culinary, health and legendary properties, Colin has developed the business and has personally become the number one garlic expert in the UK, perhaps in Europe. The shop sells plain garlic, smoked garlic, garlic planting packs and garlic in dozens of products made on the farm. These include pickles and relishes, garlic mayonnaise, garlic-infused oils and vinegars, smoked garlic honey, mint sauce with a hint of garlic, sweet garlic cloves in oil, garlic and horseradish mustard, pesto, tapénade, oak-smoked garlic butter, garlic salsa, garlic bread.......the range grows each year. The relocated farm shop is open every day all year round, and in summer visitors can relax over coffee and croissants with the papers and jazz music.

The Garlic Festival that started here in 1983 has become one of the largest annual events on the Island, attracting some 25,000 visitors in an ambience that mixes all things garlic with a country fair and a pop festival.

MERSLEY FARM SELF-CATERING

Newchurch, Isle of Wight PO36 0NR
Tel: 01983 865213
e-mail: web@mersleyfarm.co.uk
website: www. mersleyfarm.co.uk

A variety of excellent self-catering accommodation is available in converted barns and cottages on **Mersley Farm**.

Little Mersley Farmhouse, sleeping 10, was built in 1672. It stands alone in its own grounds, a fine and little altered example of an Island yeoman's house. The master bedroom is in on the ground floor, with en suite toilet and shower. There's a separate sitting room and dining room off a well-appointed kitchen. The other bedrooms are on the first floor. The Milking Parlour, sleeping 8, is a large unit first built as a threshing barn and then used for milking cows. This attractive barn conversion features a spacious, comfortable sitting room and kitchen with a vaulted ceiling. There are four bedrooms – two with double beds, one twin-bedded and one bunk-bedded; with the option of extra accommodation on a sofa bed/Z bed in the living room. Adjoining the Milking Parlour is Paddock Cottage, sleeping 2 in a double bedroom (plus an optional single bed). French windows open from the living room on to a patio and paddock. Paddock Cottage and the Milking Parlour can be rented as one. The Barn Cottage, sleeping 4, is an attractive conversion on one level with its own entrance, garden and barbecue areas with access to the farm grounds and tennis court.

Free Wi-Fi Broadband Internet access is available in all the properties.

XANADU

The Square, Godshill, Isle of Wight PO38
Tel: 01983 840949

The dictionary meaning of 'xanadu' is an id
beautiful place and I can't think of a better
this fantastic gift shop in the popular Isle o
Upon entering **Xanadu**, you will be amazed
vast range of fabulous household items, so
collectables and unusual gifts on offer, as
confectionary, preserves, biscuits and choc
is a real delight to wander round the shop,
marvelling at the assortment of traditional
unique gifts available to purchase for yours

Tom and Allison Greatorex invite you to
gifts. For him you will be spoilt for choice
clocks in vehicles, motorbikes or musical in
Yankee Candles – a huge selection of the
pot pourri. This fantastic collection is excel
will help make your house feel like home.
newcomers alike. For sweet lovers there ar
hard candies, plus imported chocolates from

You will also find an array of photo fram
babies, as well as toys, calendars, watches
mechanise and wedding gifts including keep

A Yankee Candles Loyalty Card can be
the card is stamped. When the card is full,
absolutely FREE!

weather and the place and returned
liar Broadstairs.

NTNOR

iles SW of Shanklin on the A3055

Heritage Museum   Visitor Centre

Botanical Gardens   Coastal Visitor Centre

St Boniface Down

ng the southeastern corner of the
tches a six-mile length of ragged
wn as Undercliffe. Clinging to the
s eastern end, Ventnor has been
an alpinist's town" and as "a stee
torium with the sea as the stage
moted as a spa town in the 1830
nguished visitors have included
ston Churchill and an elderly

entnor Heritage Museum
inating collection of old prin
tographs and working mode
town's history, while **Ventn**
dens shelters some 10,000
s of grounds, amongst the
exotic trees, shrubs, alpin
ulents and conifers. The
ge boost in the spring o
ning of an exciting new

made

anges

If, so

he

a little

quite incredible. Real straw was prepared in the traditional way for thatching; the church on the hill took 600 hours of work before being assembled in its position; each house has its own tiny garden with miniature trees and shrubs. The airfield is in the style of small landing strips of the 1920s and 1930s, and the little railway is modelled on the older Island systems. Things get even smaller in the model garden of the model Old Vicarage, where there is another (1/100 scale) model village with yet another Old Vicarage, and within its garden another (1/1000 scale) model village – a model of a model of a model! There's also a (full-size) tearoom here with outdoor seating.

Godshill Model Village

Also in Godshill are the **Nostalgia Toy Museum**, where 2,000 Dinky, Corgi and Matchbox toys and 1960s dolls bring back childhood memories, and the **Natural History Centre** with its famous sea-shell collection of more than 40,000 shells from both tropical and local shores. The display includes the worlds tiniest shell, most poisonous shell mollusc and the most beautiful shells.

BONCHURCH
2 miles S of Shanklin on the A3055

The poet Algernon Swinburne spent some of his childhood in this lovely hilltop village and is buried in the churchyard of St Boniface. Charles Dickens wrote part of *David Copperfield* while staying in Bonchurch. His first impressions of the place were very favourable – "I think it is the prettiest place I ever saw". He seemed likely to make it his permanent home, but he soon grew to dislike the weather and the place and returned to his familiar Broadstairs.

VENTNOR
3 miles SW of Shanklin on the A3055

🏛 Heritage Museum	🌱 Visitor Centre
🌱 Botanical Gardens	🌱 Coastal Visitor Centre
🚶 St Boniface Down	

Along the southeastern corner of the island stretches a six-mile length of ragged cliffs known as Undercliffe. Clinging to the slopes at its eastern end, Ventnor has been described as "an alpinist's town" and as "a steeply raked auditorium with the sea as the stage". Promoted as a spa town in the 1830s, its distinguished visitors have included a young Winston Churchill and an elderly Karl Marx.

Ventnor Heritage Museum houses a fascinating collection of old prints, photographs and working models relating to the town's history, while **Ventnor Botanical Gardens** shelters some 10,000 plants in 22 acres of grounds, amongst them many rare and exotic trees, shrubs, alpines, perennials, succulents and conifers. The gardens received a huge boost in the spring of 2000 with the opening of an exciting new **Visitor Centre**

BON BON

29A Pier Street, Ventnor, Isle of Wight PO38 1SX
Tel: 01983 853856

Have you got a sweet tooth and a passion for French inspired interior design? If the answer is yes, then the perfect shop for you is **Bon Bon** in the popular Isle of Wight!

It may seem like an odd combination - decorative home furnishings plus nostalgic sweets!? But it works; this speciality shop has attracted visitors from around the Island and mainland as well as adding diversity to what the town has to offer.

One half of the shop stocks lovely French Affair items such as chandeliers, mirrors, linens and garden furniture that is both practical and decorative, plus much more. The furniture, both original and in the French style, has the ability to create tranquillity in any room setting. Offering you the opportunity to feel that your home is incredibly relaxing, comfortable but above all stylish. The other half is home to speciality hand made chocolates and a fantastic range of nostalgic sweets (all made in England), bringing back childhood memories of the old favourites and all the new mouth watering goodies. New lines are being added all the time as Steve and Carol discover new ranges and find old favourites.

Sharing all these wonderful goodies is equally as satisfying as eating them all to yourself, so say it with sweets, nothing says "I love you" like delicious hand made chocolates.

It doesn't stop there; sweets make the perfect table toppers for weddings and are surely the sweetest way to promote your business. You're sure to find something to make your day a little sweeter. Bon appétit!

THE OLD STUDIO

48 High Street, Ventnor, I.O.W, PO38 1LT
Tel: 01983 853996
e-mail: info@theoldstudio.co.uk
website: www.theoldstudio.co.uk

The Old Studio is an impressive Gallery consisting of four rooms. Owners Philip and Lindy Le May have restored the shop and studio to showcase an exciting collection of contemporary art, craft, and design led objects sourced locally and from the mainland. The atmosphere is light hearted and you can choose at your leisure between a large painting inspired by the waves or fine silver jewellery and anywhere in-between.

The building was built in 1860 and became a photographers' studio in 1890. **The Old Studio - "The only gallery on the Back of the Wight"** is situated in Ventnor, a Victorian seaside town of steep terraces populated by artists, sculptors, potters, glass makers, authors, poets, musicians and, of course, crab and lobster fisherman.

The front room of the Gallery is mainly attractive cards, jewellery and antique furniture, and upstairs displays artwork by local and national artists, most of them being paintings, but there is also a high quality of photos on stretch canvases. In the back of the Gallery there's pottery, lamps and local hand painted cushions. The theme of The Old Studio is coastal based, so a lot of the designs on the pottery are sea blues, and the style of the pottery is very different to conventional designs. The Old Studio has a range of exhibiting artist such as Helen Derbyshire, Celia Wilkinson and sculptures by Fran Doherty and Dennis Fairweather.

Phil and Lindy have shared a love of art and antiques since they met in 1980, Phil has been an art dealer for many years dealing through the large auction houses and Lindy trained as a fashion designer and has had shops in Brighton since the 1970's. Their last shop on the mainland was dedicated to interiors mixing the antique with the contemporary. For many years they wanted to move to the Island and finally did so in 2004.

"We have had such fun setting up The Old Studio. Going around the country meeting artists and makers, especially young people making their first entry into the art arena, has given us such pleasure. Obviously the work is important but the human side to this business, both artist and customer, is paramount to us so that we can all share our enthusiasms."

THE OLD RECTORY B&B

Ashknowle Lane, Whitwell, Isle of Wight PO38 2PP
Tel: 01983 731242
e-mail: info@oldrectory1868.co.uk
website: www.oldrectory1868.co.uk

Having renovated and restored this fine house, Jon and
Selina Hepworth would love to welcome you to share it with
them. **The Old Rectory B&B** offers peace and tranquility
surrounded by glorious countryside and only a mile from the
sea. Set in the heart of a quiet village, it is next to the lovely
old church and a stone's throw from, reputedly, the oldest pub
on the island, which serves excellent food. The local town of
Ventnor offers a variety of places to eat, from top quality
cuisine to locally caught fresh fish served on the seafront.

This fine Old Rectory was built in 1868 in the grand
Victorian Gothic tradition. Jon and Selina have a keen eye for
detail, and the reception rooms and bedrooms are tastefully
equipped with antique furniture, blissfully comfortable beds and
luxurious fittings. The house is set in an acre of garden, and nestling in the trees is a pretty
summer house and guests have the use of the garden and sun loungers.

Beautifully prepared breakfasts made from locally sourced Island ingredients are served, and
evening meals are available on request - this is a set three course meal with a complimentary
glass of wine; guests are welcome to bring their own wine as well.

GOTTEN MANOR

Gotten Lane, Chale, Ventnor,
Isle of Wight, PO38 2HQ
Tel: 01983 551368
Mobile: 07746 453398
e-mail: cl@gottenmanor.co.uk
website: www.gottenmanor.co.uk

Gotten Manor can be found nestling beneath St Catherine's Down where a wonderful selection
of B&B and self catering accommodation are on offer.

The Old House B&B has a stunning bedroom with polished wooden floors, lime washed walls
and a beautiful rosewood bed. This peaceful location is enhanced by a sympathetic restoration
downstairs with open fires and a cosy dining room. Breakfast includes smoked salmon,
scrambled egg and full English, with all ingredients fresh and sourced locally where possible.

The Cart House is a 200 year-old stone barn converted into two self catering cottages, yet
retaining the open facade of the original building. The cottages feature a huge open plan living/
kitchen area with big, picture windows across the front and two bedrooms. The main bedroom
has a double and single bed and through into the second bedroom there are three singles. The
downstairs bathroom includes a king size shower. Both cottages have central heating, ample
parking space and a garden with a barbecue.

The Milk House is a 200 year-old stone barn converted into a delightful and very comfortable
holiday home. There are three large en-suite bedrooms and, from the third bedroom, there are
French doors that lead out onto a wooden balcony, with steps out to the garden. There are
magnificent views across unspoiled countryside to Freshwater Bay.

whose exhibits include an interactive display called The Green Planet – the Incredible Life of Plants. Many unusual varieties are for sale in the shop. There's a picnic area and children's playground, and during August the Gardens host open-air performances of Shakespeare's plays.

Back in town, the **Coastal Visitor Centre** provides a fascinating and educational insight into the island's coastal and marine environment, with special features on animal and plant life, coastal defences and living with landslides - a problem very familiar to the island as well as to many parts of England's south coast.

Ventnor Beach

Above the town, **St Boniface Down** (National Trust), at 785 feet the highest point on the island, provides some dizzying views across coast and countryside.

ST LAWRENCE
1 mile W of Ventnor on the A3055

🐟 St Catherine's Point 🔎 Studio Glass

🖉 Blackgang Chine

Nestling in the heart of the Undercliff, the ancient village of St Lawrence has a 13th-century church that once laid claim to being the smallest in Britain. It was extended in 1842 but remains diminutive, measuring just 20 feet by 12 feet.

Not far away, old farm buildings were converted into **Isle of Wight Studio Glass**, where skills old and new produce glass of the highest quality.

Lord Jellicoe, hero of Jutland, lived for some years in St Lawrence and often swam in Orchard's Bay, a small cove where Turner sketched.

The coast road continues through the village of Niton to **St Catherine's Point**, the most southerly and the wildest part of the island, and an Area of Special Scientific Interest. Steps lead down to St Catherine's lighthouse and a path leads up to the summit of St Catherine's Hill, where the remains of a much older lighthouse, known as the Pepperpot, can be seen. Close by is the Hoy Monument erected in honour of a visit by Tsar Nicholas I.

Blackgang Chine, at the most southerly tip of the island, has been developed from an early Victorian scenic park into a modern fantasy park with dozens of attractions for children. Also inside the park are two heritage exhibitions centred on a water-powered sawmill and a quayside, with displays ranging from cooper's and wheelwright's workshops to a shipwreck collection, a huge whale skeleton and a 19th-century beach scene complete with a bathing machine. The coastline here is somewhat fragile, and a large slice of cliff has been lost to storms and gales in recent years.

Blackgang

Distance: *5 miles (8.0 kilometres)*
Typical time: *140 mins*
Height gain: *165 metres*
Map: *Explorer OL 29*
Walk: *www.walkingworld.com ID:546*
Contributor: *David L White*

ACCESS INFORMATION:

Large car park, nearest bus stop 'Blackgang'. If travelling from the mainland best crossings:

Ryde/Portsmouth - Catamaran;

Ryde/Southsea - Hovercraft;

Fishbourne/Portsmouth - Car ferry

ADDITIONAL INFORMATION:

Seafaring history is evident here as may be seen in the form of the three lighthouses all built at different periods in history. The area of Blackgang and Niton featured strongly in the business of smuggling in earlier days. During the warmer weather there is an abundance of wildlife and flowering plants. Should you wish to take a short diversion from the Niton parish church further into the village, shops and a local pub may be found (the pub serves food). Opposite the church are the public toilets.

DESCRIPTION:

A walk with fabulous views over the Isle of Wight and English Channel taking in some of the local history and landmarks.

FEATURES:

Hills or Fells, Sea, Pub, Toilets, Church, Wildlife, Birds, Flowers, Great Views.

WALK DIRECTIONS:

1 | A Heritage Coast information board in the car park will tell you about the coastal area. Climb steps on seaward side of car park - follow path to cliff top. Turn left along cliff top towards Niton. Follow path past radio mast station on your left. After second stile beyond radio station, turn immediately left over another stile heading inland.

2 | From this high vantage point looking slightly Southeast, St Catherine's lighthouse may be seen. It was built in 1840 to replace the earlier lighthouses that were further inland. This coastline was famous for its many wrecks, one night it is said that there were as many as 14.

3 | Keeping fence on your right, walk across to far end of field to stile. Head across small meadow slightly to your left to stile, cross and walk through a coppice path until you reach the main road. Follow road to right, until it bears left (marked through traffic) to church. At lychgate turn left and go up Pan Lane, which eventually turns into a bridlepath. Follow path eventually turning left and you soon reach a metal gate. Follow blue arrow sign straight ahead.

4 | After passing through gate, follow track indicated by blue waymark arrow, upon reaching metal gate at other end of the field (keeping radio mast on your left). After passing through this gate, turn immediately left and climb to summit of the hill where the Old Oratory stands. Here you will see fantastic views. If you do not wish to visit Hoy's Monument ignore waymarks 5 and 6, proceed to waymark 7.

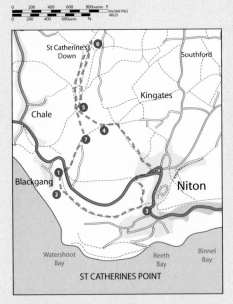

5 | To visit Hoy's Monument, instead of turning left walk across the field bearing slightly to your right towards a visible signpost, follow bridleway C6 to Hoy's monument.

6 | From Hoy's Monument return to waymark 5 by same path.

7 | The Oratory is known to locals as the Pepper Pot and is one of the original lighthouses built in 1314 and manned by a local duty monk. Also visible to the East from here is the Salt Pot, built later but, before completion, it was decided that due to mist and fog on the hills often obscuring the glow of the light, the project would be abandoned in favour of a building closer to the coast and lower down (the present St Catherine's). From the Oratory, cross field heading towards the sea where you will see a stile. Standing on the stile and looking down slightly to your left you will see your starting point car park.

WROXALL
2 miles N of Ventnor on the B3327

🏠 Appuldurcombe House

🦉 Owl & Falconry Centre 🦉 Donkey Sanctuary

Owls, falcons, vultures and donkeys all call Wroxall their home. **Appuldurcombe House**, once the grandest mansion on the whole island, with gardens laid out by Capability Brown, was badly bombed in 1943 and has never been lived in since. The building has been partly restored and visitors can stroll in the 11 acres of ornamental grounds, which provide an enchanting setting for picnics. The **Owl and Falconry Centre**, in what used to be the laundry and brewhouse, stages daily flying displays with birds of prey from around the world and holds courses in the centuries-old art of falconry.

Heaven for 200 donkeys and many other

LITTLE SPAN FARM

Rew Lane, Wroxall, Ventnor, Isle of Wight PO38 3AU
Tel: 01983 852419
e-mail: info@spanfarm.co.uk   website: www.spanfarm.co.uk

Little Span Farm in Wroxall, is an attractive stone farmhouse dating back to the 17th century, and is part of a working arable stock farm. Set in an Area of Outstanding Natural Beauty, it is ideal for walking and family holidays. Wroxall's main attraction is Appuldurcombe House and at Little Span you couldn't be any closer to this magnificent ruin since the farm used to part of the Appuldurcombe Estate. In this lovely peaceful setting Felicity Corry offers a choice of accommodation for Bed & Breakfast and self-catering guests. The Farmhouse has two en-suite double bedrooms and a double/twin with en suite shower. All have TV/video-player, beverage tray and hairdryer. The other B&B property is Harvester Cottage, located behind the farmhouse, with a

king-size double-bedded room, bunk beds, a shower room and similar amenities to the farmhouse. A hearty full English breakfast is served in the dining room in the farmhouse.

For self-catering guests The Stable has been recently converted to provide comfortable 'upside down' accommodation with a roomy farmhouse kitchen, an open-plan beamed living/dining area and a first-floor sun deck. It also has its own small-enclosed garden. The Brewhouse, sleeping four (double and bunk beds), plus extra sofa bed offers the visitor every comfort. Both these properties have spiral staircases linking the living and sleeping areas. Guests are free to roam round the farm, and children can help with feeding during the lambing season.

animals, the **Isle of Wight Donkey Sanctuary** is at Lower Winstone Farm. The rescue centre is a registered charity relying entirely on donations, and visitors have several ways of helping, including the Adopt a Donkey scheme.

SHORWELL
7 miles SW of Newport, on the B3323

🏠 St Peter's Church 🝅 Yafford Mill

Pronounced 'Shorell' by Caulkheads, as Isle of Wight natives are known, this village of thatched stone cottages has no fewer than three venerable manor houses within its boundaries. West Court, Wolverton, and North Court were built respectively during the reigns of Henry VIII, Elizabeth I, and James I. They possess all the charm you would expect from that glorious age of

English architecture, but sadly none of them is open to the public. However, you can visit **St Peter's Church** to gaze on its mesmerisingly beautiful 15th-century wall-painting and admire its 500-year-old stone pulpit covered by an elaborate wooden canopy of 1620. The church also has a real oddity in a painting on wood of the Last Supper, brought from Iceland in 1898.

This small village boasts another attraction. **Yafford Mill** is an 18th-century water mill in full working order. It's surrounded by ponds and streams where you'll find Sophie, the resident seal, and within the grounds there are paddocks which are home to rare cattle, sheep and pigs, a collection of antique farm machinery, a steam engine and narrow-gauge railway. There are also waymarked nature walks, a

---

NORTHCOURT MANOR

*Main Road, Northcourt, Shorwell,
Isle of Wight, PO30 3JG
Tel: 01983 740415
e-mail: christine@northcourt.info
website: www.northcourt.info*

The countryside village of Shorwell on the Isle of Wight is a quiet little hideaway home to some lovely thatched cottages, a historic church and 3 impressive manor houses. The largest of the three and by far most breathtaking is **Northcourt Manor**.

This historic dwelling was built in 1615 by the deputy Governor of the Island, Sir John Leigh and went on to be extended by Lord Burgh in 1905 with the addition of a music room. Once home to the poet Swinburne, this magnificent Jacobean Manor House now receives guests and provides 6 grand en-suite bedrooms. Each bedroom has been tastefully decorated and furnished, and offers central heating with views of the striking grounds.

The private gardens stretch from the stream to the terraced walks and contain many exotic and unusual plants, a garden lover's paradise! Northcourt is an ideal base to explore the local area and with its short distance to the sea, south coast and local pub The Crown, it's perfect for those who enjoy a peaceful stroll followed by a bite to eat or refreshing drink.

🏠 historic building 🏛 museum and heritage 🏚 historic site 🝅 scenic attraction 🌿 flora and fauna

playground, picnic area, gift shop, tea gardens and a licensed bar.

BRIGHSTONE
8 miles S of Newport on the B3399

 🏛 Dinosaur Farm Museum

 🌱 Mottistone Manor Garden 🚶 Mottistone Common

One of the prettiest villages on the island, Brighstone was once notorious as the home of smugglers and wreckers. Today, the National Trust runs a shop in a picturesque row of thatched cottages, and there's a little museum depicting village life down the years.

The island has long been known for its fossil finds, especially relating to dinosaurs. On a clifftop near the village the bones of a completely new species of predatory dinosaur were unearthed. The 15ft carnivore, which lived in the cretaceous period about 120 million to 150 million years ago, has been named *cotyrannus lengi* after Gavin Leng, a local collector who found the first bone. On Military Road (A3055) near Brighstone, the **Dinosaur Farm Museum** came into being following the unearthing in 1992 of the skeleton of a brachiosaurus, at that time the island's largest and most spectacular dinosaur discovery. This unique attraction follows the tale of this and other finds. Visitors are invited to bring their own fossils for identification, and the farm also organises guided fossil tours at various locations on the Island.

A mile or so west of Brighstone, the National Trust is also responsible for **Mottistone Manor Garden**, a charming hillside garden alongside an Elizabethan manor house. The garden is particularly well known for its herbaceous borders and terraces planted with fruit trees. The Mottistone Estate extends from Mottistone Down in the north to the coast at Sudmoor. On **Mottistone**

Common, where New Forest ponies graze, are the remains of a neolithic long barrow known as the Longstone.

FRESHWATER
11 miles W of Newport, on the A3055

 🏛 Church of All Saints 🏛 Dimbola Lodge

 🏛 Old Battery 🚶 Tennyson Down 🚶 Farringford

 🚶 Tennyson Trail 🚶 The Needles

 🌿 Needles Pleasure Park

Freshwater and the surrounding area are inextricably linked with the memory of Alfred, Lord Tennyson. In 1850, he succeeded Wordsworth as Poet Laureate, married Emily Sellwood, and shortly afterwards moved to **Farringford,** just outside Freshwater. The house, set in 33 acres of parkland, is now a hotel where visitors can relax in the luxuriously appointed drawing room with its delightful terrace and views across the downs. Tennyson was an indefatigable walker and however foul the weather would pace along nearby High Down dramatically arrayed in a billowing cloak and a black, broad-brimmed sombrero. After his death, the area was re-named **Tennyson Down** and a cross erected high on the cliffs in his memory.

There are more remembrances of the great poet in the **Church of All Saints** in Freshwater town where Lady Tennyson is buried in the churchyard and a touching memorial inside commemorates their son Lionel, "an affectionate boy", who died at the age of 32 while returning from India. As Tennyson grew older, he became increasingly impatient with sightseers flocking to Farringford hoping to catch sight of the now-legendary figure. He moved to his other home at Blackdown in Sussex where he died in 1892.

About a mile south of the town, Freshwater

BRAEWOOD FRESHWATER BAY

Afton Road, Freshwater, Isle of Wight, PO40 9TP
Tel: 01983 759910

Braewood is a late Victorian house situated in a semi-rural location on the outskirts of Freshwater Village and Freshwater Bay and only five minutes drive from Yarmouth.

It offers guests a relaxing stay with full access to all the facilities at all times of the day. The accommodation is excellent, luxurious and immaculate with extremely comfortable beds and a very warm welcome.

Prices include an excellent breakfast (fresh eggs from our own chickens). Delicious home cooked evening meals (made from fresh local produce) are available on request from £12.50 per head.

All rooms have colour television with free view and tea/coffee making facilities.

There is a beautiful, well-maintained English country garden leading down to the River Yar with a wildlife reserve at the bottom of the garden. Guests are welcome to make use of the garden and to enjoy the amazing abundance of wildlife on the riverbank; feed the ducks or watch the red squirrels.

SEAHORSES

Victoria Road, Freshwater,
Isle of Wight PO40 9PP
Tel/Fax: 01983 752574
e-mail: seahorses-iow@tiscali.co.uk
website: www.seahorsesisleofwight.com

Seahorses Bed and Breakfast is a warm, friendly and spacious former rectory, from which to explore the local landscape of West Wight - a wonderful walking area. The Freshwater Way runs through the large garden and leads on to Freshwater Bay, Tennyson Downs and the Needles (dogs are welcome at no extra charge).

The spacious rooms offer comfortable accommodation for families and just a short drive in any direction leads to a beach for children to enjoy. There is ample parking space at the front of the house, and a safe place for cyclists to lock their bikes at night. For people without transport there are bus stops at the entrance to the driveway.

At Seahorses there is an opportunity to do some art and craft, beginners are welcome. Depending on your time there are various activities from T-shirt printing to sculpting. Prices vary according to materials used.

Bay was once an inaccessible inlet, much favoured by smugglers. Today, the bay is the start point of the 15-mile **Tennyson Trail**, which ends at Carisbrooke and its scenic beauty attracts thousands of visitors every year. They also flock in their thousands to **Dimbola Lodge** (see panel below), one of the most important shrines in the history of early photography. It was the home of Julia Margaret Cameron (1815-1879) who bought it in 1860 to be close to her friend, Tennyson. Three years later, she was given a camera and immediately devoted herself with her usual energy to mastering the technical and artistic aspects of what was then called the "Black Art". (Because handling the chemicals involved usually left the photographer's hands deeply stained.) The coal-house at Dimbola Lodge was turned into a dark room and within a year, Julia had been elected a member of the Photographic Society of London. She photographed most of the leading lights of the artistic community of the time including Thackeray, Darwin, GF Watts and his wife the actress Ellen Terry, who all at some time lived locally. Perhaps the most famous of her images is the classic portrait of Tennyson himself, a craggy, bearded figure with a visionary gaze. Dimbola Lodge was acquired by the Julia Margaret Cameron Trust in 1993 and it has been converted into a museum and galleries devoted to her photography. There's also a gift shop, antiquarian bookshop, and vegetarian restaurant.

From the bay itself, there are regular cruises around the island's most spectacular natural feature, the dreaded **Needles**. The boat trip takes you through the swirling waters around the lighthouse, and past the line of jagged slabs of gleaming chalk towering some 200ft high. The sea has gouged deep caves out of the cliffs. Two of them are known as Lord Holmes' Parlour and Kitchen, named after a 17th-century Governor of the Island who once entertained his guests in the 'Parlour' and kept his wines cool in the 'Kitchen'.

The Needles are undoubtedly at their most impressive when viewed from the sea, but they are still a grand sight from the land. There are some particularly striking vistas from the **Needles Old Battery** (National Trust), a Victorian coastal fort standing 250ft above the sea. Visitors pass through a 200ft long tunnel and emerge onto a platform with

Dimbola Lodge

Terrace Lane, Freshwater Bay,
Isle of Wight PO40 9QE
Tel: 01983756814 Fax: 01983755578
website: www.dimbola.co.uk

This historic house is the former home of internationally known 19th century photographer Julia Margaret Cameron, and contains a museum and galleries. There is a permanent display of Cameron's images and contemporary revolving photographic exhibitions, lectures, photographic courses and musical performances. The Lodge is also available for hire, book launches, etc.

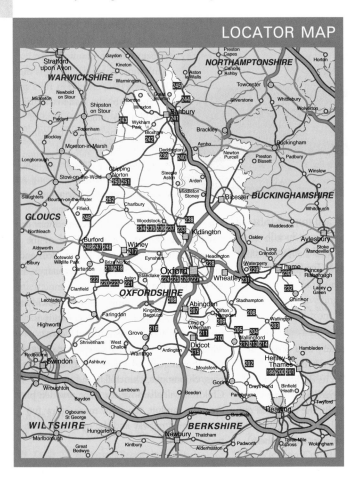

LOCATOR MAP

ADVERTISERS AND PLACES OF INTEREST

🏠 historic building   🏛 museum and heritage   🏛 historic site   ♨ scenic attraction   🌱 flora and fauna

8 Oxfordshire

Oxfordshire is a county covering about 1,000 square miles, contained largely within the Thames Basin. Between Henley and Wallingford lie the beginnings of the Chiltern Hills, while in the north are the most easterly hills of the Cotswolds as well as rich farmland based on the clay soil that stretches up from Oxford to the Midlands. In the east, Henley is one of many attractive Thames-side settlements, towards the west are Faringdon and Witney, and in the north Bicester, Chipping Norton and Banbury. The county is of course dominated by its capital, Oxford, which from the 12th century grew from a small and little known market town into one of the major seats of learning in the world. It also prospered as a central point of communication, first as a stopping point on coaching routes and later with the coming of the canals and the railways. Industry grew, too, and in the suburb of Cowley, Lord Nuffield's Morris car works were a major employer. Many palaeolithic, mesolithic and neolithic finds have been made in the county, but the most eyecatching early archaeological feature is the Uffington White Horse from the Iron Age. Dorchester and Alchester were the most important sites in Roman Oxfordshire, the Saxons built many settlements along the Thames, and the Danes overran the area in the 10th and 11th centuries. The county was heavily involved in the Civil War (1642-1651) and the towns of Oxford (for three years the Royalist headquarters), Banbury and Wallingford were all besieged by Parliamentary forces during the conflict.

ADVERTISERS AND PLACES OF INTEREST

📺 stories and anecdotes 🦜 famous people 🎨 art and craft 🏅 entertainment and sport 🚶 walks

THE LEMONGROVE GALLERY

10 Duke Street, Henley-on-Thames, Oxfordshire, RG9 1UP
Tel: 01491 577215
e-mail: henley@thelemongrovegallery.co.uk
website: www.thelemongrovegallery.co.uk

If you are looking for inspiring artwork from some of the world's most celebrated artists, **The Lemongrove Gallery** is a haven in the middle of Henley-on-Thames. The Town is overlooked by the rolling Chiltern Hills and is nestled next to a beautiful stretch of the Thames. The Lemongrove is the area's premier contemporary art gallery. They have an unrivalled range of original paintings, limited editions and sculptures from award winning international stars such as Henderson Cisz, Sherree Valentine Daines and Doug Hyde as well as household names like Jack Vettriano and Rolf Harris.

Upon entering the gallery you will be captivated by the outstanding paintings that adorn the walls. It offers art lovers a rich experience of carefully selected paintings and sculptures in a range of genres and styles; from landscapes to still life, to traditional and contemporary styles. The works displayed have been chosen for their artistic merit by the professional gallery team.

The gallery is characterised by a welcoming and unpretentious atmosphere and offers customers a superb range of services to make their art buying experience more pleasurable including Bespoke Framing, Home Consultation, Wedding Gift List, Loyalty Card and Interest Free Credit to name but a few.

In the workplace, art is not merely decoration. In the business environment a picture does really mean a thousand words, reflecting your core ideals and philosophy. One of the experts from the gallery can visit your office, restaurant or hotel to help you select the kind of art that will enhance your company's image and ensure it oozes energy and style.

Whether you are in the gallery or searching for that ideal piece from the comfort of your own home of via the internet, the Lemongrove staff are a friendly and helpful team and will be delighted to advise you on your choice of artwork and sculpture to fit any budget.

The Lemongrove Gallery has three locations within the UK, Henley-on-Thames, Reading and now Chiswick.

🏚 historic building   🏛 museum and heritage   🏛 historic site   ⌘ scenic attraction   🐦 flora and fauna

Henley-on-Thames

🏠 Greys Court 🏛 River & Rowing Museum

🏛 Fawley Court Museum 🏊 Regatta

Reputed to be the oldest settlement in Oxfordshire, this attractive riverside market town has more than 300 listed buildings from various periods. The Thames has always played an important role in its life; in 1829 the first varsity boat race, between Oxford and Cambridge, took place here on the river and, within a decade, the event was enjoying royal patronage. First held in 1839, the **Henley Regatta** takes place every year in the first week of July, is a marvellous and colourful event with teams from all over the world competing on the mile long course. Scores of tents and striped marquees are erected on the Berkshire side of the river and champagne flows freely.

Opened in 1998, the **River and Rowing Museum** is a fascinating place that traces the rowing heritage of Henley, the river's changing role in the town's history, and even provides the opportunity to 'walk' the length of the River Thames, from source to sea, taking in all the locks. Housed in spacious, purpose-built premises designed by the award-winning architect, David Chipperfield, its exhibits include the boat in which the British duo, Steve Redgrave and Matthew Pinsent, won their gold medals at the 1996 Olympics. A major new attraction re-creates Kenneth Grahame's much-loved tale *The Wind in the Willows*. In a spectacular walk-

JAM FOR TEA

12 Friday Street, Henley-on-Thames,
Oxfordshire RG9 1AH
Tel: 01491 411414
e-mail: ask@jamfortea.co.uk
website: www.jamfortea.co.uk

Just a short walk from the river, **Jam for Tea** on Friday Street is unmistakable with its corner position and large window housing an eye-catching display of beautiful furniture.

Lisa McLaughlin realised a long standing love of French style by opening Jam for Tea after moving to Henley from London. This gem of a shop has become a favourite destination for French antiques, decorative mirrors, vintage hand-painted furniture, Scandinavian textiles, antique linen and home accessories. Vintage hand woven French linens and faded floral cushions can bring a softness to a room or for a contemporary feel maybe add some brightly printed Scandinavian textiles. "Although we have an obvious passion for all things vintage, we believe that by taking the best from the past and mixing it with the new, it's possible to create a totally unique style", says Lisa.

Jam for Tea also stock a range of giftware including designer jewellery, scented candles, aromatherapy products and unique hand crafted gifts sourced locally.

Jam for Tea believe in good old fashioned customer service and will often source French furniture and mirrors for clients who are looking for something special.

DOWN-TO-EARTH

40a Bell Street, Henley-on-Thames, Oxfordshire RG9 2BG
Tel: 01491 575858
e-mail: andrewelias@hotmail.com
website: www.down-to-earth-online.co.uk

The family run **Down-to-Earth** home and gift shop is a must for any visitor to Henley on Thames. The shop is well located on Bell Street in the middle of the town centre and offers a wonderful array of designer gifts and homeware.

Down-to-Earth are large stockists of the fabulous Cath Kidston designer homeware range and have all sorts of products with beautiful and bright patterns that give the shop a lovely and uplifting feel. They also stock Greengate, a Danish designer offering products for the home full of Nordic charm and style.

The shop sells luxury natural body products and candles from companies such as Dr. Hauschka and Natural Magic Luxury Organics allowing one to treat one's self as well as others!

Down-to-Earth have their flagship store 15 minutes away from Henley at 35 – 36 St. Martin's Street, Wallingford, Oxfordshire. Here you will find all of the same wonderful designer homeware as well as a local food shop selling homemade cakes, local meats and other delicious foods.

through exhibition visitors can meet all the familiar characters and places in the book, with E H Shepard's illustrations brilliantly brought to life.

Henley was the site of Rupert's Elm, where Prince Rupert is said to have hanged a Roundhead spy. A portion of the tree is preserved in this museum. Also situated on the riverbank, beside the town's famous 18th-century five-arched bridge decorated with the faces of Father Thames and the

goddess Isis, is the Leander Club, the headquarters of the famous rowing club.

Apart from the boating, which is available throughout the summer, and the pleasant

Henley Bridge

🏛 historic building 🏛 museum and heritage 🏛 historic site ⚘ scenic attraction ❦ flora and fauna

walks along the riverbanks, there are many interesting shops, inns, and teashops in the town. Buildings of note include Speaker's House, home of Speaker Lenthall of the Long Parliament who lived there in the 17th century, some attractive almshouses around the churchyard, and Chantry House, which dates from the 14th century and is believed to be the oldest building in Henley.

Just down river from the town centre lies **Fawley Court**, a wonderful private house that was designed by Christopher Wren and built in 1684 for a Colonel Freeman. Now owned by the Marian Fathers, the **Museum** it contains includes a library, documents relating to the Polish kings, and memorabilia of the Polish army. The house, gardens, and museum are open to the public from March to October.

Greys Court, Henley

To the northwest of Henley, at Rotherfield Greys, is another interesting house, **Greys Court** (National Trust), dating originally from the 14th century, but much altered down the years; a beautiful courtyard and a tower survive from the earliest building. A Tudor wheelhouse is among the interesting outbuildings, and the gardens offer many delights, notably old-fashioned roses and wisterias, an ornamental vegetable garden, a ha-ha, an ice-house and the Archbishop's Maze, which was inspired, in 1980, by Archbishop Runcie's enthronement speech. The house is closed throughout 2008 for major maintenance and refurbishment but the gardens remain open.

Around Henley-on-Thames

SONNING COMMON
3½ miles SW of Henley on the B481

Sonning Common was originally part of the manor of Sonning-on-Thames with the livestock driven from the flooded riverside pastures to winter on the higher ground.

Widmore Pond, on the edge of the village, is said to have been a Roman silver mine: according to a 17th-century account, when the pond was emptied for cleaning out, upturned oak tree stumps were found in the bottom of the pond along with stag antlers and Roman coins.

MAPLEDURHAM
6½ miles SW of Henley off the A4074

🏠 Mapledurham House 🏠 Church of St Margaret

🏠 Watermill

A narrow winding lane leads to this famously picturesque village set beside the Thames. The

🎭 stories and anecdotes 🎭 famous people ⚲ art and craft ✍ entertainment and sport 🚶 walks

PHILIP KOOMEN FURNITURE

Wheelers Barn, Checkendon, nr Henley-on-Thames,
Oxfordshire, RG8 0NJ
Tel: 01491 681122
e-mail: furniture@koomen.demon.co.uk
website: www.philipkoomen.co.uk

Philip Koomen Furniture, a team of designers and makers, was established by Philip Koomen in 1975 to create enduring furniture for people who enjoy and appreciate fine craftsmanship, thoughtful design and beautiful woods.

The designs are rooted in the craft tradition of the Arts & Crafts philosophy yet maintain a contemporary edge. Clients either commission a bespoke version of one of Philip's designs or an entirely new design is developed. Selection of woods is a key aspect of the furniture design and making process: grain, colour and character all influence and enrich the designs. Increasingly the timber used comes from woodlands and estates in Oxfordshire.

The 19th century flint and brick workshop and showroom are open during the week and by appointment at weekends. Visitors are able to view furniture and extensive portfolios in their own time. Every year open days are held over two weekends during Oxfordshire Artweeks in May.

The workshop is set in the beautiful Chilterns countryside, only one hour from London, thirty minutes from Oxford and fifteen minutes from Reading and Henley-on-Thames. Details can be found on the website or contact Philip Koomen.

THE GRANARY DELICATESSEN

30 High Street, Watlington, Oxfordshire OX49 5PY
Tel: 01491 613585
e-mail: granarydeli@btinternet.com
website: www.granarydeli.co.uk

The residents of Watlington and the surrounding area have every reason to be grateful for the efforts of Robin and Francesca Holmes-Smith, who saved **The Granary Delicatessen** from closure in 2002. Always a cheese shop at heart, it stocks an impressive selection of some 170 cheeses, mainly from the UK (many of them award winners), but with prime varieties also from France and Italy.

The shop hosts cheese tasting on Fridays and Saturdays. Cheese related items such as knives and scoops are always available, and other produce includes preserves, olive oil and olives, pickles and chutneys, biscuits, bread from two local bakeries, coffees, organic wines and store cupboard basics. The Granary can make up hampers for any occasion.

A trip to Granary Deli will not disappoint!

WATLINGTON
8 miles NW of Henley off the B480

🌿 Watlington Hill

There are superb views over the surrounding countryside from **Watlington Hill**, which rises 700ft above Watlington Park with its woods of beech and yew. Watlington Hill and its neighbour Pyrton Hill are designated a Site of Special Scientific Interest and are home to over 30 species of butterflies and a wide variety of chalk-loving plants.

EWELME
9 miles NW of Henley off the B4009

At the centre of this pretty village is a magnificent group of medieval buildings, including the church, almshouses and school,

Almshouses, Ewelme

which were all founded in the 1430s by Alice Chaucer, granddaughter of the poet Geoffrey, and her husband, the Duke of Suffolk. There is a wonderfully elegant alabaster carving of Alice inside the church and under this effigy is another rather macabre carving of a shrivelled cadaver. In the churchyard is the grave of

EWELME POTTERY

Parsons Lane, Ewelme, Wallingford,
Oxfordshire, OX10 6HP
Tel: 01491 835633
e-mail: harrietcoleridge@aol.com

The Ewelme Pottery is at the heart of Ewelme, an historic village well known for its fifteenth century church and school. The Pottery was started in 2001 by Harriet Coleridge who trained as a potter under Alan Caiger Smith, at Aldermaston, in the 'eighties.

She makes decorative ceramics for the house and the garden, ranging from tableware designed for daily use and special occasions, bottles tall and round, bowls tiny and garguantuan to more individual pieces such as long serpentine boats for shots, life sized fish- sea green and foamy- for the wall, tiled tables, birdbaths and chess boards.

Having spent twenty years making tin glazed earthenware decorated with elaborately stylised flowers and animals, she now works with stoneware and porcelain. The work is glazed and reduction fired in a gas kiln to 1280 degrees centigrade. She uses a variety of glazes – from quiet translucent celadon blues to burnished copper reds and fiery black and amber carbon trap shinos. These last are dramatic in their effects and their variety- but the drama comes more from the fire than the brush. There is also a range of pots that have been fired in an anagama kiln which have been decorated entirely by flame and ash in a firing that might last five days.

The sizes range from 2" shots to 20" bottles and the prices from £5.00 to £500.00.

🎭 stories and anecdotes 🐦 famous people 🎨 art and craft 🎟 entertainment and sport 🚶 walks

KELSO

41 Stert Street, Abingdon, Oxfordshire OX14 3JF
Tel: 01235 521000
e-mail: kelsostyle@hotmail.co.uk
website: www.kelsostyle.co.uk

Liz Fletcher has a well established skill in leather craft. After training as a saddler, she studied at the London College of Fashion and from there her interest in style and enjoyment from working with leather led her to open **Kelso** in 2007.

The shop has a clean and contemporary feel to it and is divided into two rooms. As you enter the shop, the first room is an eye-catching display of glass cabinets beautifully showcasing all the items available to purchase. First and foremost is the extensive range of leather goods made by Liz herself in the second room of the premises. The collection comprises of many hand-crafted bags in a variety of different colours and sizes and intricately detailed belts. Other cabinets house vintage and modern jewellery including Lea Stein brooches, pendants by Chelsea Pink and pretty, delicate pieces by Flutterby. There are hats by Helen Berman, bright and colourful bags from Miss Foxglove alongside ranges of clothing from Fever of London and Palace of London.

With a range of fretwork and mosaic pottery, Kelso is the perfect place to find that unique gift for a loved one or that special accessory to set off any outfit.

---

more elaborate building. With its five aisles, it is now broader than it is long. The main glory of the church, the painted ceiling of the Lady Chapel, has been retained from the 14th century. Beside the churchyard, which contains a curious small building that was the blowing chamber for the church organ, are three sets of almshouses. The oldest, Christ's Hospital, was founded in 1446 while the other two, Twitty's Almshouses and Brick Alley Almshouses, date from the early 1700s.

Around Abingdon

DORCHESTER

5 miles SE of Abingdon off the A4074

🏛 Abbey Church 🏛 Abbey Museum

This charming little town, situated on the River Thame just before it flows into the River Thames, has been described as 'the most historic spot in Oxfordshire', since it was here that Christianity was established in the southwest of England by St Birinus. Known as the Apostle of the West Saxons, Birinus was consecrated in Genoa, landed in Wessex in 634AD, and converted King Cynegils of Wessex in the following year. As a mark of his devotion to the church, Cynegils gave Dorchester to Birinus and the church he built here became the cathedral of Wessex.

The **Abbey Church of St Peter and St Paul** was built in 1170 on the site of that Saxon church and greatly extended during the next two centuries. Its chief glory is the 14th-century choir and the huge Jesse window, showing the family tree of Jesus, which has retained its original stained glass. The story of

---

🏛 historic building 🏛 museum and heritage 🏛 historic site 🌿 scenic attraction 🌿 flora and fauna

Abbey Church, Dorchester

the abbey, along with the history of settlement in the area going back to neolithic times, is told in the **Abbey Museum**, which is housed in a classroom of the former Grammar School, built in 1652.

The town itself has some attractive old houses with overhanging upper stories, a fine Georgian coaching inn, and there's a pleasant footpath that crosses fields to the bank of the Thames.

LITTLE WITTENHAM
5 miles SE of Abingdon off the A4130

🏛 Wittenham Clumps 🏛 Pendon Museum

This village, which has a number of pretty cottages, lies beneath the **Wittenham Clumps**, which for centuries formed an important defensive position overlooking the Thames. In the village church of St Peter are

THE MERRY MILLER

Cothill Road, Dry Sandford, nr Abingdon, Oxfordshire OX13 6JW
Tel: 01865 390390
e-mail: rob@merrymiller.co.uk   website: www.merrymiller.co.uk

Dry Sandford is set in an area of small, pretty Oxfordshire villages and lovely countryside, close to the attractive market town of Abingdon. It is here that you will find **The Merry Miller**, a traditional village pub offering a warm welcome and impeccable service. If you are after a local ale, glass of wine, light bite or somewhere to dine of an evening, The Merry Miller is the place to visit.

The menu is endless and each dish is equally as tempting with starters such as; Curried Whitebait, main courses such as Beef Pie with Guinness, Wild Mushroom & Baby Onion and tempting desserts such as Belgium Chocolate & Rum Torte and Morello Cherry Bakewell Tart. The children are also catered for with a delightful kids menu offering wholesome home cooked food. To quench your thirst The Merry Miller provides a good selection of real ales and guest beers including Tiger and Davenport and the wine list is no different providing a large selection of white, red, rose and champagnes. A Traditional Sunday Roast is freshly prepared and cooked every week with red meats, homemade Yorkshire pudding and seasonal vegetables. Every Tuesday is Curry and a Pint night with a selection of homemade curries to choose from varying from mild to spicy (booking is recommended).

The Merry Miller will also cater for large groups, providing a range of set menus to cater for all palates and budgets. There is ample parking available and disabled access throughout.

🎭 stories and anecdotes 🍴 famous people 🎨 art and craft 🚶 entertainment and sport 🥾 walks

OCCASIONS UNLIMITED

13 Market Place, Wallingford, Oxfordshire OX10 0AD
Tel: 01491 652300
e-mail: cardsofcharacter@aol.com   website: www.cardsofcharacter.com

Situated at 13 Market Place in the historic town of Wallingford; **Occasions Unlimited** is a treasure trove of gifts and cards for the discerning buyer. Packed full of quality gifts for that somone special or maybe just a treat for yourself you will be guaranteed to find what you are looking for in this delightful shop.

Bright character china mugs sit alongside handcrafted ornaments. Colourfully painted piggybanks nestle with notebooks and novelty plates . Peeping out from the dressers are Steiff and Deans Bears, all this along with top quality interior items from Gisela Graham and Junction 18, perfect gifts from East of India and Yankee Candle and not forgetting the popular Willow Tree Figurines as well as breaktaking jewellery from Sea Gems.

Occasions Unlimited are also very proud to introduce our own range of Greeting Cards. Based around a timeless, nostalgic feel and produced using genuine old photographs, these cards appeal to all ages, and with over 95 in the range, you are bound to find the perfect card, whatever the occasion.

Not only do we provide our cards to our very loyal customer base here at the shop, we are also delighted to supply our greeting cards to other independant retailers all over the country. The popularity of our cards speaks for itself and we have provided our trade buyers with over 16,000 cards in the last four months.

Occasions Unlimited prides itself on its customer service and product knowledge. We would be delighted to help you and with our mail order service going from strength to strength you can confidently purchase your gift items safe in the knowledge that every last detail will be taken care of. Please do pop in and visit us, or give us a call. A warm welcome awaits you at Occasions Unlimited, the shopping experience, as it should be!

WALLINGFORD

8 miles SE of Abingdon on the A4130

A busy and prosperous town, Wallingford has been a strategic crossing point of the Thames since ancient times. Alfred the Great first fortified the town, against the Danes, and the Saxon earth defences can still be seen. It was here that William the Conqueror crossed the river on his six-day march to London. Wallingford was also an important trading town; it received its charter in 1155 and for several centuries had its own mint. During the Civil War, the town was a Royalist stronghold defending the southern approaches to Oxford, the site of the Royalist headquarters. It was besieged in 1646 by the Parliamentary

Wallingford Castle

forces under Sir Thomas Fairfax and its walls were breached after a 12-week siege; it was the last place to surrender to Parliament. The castle built by William the Conqueror was destroyed by Cromwell in 1652, but substantial earthworks can still be seen and

ILLUMIN-NATION LTD

5 St Peters Place, Wallingford, Oxfordshire OX10 0BG
Tel: 01491 833505 Fax: 01491 833806
e-mail: info@illumin-nation.co.uk
website: www.illumin-nation.co.uk

In 2000, Trevor Priddle, an experienced electrician, decided that Wallingford needed a shop providing good quality lighting and lighting accessories, so in 2001, along with his brother Allan and sister Karen, Trevor opened **Illumin-nation**.

The dazzling showroom is an extensive and varied cross section of traditional and contemporary styles of interior lighting including table and floor lamps, ceiling fittings and wall lights, cabinet and bathroom lighting. All products are of a high standard from manufacturers such as Firstlight and Elstead. Illumin-nation ltd also provides many exterior lighting solutions with flood lighting and security lights together with post lights not only to brighten but also to decorate and add safety to gardens and driveways.

Ceiling and floor fans are amongst other products available which also include light bulbs, light sockets and switches and vacuum cleaner bags.

This friendly, family run business allows each customer a personal and thorough service, if you can't find exactly what you need in the showroom than they will endeavour to order it for you. A repair service is also available for all lighting products and switches.

🎭 stories and anecdotes 🦢 famous people 🎨 art and craft ✒ entertainment and sport 🚶 walks

Witney & District Museum

Gloucester Court Mews, High Street, Witney,
Oxfordshire 338OX8 6LR
Tel: 01993 775915
website: www.witneymuseum.com

Opened in 1996, the **Witney & District Museum** is situated in a traditional Cotswold stone building at the northern end of Witney High Street. The ground floor gallery houses permanent displays reflecting the industrial, military and social history of Witney and the surrounding area, while the upper floor incorporates a large gallery which is used for art exhibitions and temporary displays. Other exhibits include a display of historic toys and a typical Witney domestic kitchen of circa 1953. The museum is open from April to October, Wednesdays to Saturdays 10am - 4pm, and Sundays 2pm - 4pm. Admission is £1.00 for adults and free for children.

those who worked the surrounding land down the centuries. The farm itself is home to traditional breeds of farm animals; there's walled kitchen garden, a riverside walk, gift shop and tearoom.

Nearby St Mary's Church, Cogges, has a curious tower that is square at the base but then becomes octagonal and is surmounted by a stone pyramid.

The story of the blanket trade and other local industries, including brewing and glove-making, is recounted at the **Witney and District Museum** (see panel above), housed in a traditional Cotswold stone building in a courtyard just off the High Street.

Real-life brewing can be seen at the Wychwood Brewery, which produces more than 50,000 barrels of ale each year using traditional methods. Guided tours for groups of up to 20 people are available on Saturday afternoons. The 45-minute tour concludes with a tutored tasting in the Cellar Bar.

St Mary's Church is notable for its soaring spire, which is all the more striking set amidst the surrounding level fields. Built on the scale of a mini-cathedral, the church and spire are

13th century; as Witney's wool trade prospered in the 14th and 15th centuries, chapels and aisles were added; but the interior is marred by over-enthusiastic restoration in Victorian times.

By 1278, Witney had a weekly market and two annual fairs, and in the centre of the market place the charming Buttercross still stands. Originally a shrine, the cross has a steep roof with 12 rustic-looking stone columns; its precise date is unknown.

Around Witney

STANTON HARCOURT
4 miles SE of Witney off the B4449

🏠 Stanton Harcourt Manor

🏠 Church of St Michael 🛕 Pope's Tower

This beautiful village is noted for its historic manor house **Stanton Harcourt Manor**, which dates back to the 14th century. Famed for its well-preserved medieval kitchen, one of the most complete to survive in this country, the house is also renowned for its fine collection of antiques and the tranquil

---

🏠 historic building 🏛 museum and heritage 🏚 historic site 🛕 scenic attraction � flora and fauna

Pope's Tower

gardens. It was while staying here, from 1717 to 1718, that Alexander Pope translated Homer's great work, the *Iliad*. He worked in the tower, part of the original manor house and now referred to as **Pope's Tower**.

While the manor house draws many people to the village, the splendid Norman **Church of St Michael** is also worthy of a visit.

Naturally, the Harcourt chapel dominates, but there are other features of interest, including an intricate 14th-century shrine to St Edburg.

STANDLAKE
5 miles SE of Witney on the A415

🏛 Newbridge

A little way south of the village is the three-arched **Newbridge,** built in the 13th century and now the second oldest bridge across the Thames. Newbridge saw conflict during the Civil War and the Rose Revived pub was used by Cromwell as a refreshment stop.

BRIZE NORTON
3 miles SW of Witney off the A40

Best known for its RAF transport base, Brize Norton village lies to the north of the airfield. It's a long straggling village of old grey stone houses and a Norman church, which is the

CASWELL HOUSE

Brize Norton, Oxfordshire OX18 3NJ
Tel: 01993 701064
Fax: 01993 774901
e-mail: stay@caswell-house.co.uk
website: www.caswell-house.co.uk

Caswell House is a wonderful late 15th-century Cotswold stone building reached up a sweeping drive. Well off the beaten track, but easy to find, it stands a mile out of Brize Norton on the Curbridge road just south of Witney. Richard and Amanda Matthews are the fourth generation to have lived on this 500-acre farm, which includes streams, ponds, gardens, orchards and lawns that reach down to the ancient moat. They offer a choice of bed & breakfast and self-catering accommodation, both high-spec and spacious. The B&B facility comprises en suite doubles and twins, with TV/DVD players and tea/coffee trays. An excellent Aga-cooked breakfast is locally sourced and served in the dining room.

Self-catering guests have three holiday lets sleeping two, four and six respectively in the Coach House, the Granary and the Keepers Retreat, all providing additional sleeping accommodation, good living and eating space, very comfortable bedrooms and well-fitted kitchens. The area is rich in historic and scenic interest, but guests staying at Caswell House will find plenty to see and do without leaving the farm: the views, the gentle strolls, the nature trails, the full-size snooker table and much more.

THE VINES

Burford Road, Black Bourton,
Oxfordshire OX18 2PF
Tel: 01993 843559 Fax: 01993 840080
e-mail: info@vineshotel.com
website: www.vinesblackbourton.co.uk

In the picturesque village of Black Bourton, **The Vines** traditional stone exterior promises a warm Cotswold welcome within. In the spacious bar and lounge area you can relax and enjoy a drink with a light snack next to the cosy log fire in the comfort of the stylish furnishings and friendly hospitality.

The elegant restaurant was designed by John Clegg of BBC Real Rooms and the unique decor is the perfect backdrop to delight the culinary senses with a choice from the fine evening a la carte menu or the delicious lunch dishes. The acclaimed food is created using the best of fresh local and seasonal ingredients.

Accommodation at The Vines offers every modern comfort and convenience. There is a choice of double, twin and family rooms that all come with an en-suite shower, television,, desk shaver socket, hairdryer, toiletries, ironing facilities and a hospitality tray. The rooms in the new wing also have king size beds, flat screen televisions, Internet access and direct-dial telephones. The ground floor rooms have their own patio area, overlooking Black Bourton church.

The Vines is ideally located for exploring all the Beautiful Cotswolds have to offer including the lovely towns of Burford, Lechlade as well as Blenheim Palace, Kelmscott Manor, The Cotswold Wildlife Park and the Thames Path.

WEST OX ARTS GALLERY

Town Hall, Market Square, Bampton,
Oxfordshire OX18 2JH
Tel: 01993 850137
e-mail: westoxarts@yahoo.co.uk
website: www.wospweb.com

West Ox Arts is situated in a lovely, spacious gallery on the first floor of the Grade II listed Town Hall in Bampton, a picturesque Cotswold village about five miles from Witney.

The gallery holds over twelve exhibitions a year, with recent shows focusing on life drawing, landscape painting, printmaking, photography, recycled art, ceramics, weaving, and quilts. Some forthcoming shows will feature sculpture, glass, still life, animal painting, woodcut prints, and felt.

West Ox Arts is an association of enthusiastic artists and art lovers, many of whom take part in exhibitions alongside artists invited from the wider region. Talks, workshops and theatre productions are also organised.

The gallery has a shop that sells reasonably priced, handmade jewellery, ceramics, glassware and cards, and a coffee shop opposite the gallery sells refreshments. The gallery is open: Tuesday to Saturday 10.30am to 12.30pm & 2pm to 4pm; on Sunday from 2pm to 4pm.

only one in England dedicated to a little-known 5th-century French bishop, St Brice.

RADCOT
7 miles SW of Witney on the A4095

🏛 Radcot Bridge

This tiny hamlet boasts the oldest bridge across the River Thames. Built in 1154, **Radcot Bridge** represents an important crossing place and, as a result, the hamlet has seen much conflict over the centuries. To the north of the bridge are the remains of a castle where, in 1141, King Stephen battled with the dethroned Queen Matilda. In the following century King John fought his barons here before finally conceding and signing the Magna Carta.

FILKINS
8 miles SW of Witney off the A361

🏛 Cotswold Woollen Weavers

🏛 Swinford Museum

This tiny Cotswold village is now the home of a flourishing community of craft workers and artists, many of whom work in restored 18th-century barns. One of these groups operates the **Cotswold Woollen Weavers**, a working weaving museum with an exhibition gallery and a mill shop. In the same village, occupying a charming 17th-century cottage, is the **Swinford Museum** which concentrates on 19th-century domestic and rural trade and craft tools.

KELMSCOTT
9 miles SW of Witney off the A4095

🏛 Kelmscott Manor

William Morris called the village of Kelmscott "a heaven on earth", and **Kelmscott Manor**, the exquisite Elizabethan manor house he leased jointly with Dante Gabriel Rosetti, "the loveliest haunt of ancient peace that can well be imagined". Located near the River Thames, and dating from about 1570, the manor was Morris's country home from 1871 until his death in 1896. He loved the house dearly and it is the scene of the end of his utopian novel *News from Nowhere*, in which he writes of a world where work has become a sought-after pleasure. The house, which along with the beautiful garden is open to visitors during the summer, has examples of Morris's work; the four-poster in which he was born, and memorabilia of Dante Gabriel Rosetti. Rosetti is reputed to have found the village boring, so presumably the fact that he was in love with Morris's wife, Jane, drew him here. Rosetti's outstanding portrait of her, *The Blue Silk Dress*, hangs in the Panelled Room. Opening times at the manor are limited and admission is by timed ticket.

Morris is buried in the churchyard, under a tombstone designed by his associate Philip Webb on the lines of a Viking tomb house. The church itself is interesting, the oldest parts dating from the late 12th century, and the

Kelmscott Manor

Winchester, and its bell tower is one of the city's most famous landmarks.

Oxford was closely involved in the Civil War and was for three years the King's headquarters. Several of the colleges were pressed into service by the Royalists: Wadham and New College were both used as stores for arms and gunpowder; Magdalen was Prince Rupert's headquarters and the tower was used as Charles' lookout when the Earl of Essex laid siege to the city. The damage caused by Cromwell's men is dramatically illustrated by bullet holes in the statue of the Virgin in the wonderful **Church of St Mary**. It was in this church that the trial of the Protestant martyrs Hugh Latimer, Nicholas Ridley and Thomas Cranmer was held. They were found guilty of heresy and burned to death in a ditch outside the city walls. The three are commemorated by the **Martyrs Memorial**, erected in 1841 in St Giles. If Oxford was the temporary home of countless luminaries (from Wolsey, Wesley and Wilde to 12 British Prime Ministers), it is also the permanent resting place of many others. In the churchyard of St Cross are buried Kenneth Grahame (*The Wind in the Willows*), Kenneth Tynan and the composer Sir John Stainer. William Laud, 17th-century Archbishop of Canterbury, is buried in the chapel of St John's College; JRR Tolkien, Oxford professor and author of *The Lord of the Rings*, and the philosopher Sir Isiah Berlin lie in Wolvercote cemetery; and CS Lewis, critic and writer of the Nania series of books, is at rest in the churchyard of Holy Trinity, Headington.

Many of the colleges have lovely peaceful gardens, some of them open to the public at various times, and the **University Parks** are a

---

THE RIDINGS GUEST HOUSE

280 Abingdon Road, Oxford OX1 4TA
Tel: 01865 248364 Fax: 01865 251348
e-mail: stay@theridingsguesthouse.co.uk
website: www.theridingsguesthouse.co.uk

A small stylish guesthouse, **The Ridings Guest House** is situated just south of the enchanting city centre of Oxford.

The guesthouse provides four quiet, comfortable en-suite furnished bedrooms and a high standard of personal service to its guests. Rooms are bright, spacious and pleasantly furnished to ensure your stay is a comfortable one. All rooms are centrally heated and double-glazed, with tea and coffee-making facilities, a colour remote satellite television supplied and a cot available on request.

Starting the day with a great meal is important, so Ridings offers a wide range of breakfast options including a full English breakfast, a continental breakfast and a vegetarian breakfast. Children are catered for and if you have any dietary requirements you just have to ask. There is also off road parking so you can leave your car here and avoid parking problems when exploring the fascinating University City.

Oxford is a delightful city, famous for its dreaming spires, ancient University colleges and beautiful architecture. The guesthouse is twenty minutes walk (or five minutes on one of the very frequents buses) from all the major tourist attractions. It is also ideally located for transport connections to both central London and Heathrow & Gatwick airports.

BRIDGET WHEATLEY CONTEMPORARY JEWELLERY

38 Cowley Road, Oxford OX4 1HZ
Tel: 01865 722184 Fax: 01865 790858
e-mail: bridget.wheatley@ntlworld.com website: www.bridgetwheatley.com

Established in 2000, situated 10 minutes leisurely walk from the city centre Bridget Wheatley Contemporary Jewellery is a haven of creativity set within the vibrant multi cultural Cowley Road. The shop is set back slightly from the road with a light and airy interior. Customers are welcome to browse and there is a friendly service with help in finding the right piece of jewellery, either from stock or a specially made item.

Bridget creates her own ranges of jewellery within the shop and offer's a bespoke service for wedding and engagement rings. Choose from one of Bridget's collections or she will be happy to work with you to create your own design. The essence of her work is simplicity with attention to detail, influences are from Medieval and Celtic art. Within the collections and one-off pieces she likes

to use irregular shaped freshwater pearls and richly coloured gemstones including tourmaline, aquamarine, moonstone, opals, pink sapphire is a current favourite, combined with silver and gold to produce simple bold rings, elegant earrings and unusual lariat style necklaces. Wide bangles with wire detailing and a hammered finish are signature pieces.

Alongside Bridget's own work the shop has jewellery from an eclectic group of artists using diverse materials and techniques to produce a stunning array of beautiful individual pieces. Colourful and bold wrapping paper and cards, some hand-made, are the finishing touch to the perfect present. Prices of jewellery range from £18 upwards. Opening hours are Tuesday to Saturday 10am to 5pm.

perfect place for a stroll at any time. As well as the college buildings, Oxford has many interesting and magnificent places to explore.

At the city's central crossroads, unusually named Carfax and probably derived from the Latin for four-forked, is a tower, Carfax Tower, which is all that remains of the 14th-century Church of St Martin. A climb to the top of the tower offers magnificent views across the city. One of the most interesting buildings, the **Radcliffe Camera**, was built between 1737 and 1749 to a design by James Gibb.

River Cherwell, Oxford

PICKWICK'S GUEST HOUSE

15-17 London Road, Headington, Oxford OX3 7SP
Tel: 01865 750487 Fax: 01865 742208
e-mail pickwicks@tiscali.co.uk
website: www.pickwicksguesthouse.co.uk

Well known as it is, Oxford never fails to impress even its most regular visitors with something different or something new. The Bodleian Library, The Ashmolean Museum, The Botanic Gardens and Christ Church Cathedral are just a few of Oxford's world famous attractions. Boat trips or punting on the River Thames, entertaining guided walking tours and open-top bus tours take in the city's architecture and introduce Oxford's heritage.

Enjoy everything Oxford has to offer while staying at the four star AA recommended **Pickwick's Guest House**. The spacious accommodation furnished with care and to a high standard is the ideal setting to relax after a busy day out and about. Guests are assured of a warm welcome and attentive service. There are 15 rooms, each equipped with a telephone, radio alarm clock, colour TV and tea/coffee making facilities. Most rooms have en-suite showers. The memorable breakfast menu is a treat from a full English breakfast to lighter alternatives.

Whatever your tastes you're sure to find something you like.

stay. From the nearby quarries came the stone for building many of the Oxford colleges. You can enjoy a grand view of them from South Park where Parliamentary troops camped during the Civil War.

WHEATLEY
4 miles E of Oxford on the A40

🌱 Waterperry Gardens

This former quarry village retains many old buildings, of which the most interesting is a curious conical lock-up. To the west, close to the M40 (junction 8), are the famous **Waterperry Gardens** (see panel opposite) surrounding Waterperry House (the house is not open to the public). Established as a residential gardening school for women in the 1930s, Waterperry is now part pleasure garden

and part commercial garden centre. The gardens are host each year to Art in Action, which brings together many of the world's finest craftspeople.

GARSINGTON
4 miles SE of Oxford off the B480

🏛 Garsington Manor 🏛 Church of St Mary

The most distinguished building hereabouts is **Garsington Manor**, built on a hilltop of mellow Cotswold stone in the 16th century. Between 1915 and 1927, this was the home of the socialite Lady Ottoline Morrell and her husband Philip who were hospitable to a whole generation of writers, artists and intellectuals, including Katherine Mansfield, Lytton Strachey, Clive Bell, Siegfried Sassoon, DH Lawrence, TS Eliot, Rupert Brooke,

WATERPERRY GARDENS

Waterperry, Wheatley, Oxfordshire OX33 1JZ
Tel: 01844 339226
e-mail: office@waterperrygardens.co.uk
website: www.waterperrygardens.co.uk

You'll never be short of something to see or do at **Waterperry Gardens** - whatever the weather - or the time of year! Whether you're looking for a stroll around magnificent gardens, excellent home-baked teas and lunches, a gallery featuring British arts and crafts, the chance to savour a bygone age in the Museum of Rural Life or a spot of retail therapy, you can be sure Waterperry will meet your every needs.

Waterperry Gardens has an atmosphere that reflects its 1,000-year history. The magnificent gardens are close to Oxford and for the visitor - this is a chance to enjoy the beauty and peace of this special place. The gardens are well known for the herbaceous border, which flowers from May until November. You'll also find a Formal Garden, the Mary Rose Garden, a Waterlily Canal, the Long Colour Border and a recently planted small arboretum in the meadow area beyond the canal.

Waterperry Gardens are guaranteed to delight and inspire garden-lovers from across the country and the world and no visit is complete without a sumptuous, lovingly prepared lunch or tea at the Pear Tree Teashop, all freshly made from locally-sourced produce. That means you can sit back and enjoy your day out at Waterperry even more!

Bertrand Russell and Aldous Huxley. Huxley based an account of a country house party in his novel *Crome Yellow* on his experiences at Garsington, thereby causing a rift with his hostess. She found his description all too recognisable and they were estranged for some time. It seems that Lady Ottoline was not very lucky in the artists on whom she lavished her attention and hospitality. DH Lawrence also quarrelled with her after drawing a less than flattering, but clearly recognisable, portrait of life at her house in *Women in Love*.

Garsington's other claim to literary fame is that Rider Haggard was sent to the school run by the Rev HJ Graham at the rectory in 1866. The present house is later, built in 1872, but

across the road from the Church is a 16th-century gateway from the rectory he would have known. While there Haggard became friendly with a local farmer named Quartermain whom he must have remembered with affection as he used the name for his hero, many years later, in his novel *King Solomon's Mines*.

The village **Church of St Mary** is a pleasant and cosy building with fine views to the south over the Chilterns from its hill top position, but it also looks over the industrial belt to the south of Oxford. Though the interior is chiefly Victorian, the church has retained its Norman tower and inside there is an elegant memorial to Lady Ottoline.

🎞 stories and anecdotes 🐦 famous people 🎨 art and craft 🖉 entertainment and sport 🚶 walks

THE INN AT EMMINGTON

Sydenham Road, Sydenham, Chinnor,
Oxfordshire OX39 4LD
Tel: 01844 351367 Fax: 01844 355144
e-mail: theinnemmington@btconnect.com
website: www.theinnatemmington.co.uk

The Inn at Emmington is owned by David McLelland who has over 16 years experience in the licensed trade. The Inn prides itself on the exceptional quality of their food which is all cooked to order using ingredients from local sources wherever possible. The restaurant seats up to 30 people where customers can choose from an extensive menu that is constantly changing. For a lunch time snack why not choose from classics such as Home made Soup of the Day or Steak & Mushroom Pie that is also home cooked. The evening menu has an al a carte feel with tempting dishes such as Grilled Chicken Fillet stuffed with Sun Dried Tomato and Mozzarella and locally sourced Steak with blue cheese sauce. On finer days, meals and the range of Real Ales, Beers and Wines can be enjoyed in the garden that can accommodate up to 100 people.

Accommodation comprises of seven en-suite double rooms all decorated to a high standard. The rooms enjoy views of the Chiltern Hills or the Gardens and have televisions, hairdryers and Tea & Coffee making facilities.

Situated close to the Chiltern Hills, The Inn at Emmington is the ideal base for enjoying the lovely walks and local attractions.

BOAT INN

Canal Road, Thrupp, Kidlington,
Oxfordshire OX5 1JY
Tel: 01865 374279

What could be better than dining (or drinking) with friends while watching out for waterway wildlife and colourful narrowboats?

Thrupp is a pretty canal side village located to the North of Kidlington on the Oxford Canal and home to **The Boat Inn**. A 17th century tradition canal side pub, which has been little changed over the

centuries, retaining much of its genuine character, with, exposed oak beams and open fire places. It is an attractive pub with a good bar restaurant and outdoor areas set in picturesque surrounds. Meals are prepared to order by master chef, Pete Solet, who has received numerous awards. Rest assured your meal will be excellent - fresh produce, as local as possible, is used and everything from the kitchen is produced to a very high standard. The staff are friendly and look forward to your visit where you are assured of a warm welcome.

The Boat Inn is 50 metres from the canal moorings, 400 metres south of Bridge 221, and yet within a stone's throw of Oxford Airport and just two miles from Blenhem Palace. Whether on holiday or living locally make a date and visit the Boat Inn.

here and he also died at Thame. When the Civil War broke out he raised a regiment of infantry for the Parliamentary Army and fought with great bravery at Edgehill and Reading. He was wounded at the battle of Chalgrove Field in June 1643 and was carried back to Thame, where he died some days later in an inn that stood on the High Street. A plaque on a wall denotes the site.

NUNEHAM COURTENAY
5 miles S of Oxford on the A4074

🏛 Nuneham Park

When the 1st Earl of Harcourt moved his family here from Stanton Harcourt in 1756, he built the splendid **Nuneham Park**, one of the grandest mansions in Oxfordshire. The earl commissioned Capability Brown to landscape the grounds and observing the completed work deemed it "as advantageous and delicious as can be desired, surrounded by hills that form an amphitheatre and, at the foot, the River Thames."

To achieve this idyllic result, the earl had the old village moved a mile away and out of sight. It's a charming model village of 18th-century cottages facing each other in matched pairs on either side of the road. The mansion house is now a conference centre but its parkland forms the Arboretum of Oxford University and is open to the public (see under Oxford, page 347).

ELSFIELD
2 miles N of Oxford off the A40

This small village of farms and thatched cottages was the home of the author and administrator John Buchan, 1st Baron Tweedsmuir, from 1919 until 1935 when he left to take up his appointment as Governor-General of Canada. During his time at Elsfield Manor House he wrote a number of books, including *Midwinter*, written in 1923 and partly set in the vicinity. His ashes are buried by the east wall of the churchyard of St Thomas of Canterbury. RD Blackmore, author of *Lorna Doone*, lived in Elsfield as a child while his father was the vicar.

WOODSTOCK
8 miles NW of Oxford on the A44

🏛 Blenheim Palace

🏛 Oxfordshire County Museum   🌱 Secret Garden

Situated in the Glyme Valley, in an area of land that was originally part of the Wychwood Forest, the name of this elegant Georgian market town means a 'place in the woods'. To the north of the River Glyme is the old Saxon settlement, while on the opposite bank lies the town that was developed by Henry II in the 13th century to serve the Royal Park of Woodstock. There had been hunting lodges for the Kings of

Blenheim Palace, Woodstock

peaceful garden at whose entrance stand the old town stocks.

It is the magnificent **Blenheim Palace** (see panel below), one of only a handful of sites in the country to be included on the World Heritage List, which brings most people to Woodstock. The estate and the cost of building the palace was a gift from a grateful Queen Anne to the heroic John Churchill, 1st Duke of Marlborough, for his victory at the Battle of Blenheim during the Spanish War of Succession. However, the Queen's gratitude ran out before the building work was complete and the duke had to pay the remainder of the costs himself. As his architect, Marlborough chose Sir John Vanbrugh, whose life was even more colourful than that of his patron. He was at once both an architect (although at the time of his commission he was relatively unknown) and a playwright, and he also had the distinction of

having been imprisoned in the Bastille in Paris. The result of his work was the Italianate palace, built between 1705 and 1722, which is now seen sitting in a very English park that was designed by Charles Bridgeman and Henry Wise and later landscaped by Capability Brown. Unfortunately, once completed, the new house did not meet with universal approval: it was ridiculed by Jonathan Swift and Alexander Pope, and Marlborough's wife, Sarah, who seems to have held the family purse strings, delayed paying Vanbrugh as long as possible.

Blenheim is a marvellous, grand place with a mass of splendid paintings, furniture, porcelain, and silver on show. Visitors will also be interested in the more intimate memorabilia of Sir Winston Churchill. Born here in 1874, Churchill was a cousin of the 9th Duke; family name remains Churchill.

The **Secret Garden** was opened in 2004,

Blenheim Palace

Woodstock, Oxfordshire OX20 1PX
Tel: 01993 810555 Fax: 01993 810585
e-mail: shop@blenheimpalace.com
website: www.blenheimpalace.com

Situated just 8 miles from Oxford on the A44, **Blenheim Palace** was created a World Heritage site in 1987 and is the home of 11th duke of Marlborough and birthplace of Sir Winston Churchill.

The imposing scale of the Palace is beautifully balanced within, by the intricate detail and delicacy of the carvings, the hand painted ceilings and the amazing porcelain collections, tapestries and paintings displayed in each room. On the first floor 'Blenheim Palace: The Untold Story' brings to life enticing tales from the last 300 years.

Set in beautiful parkland 0f 2,100 acres, which was landscaped by 'Capability' Brown in 1760's, the Palace is surrounded by sweeping lawns and formal gardens. The Pleasure Gardens offer plenty of fun for children and adults alike, including the Marlborough Maze, a giant Chess board and Butterfly farm.

IONA HOUSE GALLERY

4 High Street, Woodstock,
Oxfordshire OX20 1TF
Tel: 01993 811464
e-mail: info@ionahousegallery.org
website: www.ionahousegallery.org

Open 7 days a week:
Monday - Saturday 10am-5.30pm
Sunday - 11am-5.00pm

A warm welcome awaits you in this beautiful gallery, situated in the heart of the picturesque market town of Woodstock on the edge of the Cotswolds.

As you wander from room to room there is an immense choice of paintings, sculpture and other decorative art, including a wide range of jewellery.

With over 300 exhibits at any one time, there is something for all tastes and budgets, whether you are looking for a painting for your home or choosing a gift for a friend.

The gallery showcases affordable contemporary work from both renowned artists and rising talent. Specialising in English, Scottish and Russian art, it holds new exhibitions every 6-8 weeks throughout the year. If you would like to be invited to these shows, just speak to a member of staff and they will add your details to the invitation list.

Initially set up in 2002 by Scottish International Relief, 'Iona House' is named after the charity's first children's home in Romania. Now privately owned, the gallery still maintains a strong link with the charity and helps fund its schools feeding project - 'Mary's Meals'.

🎞 stories and anecdotes 🐦 famous people ✗ art and craft 🖌 entertainment and sport 🚶 walks

THE BLACKS HEAD INN

Village Green, Bletchingdon, nr Kidlington,
Oxfordshire OX5 3DA
Tel/Fax: 01869 350315
e-mail: information@theblacksheadinn.com
website: www.theblacksheadinn.com

Dating back to the 17th century, **The Blacks Head Inn** was reportedly named after a slave that lived and worked in the village. With its central village location on one of the Cherwell District Councils cycle routes and being only minutes away from the A34 and M40, it is ideally placed for an easy commute to London and the Cotswolds and the perfect base to explore the local area and the history that is in abundance here.

You can expect a warm welcome and excellent service from the friendly staff at The Blacks Head Inn where a delicious meal can be enjoyed by the open log fire in the cosy dining room or a tasty snack sampled with views over the garden from the patio or conservatory. A commitment to supporting local farming ensures that all the food is home cooked using fresh local ingredients wherever possible. Vegetarian options are also available and there is an ever-changing specials board from which to choose a tempting dish. The outstanding reputation of the food at this popular pub makes booking very advisable.

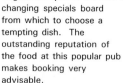

A fine selection of real ales, wines, spirits and soft drinks are served from the two bars located in the dining room and the games rooms where customers can participate in a round of darts or perhaps a diverting game of pool.

The Blacks Head Inn Bed & Breakfast accommodation occupies two areas of the pub. A newly renovated barn conversion on the Inn's grounds is ideal for families needing a little more peace and quiet than the rooms in the main part of the Inn. All rooms are decorated to a high standard with a clean, contemporary style and comprise a television, tea & coffee making facilities and fully modernised bathrooms. The pub also has a small shop selling daily newspapers etc aswell as breakfasts - full english or croissants infact what ever your heart fancies! The entire family is welcome at the Blacks Head Inn where even dogs can enjoy the gardens and the accommodation. There is also a large car-park adjoining the Inn.

the 300th anniversary of the Battle of Blenheim. The garden was originally planted in the 1950s by the 10th duke, but after his death became overgrown and virtually inaccessible. Now restored, this Four Seasons garden with its many unusual trees, shrubs and flowers offers an enchanting mix of winding paths, soothing water features, bridges, fountains, ponds and streams.

First grown by George Kempster, a tailor from Old Woodstock, the Blenheim Orange apple took its name from the palace. Though the exact date of the first apple is unknown, Kempster himself died in 1773 and the original tree blew down in 1853. The spot where the tree stood become so famous that it is said that London-bound coaches and horses used to slow down so that passengers might gaze upon it.

BLADON
1.5 miles S of Woodstock on the A4095

🌳 Churchyard

The village lies on the southern edge of the Blenheim estate and it was in the **Churchyard** here in 1965 that Sir Winston Churchill was laid to rest in a simple grave after a state funeral. Also interred here are his parents, his brother John, and his daughters. The ashes of his wife Clementine were buried in his grave in 1977.

LONG HANBOROUGH
2 miles SW of Woodstock

🏛 Oxford Bus Museum

Located next to Long Hanborough railway station, the **Oxford Bus Museum** has some 40 vehicles on display, all of which were used at one time for public transport in and around Oxford. They range from early 19th-century horse-trams to buses from the 1980s. Also on show is the double-decker bus used in the

Spice Girls movie. The museum is open at weekends and daily throughout August.

NORTH LEIGH
4.5 miles SW of Woodstock off the A4095

🏛 Roman Villa

The Saxon-towered St Mary's Church is well worth a visit, and just to the north of the village lies the **Roman Villa** (English Heritage; see walk on page 358), one of several known to have existed in this area. Little remains apart from the foundations and some mosaic flooring, but this is enough to measure the scale of the place; it had over 60 rooms, two sets of baths and a sophisticated underfloor heating system, all built round a courtyard and clearly the home of a prosperous farming family.

FINSTOCK
5 miles W of Woodstock on the B4022

A charming village with two notable literary associations. It was in 1927, at the 19th-century Holy Trinity Church, that TS Eliot was baptised at the age of 38 following his controversial conversion to Catholicism. The novelist and churchwoman Barbara Pym lived in retirement with her sister in a cottage in the village; she died in 1980 and is buried in the churchyard. A lectern in the church is dedicated to her memory.

CHARLBURY
5 miles NW of Woodstock on the B4026

🏛 Museum   🏛 Railway Station

🏛 Cornbury Park

Now very much a dormitory town for Oxford, Charlbury was once famous for its glove-making as well as being a centre of the Quaker Movement - the simple Friends' Meeting House dates from 1779 and there is

the first treated to give an impression of rich solemnity, the second with a rather more exuberant effect. The house has associations with Sir Winston Churchill, who used it as a weekend headquarters during the Second World War. Appropriately enough, given that Sir Winston had an American mother, Ditchley Park is now used as an Anglo-American conference centre and is not open to the public.

Bicester

Bicester has a traceable history that goes back for a thousand years and a settlement here was recorded in the Domesday Book. Today it is a busy market town and is now home to Bicester Village - a factory designer outlet shopping village. Because it is close to the

M40 motorway linking London with Birmingham via Oxford, the town has seen a considerable growth in size in recent years.

Flora Thompson based her trilogy *Lark Rise to Candleford* on the area north-east of Bicester, including the nearby villages of Juniper Hill, Cottisford, Fringford and Hethe.

Around Bicester

DEDDINGTON
8 miles NW of Bicester off the A423

🏛 Deddington Castle & Castle House

Visitors to this old market town might recognise it as the place that was demolished by a runaway crane in the television adaptation of Tom Sharpe's *Blott on the Landscape*. The damage was, of course, cleverly faked and

---

EAGLES FRESH FOODS

The Market Place, Deddington,
Banbury, Oxfordshire, OX15 0SE
Tel: 01869 338500
Fax: 01869 338588
e-mail: info@feaglesfreshfoods.co.uk
website: www.f.eaglesfreshfoods.co.uk

Situated in the small town of Deddington it is hard to believe that such an emporium of good food and enterprise exists, rarely seen outside the large cities, **Eagles** have established themselves as a leading name in food. Entering the shop one is immediately aware of a stunning design, which invites investigation of the multitude of goods on offer.

Fresh meat & fish, cheeses & olives, desserts and cakes, vegetables & fruits, chocolates & jams, breads & pasties, tracklements & herbs, teas & coffee, meals to dine on and fine wines to explore. The list is endless. Where does it all come from; well out the back are chefs and butchers that are creating all you see. There is nothing they will not prepare, whether it is some Bolognese sauce for supper, a Beef Wellington for a dinner party or a Fully Served Extravaganza. There are hampers for you to browse, make up your own or order to be delivered.....picnics for that opera in the park....

Trained staff carefully select all the produce; 'the best' being the brief, with welfare and food miles following close behind. Open seven days a week it is worth making a detour for........

🏛 historic building   🏛 museum and heritage   🏛 historic site   🜪 scenic attraction   🌢 flora and fauna

Deddington Castle

remains a prosperous agricultural centre with a still bustling market place. Little can now be seen of the 12th-century **Deddington Castle**. This was destroyed in the 14th century and most of the building materials were put to good use in other areas of the town. However, excavations have revealed the remains of a curtain wall, a hall and a small rectangular keep.

Close by is **Castle House**, where Piers Gaveston, Edward II's favourite, was held before his execution in 1312. The house's two towers were added later, in the 1650s, when the house was in the ownership of Thomas Appletree. A supporter of Cromwell, Appletree was ordered to destroy

Deddington, which hovers between a small town and a large village, still retains all its medieval character. Surveyed in the Domesday Book at twice the value of Banbury, the town never developed in the same way as Banbury and Bicester, but it

THE DUKE OF CUMBERLANDS HEAD

Main Street, Clifton, nr Deddington, Oxfordshire OX15 0PE
Tel: 01869 338534
e-mail: info@dukeatclifton.com   website: www.dukeatclifton.com

The Duke of Cumberlands Head is a 17th century traditional thatched Country Inn set in a beautiful village location just 16 miles from Oxford. The pub is steeped in old world charm whilst also providing the very best of modern amenities and service. The excellent reputation for food has been developed by the chef who has been an integral part of the pub for many years. All the food is cooked to a high standard on the premises with fresh ingredients sourced from good local suppliers. The menu is forever changing with daily and weekly specials that mix traditional favourites with dishes that have a more Mediterranean feel.

From the well stocked bar there is sure to be something to compliment every meal from the extensive wine list. There is also a great choice of real ales, a wide range of spirits and a large selection of whiskeys to choose from. Accommodation at The Duke of Cumberlands Head comprises of five en-suite bedrooms and one family room. All are comfortable and spacious and decorated to a high standard with tea & coffee making facilities.

For those wanting to enjoy a fine day outdoors, the large garden is the perfect place to relax as it feels the benefit of the sun all day long. Dogs are also welcome here as they are throughout the pub.

🎬 stories and anecdotes 🐦 famous people 🎨 art and craft ✍ entertainment and sport 🚶 walks

the property of Royalists and it was material from two local houses that he used in his building work.

LOWER HEYFORD
6 miles W of Bicester on the B4030

🏛 Rousham House

Situated at a ford across the River Cherwell, which was replaced in the 13th century by a stone bridge, the delightful village of Lower Heyford lies on the opposite bank from its other half - Upper Heyford.

To the south lies **Rousham House**, a fine mansion built in the mid-1600s for Sir Robert Dormer and set in magnificent gardens. The gardens as seen today were laid out by William Kent in 1738 and include many water features, sculptures and follies. Next to the house are very attractive pre-Kent walled gardens with a

parterre, herbaceous borders, a rose garden and a vegetable garden. The garden is open to the public all year round; the house has limited opening times.

Banbury

🏛 St Mary's Church   🏛 Banbury Cross

🏛 Museum & Tooley's Boatyard

Famous for its cross, cakes and the nursery rhyme, this historic and thriving market town has managed to hang on to many of its old buildings as well as become home to Europe's largest livestock market.

The famous **Banbury Cross** can be found in Horsefair where it was erected, in 1859, replacing the previous one demolished by the Parliamentarians during the Civil War. It was built to commemorate the marriage of

---

WYKHAM PARK FARM SHOP

Wykham Park Farm, Banbury, Oxfordshire OX16 9UP
Tel: 01295 262235
Fax: 01295 252323
e-mail: jhncolegrave@clara.co.uk
website: www.wykhampark.co.uk

John and Julia Colegrave and their helpful, hardworking staff run the **Wykham Park Farm Shop**, which has acquired a large and loyal clientele since opening in 2000. Angus X and Longhorn beef as well as Gloucester Old Spot Pork and grass fed lamb is produced from animals raised on the farm and butchered on the premises. Local, welfare friendly pork, veal, poultry and seasonal game are also sold in the shop.

Many of the vegetables on display are home-grown; these include quite superb asparagus, which is particularly well suited to the soil on the farm and supplied to a number of local restaurants (also available by mail order). The Farm is proud to have accreditations from Les Routiers as well as LEAF, which links environment and farming.

Other food on sale at this outstanding farm shop includes cheeses (with the emphasis on British farmhouse varieties), cakes and pastries, jams and preserves, pickles and chutneys, all of the best quality and most of it from local sources. The owners welcome visitors not just to buy the excellent provisions but for educational sessions and farm walks; school parties are welcome with a little notice.

🏛 historic building   🏛 museum and heritage   🏛 historic site   🍃 scenic attraction   🌿 flora and fauna

Queen Victoria's oldest daughter to the Prussian Crown Prince, and the figures around the bottom of the cross, of Queen Victoria, Edward VII, and George V, were added in 1914.

The town's other legendary claim to fame is its cakes, made of spicy fruit pastry, which can still be bought. Banbury was also, at one time, famous for its cheeses, which were only about an inch thick. This gave rise to the expression 'thin as a Banbury cheese'.

On the east side of the Horsefair stands **St Mary's Church**, a classical building of warm-coloured stone and hefty pillars, which are pleasantly eccentric touches. The original architect was SP Cockerell, though the tower and portico were completed between 1818 and 1822 by his son, CR Cockerell. The style reflects the strong influence on English architecture of Piranesi's *Views of Rome*, using massive shapes and giving stone the deliberately roughened appearance, which comes from the technique known as rustication.

Banbury Museum (free) tells the story of the town's development, from the days when it came under the influence of the bishops of

Lincoln, through the woollen trade of the 16th century, to the present day. Adjoining the striking modern museum is **Tooley's Boatyard**, a scheduled ancient monument that can be visited as part of a guided tour. Established in 1790 and in continuous use ever since, Tooley's is the oldest working dry dock in the country. It was designed to build and repair canal barges and narrowboats.

Around Banbury

BROUGHTON
2½ miles SW of Banbury on the B4035

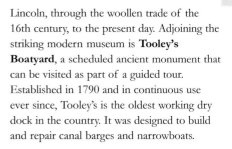 Broughton Castle

Arthur Mee considered **Broughton Castle** "One of the most fascinating buildings in the county". As you cross the ancient bridge over a moat and approach the sturdy 14th-century gatehouse, it becomes clear that it is indeed something special, the perfect picture of a great Tudor mansion. The house has been owned by the Broughton family since 1451 – Nathaniel Fiennes, 21st Lord Saye and Sele is the present occupant. Over the years, there have been several royal visitors including Queen Anne of Denmark, wife of James I. Both James I and Edward VII used the aptly named King's Chamber, with its hand-painted Chinese wall paper. The house also played a part in the Civil War as it has a secret room where leaders of the Parliamentary forces laid their plans. Arms and armour from that period are displayed in the castle's grandest room, the Great Hall, which is also notable for its dazzling plaster ceiling installed in 1599. The castle has a walled garden, café and picnic area.

Tooley's Boatyard, Banbury

LEGACY

COUNTRY HOUSE GIFTS

51 High Street, Burford, Oxfordshire OX18 4QA
Tel: 01993 823172
e-mail: countryhousegifts@talktalkbusiness.net

Situated on the picturesque main street of the 'Gateway to the Cotswolds', **Country House Gifts** stocks an impressive selection of items for the home along with gifts for all occasions.

Owners Tina and Malcolm Mustoe have put their personal seal of approval on an amazing emporium that ranges from 'melt in the mouth' Belgian and English chocolates to a fine selection of William Morris English linen. They have put a lot of time and effort into choosing a stock that will offer something for everyone and this is clearly visible upon entering.

Not only are there plenty of gifts for the 'grown ups' but they also supply a great range of items for children ranging from soft toys to Beatrix Potter clothing. This shop has so much to delight the eye that you are sure to leave with not only more than you intended but also with the satisfaction of your individual purchase. If it's a gift for someone you love, an accessory for the home or a birthday present for a niece you are sure to find it here with even the gift wrap and card taken care of.

placed under guard in the church. The next day a court martial was held and three of the rebels were shot as an example to the rest, who were made to watch the executions. They were spared similar punishment when their leader recanted in a sermon.

The town's old court house, built in the 16th century with an open ground floor and a half-timbered first floor, is now home to the **Tolsey Museum**. An interesting building in its own right, its displays cover the history of the town and the surrounding area. Other buildings worth seeking out include the 16th-century Falkland Hall, the home of a local wool and cloth merchant Edmund Sylvester, and Symon Wysdom's Cottages, which were built in 1572 by another of the town's important merchants.

The 160 acres of park and garden that make up **The Cotswold Wildlife Park** are home to a whole host of animals, many of

whom roam freely in the wooded estate. Rhinos, zebras, ostriches and tigers are just some of the animals in the spacious enclosures, while tropical birds, monkeys, reptiles and butterflies are all given the chance to enjoy the warmth of their natural habitat by staying indoors. With an adventure playground and a narrow-gauge railway, the park has something to offer all the family.

Around Burford

TAYNTON
1.5 miles NW of Burford off the A424

Up until the end of the 19th century, Taynton was a quarrying village, with the limestone taken from the quarries used in the construction of Blenheim Palace, Windsor Castle and St Paul's Cathedral as well as many Oxford colleges and local buildings.

🏛 historic building 🏛 museum and heritage 🏛 historic site 🏞 scenic attraction 🌱 flora and fauna

CHASTLETON
10 miles N of Burford off the A44

 Chastleton House

Chastleton is home to one of the best examples of Jacobean architecture in the country. In 1602, Robert Catesby, one of the Gunpowder Plot conspirators, sold his estate here to a prosperous wool merchant from Witney, Walter Jones. A couple of years later, Jones pulled the house down and built **Chastleton House**, a splendid Jacobean manor house with a dramatic five-gabled front and a garden where the original rules of croquet were established in 1865. Until it became a National Trust property, Chastleton had been inhabited by the same family for more than 400 years. They became increasingly impoverished over the years and were unable to upgrade or update the property or its fixtures and fittings. By the time the

National Trust acquired the house in 1991, it had become a virtual time capsule. For the first time in its history, the Trust decided to keep the house 'as found' rather than restore it to its former state of grace. One of the finest and most complete Jacobean houses in England, it is filled with a remarkable collection of furniture, textiles and items both rare and everyday. Visits by appointment only.

SWINBROOK
2 miles E of Burford off the A40

The Fettiplace family lived in a great manor house in this peaceful village in the valley of the Windrush. The manor has long gone, but the family is remembered in several impressive and highly distinctive monuments in the Church of St Mary. The family home of the Redesdales was also at Swinbrook, and in the churchyard are the graves of three of the six Mitford sisters, who were the daughters of the 2nd Baron Redesdale. Nancy, Unity and Pamela are buried here.

MINSTER LOVELL
4.5 miles E of Burford off the B4047

 Minster Lovell Hall

One of the prettiest villages along the banks of the River Windrush, Minster Lovell is home to the ruins of a once impressive 15th-century manor house. **Minster Lovell Hall** was built in the 1430s and was, in its day, one of the great aristocratic houses of Oxfordshire, the home of the Lovell family. However, one of the family was a prominent Yorkist during the Wars of the Roses. After the defeat of Richard III at Bosworth Field, he lost his lands to the Crown. The house was purchased by the Coke family in 1602,

Chastleton House

GOSSIP

2 West Street, Chipping Norton,
Oxfordshire OX7 5AA
Tel: 01608 646871

Gossip is a must stop when you are clothes shopping in Chipping Norton. The space itself is wonderful, light and airy. With a selection of clothes for age twenty and beyond reflecting the great taste of the owner, Sarah and is a well-edited selection of labels including Noa Noa, Nougat, Sandwich, Bandolera, Jonny Q Jeans, Out-Of-Xile, Avoca, Sarah Pacini and occasional newcomers which keep things interesting and fresh. Fashionable pieces of high quality and distinction, as well as timeless classics. To compliment the clothes Gossip also offers handbags, gloves, hats, scarves from Dents; shoes from Unisa and a wonderful range of homemade jewellery. There are also interiors pieces that combined with everything else help to create and complete their 'country living' image.

Shoppng here is an enjoyable and relaxed experience as the 'girls' are very friendly and helpful and give you an honest opinion. Sarah, herself, studied Art & Fashion & Design at Oxford and worked as a window dresser and visual merchandiser for 'Miss Selfridge' and a designer/ dressmaker for private clients - styling women in evening and wedding dresses. During this period she also created a small range of clothes for an independent clothes shop in Witney, which she eventually took over and named 'Gossip' – incorporating all her talents under one roof! That was 17 years ago, today Gossip stands in a fabulous location in Chipping Norton.

Chipping Norton - or "Chippy" as the locals call it is still the kind of town with "real" shops where the lady in the bank is the wife of the hairdresser who is the brother of your builder. There's a lot going on in the town and this fantastic boutique lives up to its name and is a 'fountain of information' for its customers. "Chippy" is a gem. Worth catching while it stays real.

With a great sense of community and personal service awaiting, you will have a memorable shopping experience with Sarah, Linda and Julie at Gossip in "Chippy"...Happy shopping!

CHADLINGTON QUALITY FOODS

The Gables, West End, Chadlington,
Oxfordshire, OX7 3NJ
Tel: 01608 676 675
website: www.chadlington.com
e-mail: shop@chadlington.com

A proud fixture on the Oxfordshire food scene for many years, **Chadlington Quality Foods** is a true village store, in that is owned by the villagers. Re-invigorated by the arrival of Nick Burgess seven years ago, this Cotswold gem stocks a full range of grocery items and wines/spirits wonderfully laid out in the traditional grocers' of past style. Locally grown vegetables are spread over flat surfaces and the shelves are piled with cans of gourmet fruit. Quality pies, quiches and cakes are all homemade on the premises in the newly refurbished kitchen at the back of the shop. You'll also find on offer not so local foodstuffs – continental cheeses and Cornish strawberries.

Burgess and the friendly, welcoming staff are extremely passionate about what they do and if you would like to express your interest and help them to keep the shop running for the village, they have created the 'Friends of Chadlington Quality Foods', membership is FREE and you will receive regular newsletters. If you would like to join, please email the above address with your Name, Address and Postcode.

Still very much a market town today - the market is held on Wednesdays - Chipping Norton has been little affected by the influx of visitors who come to see this charming place. The **Chipping Norton Museum** is an excellent place to start any exploration and the permanent displays here cover local history from prehistoric and Roman times through to the present day.

Found just to the west of the town is **Bliss Tweed Mill**, an extraordinary sight in this area as it was designed by a Lancashire architect, George Woodhouse, in 1872 in the Versailles style. With a decorated parapet and a tall chimney, which acts as a local landmark, this very northern-looking mill only ceased operation in the 1980s. It has since been converted into luxury apartments.

LITTLE ROLLRIGHT

13 miles NE of Burford off the A3400

🏛 Rollright Stones

To the northwest of Over Norton are the **Rollright Stones** - one of the most fascinating Bronze Age monuments in the country. These great gnarled slabs of stone stand on a ridge that offers fine views of the surrounding countryside. They all have nicknames: the **King's Men** form a circle; the **King Stone** is to the north of the circle; and, a quarter of a mile to the west, stand the **Whispering Knights**, which are, in fact, the remnants of a megalithic tomb. Naturally, there are many local legends connected with the stones and some say that they are the petrified figures of a forgotten king and his men that were turned to stone by a witch.

Westbury

🏛 White Horse 🛡 Woodland Park

🛡 Salisbury Plain 🏰 All Saints Church

Westbury, at the western edge of the chalk downlands of **Salisbury Plain**, was a major player in the medieval cloth and wool trades, and still retains many fine buildings from the days of great prosperity, including some cloth works and mills. Westbury was formerly a rotten borough and returned two MPs until 1832, when the Reform Bill put an end to the cheating. Scandal and corruption were rife, and the Old Town Hall in the market place is evidence of such goings-on, a gift from a grateful victorious candidate in 1815. This was Sir Manasseh Massey Lopes, a Portuguese financier and slave-trader who 'bought' the borough to advance his political career.

All Saints Church, a 14th-century building on much earlier foundations, has many unusual and interesting features, including a stone reredos, a copy of the Erasmus Bible and a clock with no face made by a local blacksmith in 1604. It also boasts the third heaviest peal of bells in the world.

On the southern edge of town is another church well worth a visit. Behind the simple, rustic exterior of St Mary's, Old Dilton, are a three-decker pulpit and panelled pew boxes with original fittings and individual fireplaces.

To the west of the town, at Brokerswood, is **Woodland Park and Heritage Centre**, 80 acres of ancient broadleaf woodland with a wide range of trees, plants and animals, nature trails, a lake with fishing, a picnic and barbecue area, a tearoom and

gift shop, a museum, a play area and a narrow-gauge railway.

By far the best-known Westbury feature is the famous **Westbury White Horse**, a chalk carving measuring 182 feet in length and 108 feet in height. The present steed dates from 1778, replacing an earlier one carved to celebrate King Alfred's victory over the Danes at nearby Ethandun (Edington) in 878AD. The White Horse is well looked after, the last major grooming carried out in 2006. Above the horse's head are the ruins of Bratton Castle, an Iron Age hill fort covering 25 acres.

Around Westbury

WARMINSTER
4 miles S of Westbury on the A350

🖼 Dewey Museum 🏛 Cley Hill

🛡 Arn Hill Nature Reserve

Warminster is a historic wool, corn-trading and coaching town with many distinguished buildings, including a famous school with a door designed by Wren. In addition to the 18th- and 19th-century buildings, Warminster has a number of interesting monuments: the Obelisk with its feeding troughs and pineapple

Cley Hill, Warminster

top erected in 1783 to mark the enclosure of the parish; the Morgan Memorial Fountain in the Lake Pleasure Grounds; and *Beyond Harvest*, a statue in bronze by Colin Lambert of a girl sitting on sacks of corn. Warminster's finest building is the Church of St Denys, mainly 14th century but almost completely rebuilt in the 1880s to the design of Arthur Blomfield. The **Dewey Museum**, in the public library, displays a wide range of local history from Iron Age times to the present day, and includes the Victor Manley collection of geology.

To the west of town is the 800ft **Cley Hill**, an Iron Age hill fort with two Bronze Age barrows. Formerly owned by the Marquess of

SERENDIPITY

18 Market Place, Warminster, Wiltshire BA12 9AN
Tel: 01985 219907

There's an art to finding something when you're not looking for it. **Serendipity** is not only a beautiful word it is a very beautiful thing, and now lends itself to a very wonderful shop in the heart of Warminster. The word itself was first coined by Horace Walpole in 1754 and is derived from an Old Persian fairy tale called The Three Princes of Serendip. In this fairy tale the three Princes are constantly making discoveries and coming across stuff they never set out to find.

More of an experience than a store, **Serendipity** is your destination for extraordinary gift giving and quality items of relaxed elegance for your everyday living. Though only a small shop it is packed full of interesting and unusual gifts, clothing and jewellery, brands include; *East of India*, beautiful white washed and pastel wooden hearts, boxes and plaques; *Uttam*, a range of funky clothing with bright bold prints and *Nomad*, Fairtrade clothing line.

The shop changes constantly. The only thing that remains the same is that it is always full of colour! So any time it is really grey outside pay them a visit.

STARRS FARM STABLE COTTAGE

The Green, Crockerton, Warminster, Wiltshire BA12 8AX
Tel: 01985 213450

Situated close to Longleat Estate, this charming cottage sleeps 2-3 persons and provides a very convenient, central base for exploring this part of southern England. Longleat House and Safari Park, the historic cities of Bath and Salisbury, the fine landscaped gardens of Stourhead (National Trust) and prehistoric Stonehenge are all just a short drive away. Converted from an old stable 20 years ago, it retains some of its original character (beamed ceilings, and stonewall interior) combined with a high degree of comfort. Local outdoor pursuits include golf at Warminsterand woodland walks & coarse fishing at nearby Shearwater Lake where there is also a small thatched tearoom.

route. A statue near the bridge over the River Wylye (from which the village, Wilton and, indeed, Wiltshire get their names) commemorates a brave postboy who drowned here after rescuing several passengers from a stagecoach that had overturned during a flood.

Above the village is the little-known **Yarnbury Castle**, an Iron Age hill fort surrounded by two banks and an outer bank. To the west is a triangular enclosure from Roman times, which could have held cattle or sheep. From the 18th century to the First World War, Yarnbury was the venue of an annual sheep fair.

IMBER
5 miles E of Westbury off the B3098

The part of Salisbury Plain containing the village of Imber was closed to the public in 1943 and has been used by the Army ever since as a live firing range. The evicted villagers were told that they could return to Imber after the war, but the promise was not kept and the village remains basically inaccessible. A well-marked 30-mile perimeter walk skirting the danger area takes in Warminster, Westbury, Tilshead in the east and Chitterne in the south.

LONGLEAT
7 miles SW of Westbury off the A362

🏛 Longleat House   🐾 Safari Park

2009 sees the 60th anniversary of the opening of **Longleat House** (see panel on page 383) to the public. The magnificent home of the Marquess of Bath was built by an ancestor, Sir John Thynne, in a largely symmetrical style, in the 1570s. The inside is a treasure house of old masters, Flemish tapestries, beautiful furniture, rare books and Lord Bath's racy murals. The superb grounds of Longleat

House were landscaped by Capability Brown, and now contain one of the country's best known venues for a marvellous day out. In the famous **Safari Park** the Lions of Longleat, first introduced in 1966, have been followed by a veritable Noah's Ark of exotic creatures, including rhinos, zebras and white tigers. The park also features safari boat rides, a narrow-gauge railway, children's amusement area, garden centre and the largest hedge maze in the world.

STOURTON
13 miles SW of Westbury off the B3092

🏛 Stourhead   🏛 King Alfred's Tower

The beautiful National Trust village of Stourton lies at the bottom of a steep wooded valley and is a particularly glorious sight in the daffodil season. The main attraction is, of course, **Stourhead** (see panel opposite), one of the most famous examples of the early-18th century English landscape movement. The lakes, the trees, the temples, a grotto and a classical bridge make the grounds, laid out by Henry Hoare, a paradise in the finest 18th-century tradition. The gardens are renowned for their striking vistas and woodland walks, as well as a stunning selection of rare trees and specimen shrubs, including tulip trees, azaleas and rhododendrons. The house itself, a classical masterpiece built in the 1720s in Palladian style for a Bristol banker, contains a wealth of Grand Tour paintings and works of art, including furniture by Chippendale the Younger and wood carvings by Grinling Gibbons. On the very edge of the estate, some three miles by road from the house, the imposing **King Alfred's Tower** stands at the top of the 790ft Kingsettle Hill. This 160ft triangular redbrick folly was built in 1772 to

---

🏛 historic building   🏛 museum and heritage   🏛 historic site   🌳 scenic attraction   🌿 flora and fauna

Stourhead

Stourhead Estate Office, Stourton,
Warminster, Wiltshire BA12 6QD
Tel: 01747 841152
website: www.nationaltrust.org.uk

Often referred to as 'Paradise', lying
in secluded privacy in its own valley,
Stourhead is one of the finest
landscape gardens in the world.
Stourhead's 18th century garden
was created by Henry Hoare II. Inspired by the views
of Italy captured by artists in paint, he decided to
create a landscape garden with temples and Gothic
ruins that would bring art to life. Sitting majestically
above the garden and surrounded by delightful lawns
and parkland is Stourhead House: a fine Palladian
mansion built by Colen Campbell, home to a unique
collection of Chippendale furniture, magnificent
paintings and an exquisite Regency library.

The magnificent lake is central to this iconic
garden of classical temples and follies. Its
lakeside paths and backdrop of colourful, rare and
exotic trees reveal many beautifully contrived
vistas, capturing the imagination of visitors for
over two centuries. The House and Garden are at
the heart of a 1,072 hectare (2,650 acre) estate.

Two Iron Age hill forts can be discovered, and
from the top of King Alfred's Tower, a 50m-high
red brick triangular folly, visitors will experience spectacular views
across three counties.

commemorate the King, who reputedly
raised his standard here against the Danes
in 878AD.

MERE

14 miles SW of Westbury off the A303

🏛 Museum 🏰 Castle Hill

A small town nestling below the downs near
the borders with Dorset and Somerset. The
town is dominated by **Castle Hill**, on which
Richard, Earl of Cornwall, son of King John,
built a castle in 1253. Nothing of the castle

remains, though many of the stones were
used in building Mere's houses. The High-
Gothic-style Church of St Michael the
Archangel features some fine medieval and
Victorian stained glass, carved Jacobean
pews, an unusual octagonal font and a 12th-
century statue of St Michael slaying a dragon.
Mere Museum, in the public library in
Barton Lane, is principally a local history
collection with a good photographic archive.
Displays are changed regularly, but a
permanent feature is a large, detailed map of

🎭 stories and anecdotes 🕊 famous people 🎨 art and craft ✒ entertainment and sport 🚶 walks

been converted into a cinema and has been fitted with a sign proclaiming ODEON in Gothic script.

A short drive takes visitors to the ruins of **Old Sarum** (English Heritage), abandoned when the bishopric moved into the city. Traces of the original cathedral and palace are visible on the huge uninhabited mound, which dates back to the Iron Age. Old Sarum became the most notorious of the rotten boroughs, returning two Members of Parliament, despite having no voters, until the 1832 Reform Act stopped the practice. A plaque on the site commemorates Old Sarum's most illustrious MP, William Pitt the Elder who, of course, was elected by the rotten borough procedure.

Salisbury Racecourse, a short drive west of the city, is one of England's oldest racecourses - racing has taken place at this picturesque downland course since the 1500s. The course stages a number of flat racing meetings during the summer months.

Eyre's Folly, Lover

and it was in commemoration of that ancient parliament that the present **Moot House** was built on the foundations of the old castle. The building and its garden stand opposite a small 18th-century amphitheatre built to resemble the Saxon moot. In 1955, a Roman villa comprising seven rooms and a bath house was discovered nearby.

Around Salisbury

BRITFORD
1 mile S of Salisbury on the A338

Lying within branches of the Wiltshire River Avon, Britford has a moated country house and a fine Saxon church with some early stone carvings. An ornate tomb is thought to be that of the Duke of Buckingham, who was beheaded in Salisbury in 1483.

DOWNTON
5 miles S of Salisbury off the A338

🏛 Moot House

The Saxons established a meeting place, or moot, on an earlier earthwork fortification,

LOVER
6 miles SE of Salisbury off the A338

🔾 Pepperbox Hill

In the vicinity of this charmingly named village is the National Trust's **Pepperbox Hill**, topped by an early 17th-century octagonal tower known as **Eyre's Folly**. Great walking, great views, and a great place for nature-lovers, with a variety of plant and bird life.

WILTON
3 miles W of Salisbury on the A30

🔾 Carpet Factory   🏛 Wilton House

🏛 Church of St Mary & St Nicholas

The third oldest borough in England and once

🏛 historic building   📷 museum and heritage   🏛 historic site   🔾 scenic attraction   ☘ flora and fauna the capital of Saxon Wessex. It is best known for its carpets, and the **Wilton Carpet Factory** on the River Wylye continues to produce top-quality carpets, maintaining a worldwide reputation for quality that goes back 300 years. Wilton carpets as we know them today were created by a French carpet weaver who was brought to England by the Earl of Pembroke in the early 1700s to teach the local weavers his skills. In 1835, redundant handlooms were brought from the Axminster factory in Devon and set up in Wilton. Luxurious hand-knotted Axminsters, with each tuft individually tied by hand, were made alongside traditional Wiltons up to 1958. Situated beside the factory, the Wilton Shopping Village offers high-quality factory shopping in a traditional rural setting.

Wilton House is the stately home of the Earls of Pembroke. When the original house was destroyed by fire in 1647, Inigo Jones was commissioned to build its replacement. He designed both the exterior and the interior, including the amazing Double Cube Room. The house was further remodelled by James Wyatt. The art collection is one of the very finest, with works by Rembrandt, Van Dyke, Rubens and Tintoretto; the furniture includes pieces by Chippendale and Kent.

There's plenty to keep children busy and happy, including a treasure hunt quiz and a huge adventure playground. There's a Tudor kitchen, a Victorian laundry, and 21 acres of landscaped grounds with parkland, cedar trees, water and rose gardens, and an elegant Palladian bridge.

The **Church of St Mary and St Nicholas** is a unique Italianate church built in the style of Lombardy by the Russian Countess of

TISBURY

12 miles W of Salisbury off the A30

🏛 Tithe Barn 🏛 Old Wardour Castle

Tisbury is the most prominent of the villages strung along the River Nadder. It has a fine parish church that has a 15th-century clerestory and used to have a lofty spire. This was hit by lightning in 1742, rebuilt, and then struck by lightning again 20 years later. At this point the parishioners gave up. In the churchyard is a venerable yew tree, which carbon dating, has established is 4,000 years old.

To the east of the village stands the magnificent gateway of Place Farm. It was built for the abbesses of Shaftesbury in the late 14th- and early 15th-centuries and gives a clear idea of the splendour of the farm at that time. The only building that remains is the huge **Tithe Barn**, believed to be the largest in England. Built of local stone, it has a thatched roof that was originally covered by stone tiles.

Notable sons of the village include Thomas Mayhew, a prosperous mercer in the early 1600s who

Tithe Barn, Tisbury

KATE GOOD POTTERY

High Street, Tisbury, nr Salisbury, Wiltshire SP3 6HD
Tel: 01747 870367

Founder of **Kate Good Pottery**, Kate Good studied at London's Central School of Arts and has lived in Wiltshire for 35 years and the Tisbury area for nearly 25 years now. Visitors to her shop will find a selection of more than 150 items of fine household and decorative stoneware pottery. Everything in Kate's repertoire is thoughtfully designed and expertly finished, the final glaze firing reaches 1280°C, producing pottery with a unique translucent though surprisingly robust finish.

Many of the items in the range of practical cookware and tableware are available plain or decorated and besides the plates, dishes and bowls there are storage jars, table lamps, candlesticks and candle holders, plant pots, money pigs and cats, along with unusual items such as egg cups small enough for bantam eggs or large enough for goose eggs. Kate also produces a series of durable, colourful mosaic tiles that are suitable for indoor or outdoor use, as well as oil burners in exquisite new designs. All items will delight you for many years and are suitable for oven, dishwasher, freezer and microwave use (plus of course everyday wear and tear). Kate also takes great pride in producing commemorative and personliased items to mark special occasions such as weddings and christenings etc.

New for 2008 is the leaf tableware (see picture), this stunning collection takes inspiration from leaves Kate has collected from all around the world, the sensitive but striking use of colour and textural effects complete the look.

🏛 historic building 📷 museum and heritage 🏚 historic site 🏞 scenic attraction 🐾 flora and fauna

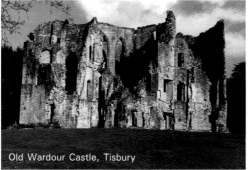
Old Wardour Castle, Tisbury

in Hindon Lane, and wrote much of his novel *Kim* while staying in Tisbury.

To the south, **Old Wardour Castle** (English Heritage) was the scene in 1643 of a bloody battle when Parliamentarian forces besieged the castle for several weeks, causing great loss of life and extensive damage to the building. The landscaped grounds in which the castle stands include an elaborate rockwork grotto.

emigrated to New England where he acquired the off-shore islands of Martha's Vineyard and Nantucket. He and his family also helped establish the township of Tisbury.

In the churchyard of the Wiltshire Tisbury, John Lockwood and Alice Kipling, the parents of the author Rudyard Kipling are buried. He often visited them at their home, The Gables

WOODFORD VALLEY

6 miles N of Salisbury off the A345

🌱 Heale Garden & Plant Centre

A seven-mile stretch between Salisbury and Amesbury contains some of the prettiest and most peaceful villages in the county, among them Great Durnford with its Norman church

---

THE WALNUT TREE GALLERY

52 High Street, Sixpenny Handley, Salisbury, Wiltshire SP5 5ND
Tel: 01725 552836
e-mail: info@thewalnuttreegallery.co.uk
website: www.thewalnuttreegallery.co.uk

At **The Walnut Tree Gallery** you will find sumptuous and colourful gifts for friends, family and colleagues – or even for yourself!

Set in the village of Sixpenny Handley, The Walnut Tree Gallery is light, airy and welcoming. The shop is warm, contemporary and unpretentious – more of an emporium than a shop. Run by artist Brady Turner, the shop provides an opportunity to discover the best of Wiltshire's arts, crafts and designs. Works featured include pottery from White Horse Pottery, Corfe Castle Pottery and Loudware by Jane Willingale. There are decorative textiles for the home, wooden items by local craftsmen and timeless paintings and prints by Sarah Ross-Thompson and Krystyna Evans.

The jewellery is simply extraordinary, consisting of contemporary sterling silver pieces by Wendy Nutt of Poole and Frances Gascoigne in Seattle, glass pendants by Linda Rowe and colourful button necklaces by Dunja Wood. Greetings cards are by Woodmansterne, Canns Down Press and Museums & Galleries. The gallery is also an outlet for Dr Hauschka skincare products. And with the advent of the online store, The Walnut Tree Gallery is now able to offer a large selection of items to customers who live further afield. This is simply shopping as it should be – inspiring, original and local!

POULTON GRANGE

Poulton Farm Estate, Marlborough, Wiltshire SN8 2LN
Tel: 01672 516888
e-mail: sheppard@poultongrange.com
website: www.poultongrange.com

Your Journey begins here... Wiltshire, England - a county of contrasts and diversity. Steeped in history, yet alive to the present. Explore the lively market town of Marlborough, rolling open scenery, stately homes and magnificent gardens plus experiencing the traditional values and warm welcome that is certain at **Poulton Grange Farmhouse Bed and Breakfast**. Be treated as 'one of the family' whilst enjoying the enticing combination of rural tranquility, heartening homemade food produced from the farm and a standard of comfort to rival the best hotels around!

has a ledge where churchgoers would leave their pattens before entering. Other buildings of interest include those clustered round The Green (originally a Saxon village, and the working-class quarter in the 18th and 19th

Merle Barrow, Marlborough

centuries); the turn-of-the-century Town Hall looking down the broad High Street; and the ornate 17th-century Merchant's House, now restored as a museum.

Marlborough College was founded in 1843 primarily for sons of the clergy. The Seymour family hbuilt a mansion near the site of the Norman castle, which was replaced in the early 18th century by a building that became the Castle Inn and is now C House, the oldest part of the College. A mound in the private grounds of the school is linked with King Arthur's personal magician, Merlin. It was said that he was buried under this mound and gave the town its name, **'Merle Barrow'**, or Merlin's Tomb. Among the many

FISHERMAN'S HOUSE

Mildenhall, nr Marlborough, Wiltshire, SN8 2LZ
Tel: 01672 515390
email: heathercoulter610@btinternet.com
website: www.fishermanshouse.co.uk

In an area of outstanding beauty on the River Kennet, The **Fisherman's House's** owners, Heather and Jeremey Coulter, look forward to welcoming you to their tranquil Georgian home. It is the perfect place to relax, recharge and kick back for a while. All the attractively furnished bedrooms have TV and tea/coffee making facilities. The garden is a delight to enjoy, ducks even venture up the lawn greeting you in the morning. Pretty as a picture - The Fisherman's House is proud to have been featured on the cover of The English Home magazine USA.

🏛 historic building 🏛 museum and heritage 🏛 historic site ⚜ scenic attraction �${}$ flora and fauna

CUNETIO RIDING AND B&B

Warren Farm Cottage, Mildenhall, Marlborough,
Wiltshire SN8 2NJ
Tel: 01672 841171
e-mail: rideout@cunetioriding.co.uk
website: www.cunetioriding.co.uk

Farmhouse Bed and Breakfast

Join us for a short break in our farmhouse
cottage in a fabulous, rural location yet only
two miles from the market town of
Marlborough. We are perfectly situated for
walking and cycling breaks. We have free range
hens, geese, ducks and pigs, and welcome well-
behaved dogs.

Riding Breaks

At Cunetio Stables in the village of Mildenhall,
we run a yard of fit, young horses and
experienced riders are invited to join us on our
exciting hacks to Barbury Castle, Avebury, the
Valley of the Stones and beyond. For those
wishing to bring their own horses we offer stabling/turn out and can map out local routes.

notable former pupils of the college were
William Morris and John Betjeman.

Around Marlborough

SAVERNAKE FOREST
2 miles E of Marlborough off the A346

🐾 Savernake Forest

The ancient woodland of **Savernake Forest**
is a magnificent 4,500-acre expanse of
unbroken woodland, open glades and bridle
paths. King Henry VIII hunted wild deer here
and the family home of his third wife, Jane
Seymour, was nearby. Designated a Site of
Special Scientific Interest, the forest is home
to abundant wildlife, including a small herd of
deer and 25 species of butterfly. One day each
winter the forest is closed to prevent rights of
way being established.

GREAT BEDWYN
6 miles SE of Marlborough off the A4

🏛 Lloyds Stone Museum

In the chancel of the 11th-century Church of
St Mary the Virgin is the tomb of Sir John
Seymour, the father of Henry VIII's third wife
Jane. Nearby is **Lloyds Stone Museum**, a
monument to the skills of the English
stonemason. Great Bedwyn was the base of
the Lloyd family of stonemasons who have
been working in stone for some 200 years.
The Bedwyn Stone Museum is based on their
mason's yard and among the items on display
are an assortment of tombstones and a stone
aeroplane with an 11ft wingspan.

To the east of Great Bedwyn and four miles
south of Hungerford off the A338 at Rivar
Hill Airfield is the home of Shalbourne
Soaring Society. It is a popular gliding club,
which offers affordable flying. Why not take a

THE OLD BEAR INN

101 High Street, Cricklade, Wiltshire SN6 6AA
Tel: 01793 750005
e-mail: theoldbear@sky.com

The Old Bear Inn enjoys a prominent position on the main street of the historic Saxon town of Cricklade, the only Wiltshire town on the River Thames. The pub is in the excellent care of Teresa and Steve Cleverly, who have the warmest of welcomes for their customers, whether they've popped in for a quick drink or are taking an overnight or longer break while touring the region.

The lounge and public bars are convivial spots for enjoying a glass of well kept Arkell's or one of the guest ales such as Moonlight or Organic. Take a drink in the sun and admire the fantastic garden which won a Gold Award in Britain Bloom 2007.

For guests staying overnight, The Old Bear has comfortable accommodation in the converted stables. All rooms have colour televisions and a courtesy tray with tea & coffee provided. Everyone is made welcome with the entire pub being dog friendly and a heated smoking area is also provided.

The pub is thought to have got its name from a performing bear that was part of a touring Russian circus that used to visit Cricklade in the 18th century. The circus left town long, long ago but there's plenty to interest today's visitors, and those wanting to make the most of the local scenery, for it is the first town on the Thames Path Walk.

THE VALE HOTEL

32 High Street, Cricklade, Wiltshire SN6 6AY
Tel: 01793 750223
e-mail: adywys@yahoo.co.uk

Cricklade an Old Saxon town set on the edge of the Cotswold Water Parks boasts many attractive historical buildings dating back beyond the 17th century and a community atmosphere supported a High Street that has always formed a tight focus around which the town could grow. Situated on the High Street **The Vale Hotel** is a charming 15-bedroom hotel where the service is personal, the rooms very comfortable and the restaurant excellent. The big draw here though is the food. Pick up either the bar or à la carte and your in for a real treat, bar staples include award winning Cricklade sausages with mash and homemade burgers with handcut chips. Or you can choose from the à la carte menu which features Rainbow trout on wilted spinach, almond potato and a caper and sultana puree...Delicious! Produce is sourced from local suppliers where possible and is guaranteed to be of the highest quality.

In this ancient environment you can enjoy lingering walks across the famous 150-acre North Meadow, a National Nature Reserve which is home to the rare Snakeshead Fritillary and two of the most magnificent churches in the South, references to St Sampson's (the oldest and largest of the two churches) can be found from as early as 983.

Steeped in history and stunning views as a backdrop make it well worth a visit.

🏛 historic building 🏛 museum and heritage 🏚 historic site ⚘ scenic attraction 🌱 flora and fauna

is a National Nature Reserve where the rare snakeshead fritillary grows.

HIGHWORTH

5 miles NE of Swindon on the A361

⚲ Highworth Hill

The name is appropriate, as the village stands at the top of a 400ft incline, and the view from **Highworth Hill** takes in the counties of Wiltshire, Gloucestershire and Oxfordshire. There are some very fine 17th- and 18th-century buildings round the old square, and the parish church is of interest: built in the 15th century, it was fortified during the Civil War and was attacked soon after by Parliamentarian forces under Fairfax. One of the cannonballs that struck it is on display outside. The church contains a memorial to Lieutenant Warneford, who was awarded the VC for destroying the first enemy Zeppelin in 1915.

WROUGHTON

3 miles S of Swindon on the A4361

🦋 Butterfly World 🦋 Clouts Wood Nature Reserve

🏛 Barbury Castle ✍ Craft Village

Wroughton Airfield, with its historic Second World War hangars, now serves as a Science Museum, Swindon's storage facility for larger objects. It is only open for pre-booked tours and special events.

A popular attraction in Wroughton is **Butterfly World** at Studley Grange Garden & Leisure Park. Visitors can get close to some of the largest and most spectacular insects on the planet. They fly freely against a backdrop of tropical plants, skimming over fish-filled pools. The 'mini-beasts' house is home to a fascinating display of spiders, scorpions, mantis and other creepy crawlies. Also within the Park is a **Craft Village** where craftspeople

Barbury Castle, nr Wroughton

make and sell their work, which ranges from stained glass to silk flowers, from ceramics to crystals and jewellery.

Nearby, **Clouts Wood Nature Reserve** is a lovely place for a ramble, and a short drive south, by the Ridgeway, is the site of **Barbury Castle**, one of the most spectacular Iron Age forts in southern England. The open hillside was the scene of a bloody battle between the Britons and the Saxons in the 6th century; the Britons lost and the Saxon kingdom of Wessex was established under King Cealwin. The area around the castle is a country park.

BROAD HINTON

5 miles S of Swindon off the A4361

In the church at Broad Hinton is a memorial to local bigwig Sir Thomas Wroughton, who returned home from hunting to find his wife reading the Bible instead of making his tea. He seized the Bible and flung it into the fire; his wife retrieved it but in doing so severely burnt her hands. As punishment for his blasphemy Sir Thomas's hands and those of his four children withered away (very hard on the children, surely). The monument shows the whole handless family and a Bible with a corner burnt off.

LYDIARD TREGOZE
2 miles W of Swindon off the A3102

🏛 Lydiard Park

On the western outskirts of Swindon, **Lydiard Park** is the ancestral home of the Viscounts Bolingbroke. The park is a delightful place to explore, and the house, one of Wiltshire's smaller stately homes, is a real

Wootton Bassett Market House

gem, described by Sir Hugh Casson as "a gentle Georgian house, sunning itself as serenely as an old grey cat". Chief attractions inside include the little blue Dressing Room devoted to the 18th-century society artist Lady Diana Spencer who became the 2nd Viscountess Bolingbroke. She shared a common ancestry and a remarkable physical resemblance to the late Diana, Princess of Wales. Lydiard Park's grounds contain a recently restored walled garden, originally built in the 1740s; an excellent children's play area, and a café.

St Mary's Church, next to the house, contains many monuments to the St John family, who have lived here from Elizabethan times. The most striking is the Golden Cavalier, a life-size gilded effigy of Edward St John in full battledress (he was killed at the second Battle of Newbury in 1645).

WOOTTON BASSETT
3 miles W of Swindon off the A3102

A small town with a big history, its records go back to the 7th century. In 1219, Henry III granted Wootton Bassett a market charter (the market is still held every Wednesday). The town boasts some fine Georgian buildings, a good range of family-run businesses – including a butcher, baker, greengrocer and ironmonger – and some good eating places. You can eat al fresco across from the striking Old Town Hall, which stands on a series of stone pillars, leaving an open-sided ground-floor area that once served as a covered market. The museum above, open on Saturday mornings, contains a rare ducking stool, silver maces and a mayoral sword of office.

A section of the Wilts & Berks Canal has been restored at Templars Fir. Opened in May 1998, about 50 boats of all kinds were launched on the canal and a day of festivities was enjoyed by all. The railway station, alas, has not been revived after falling to the Beeching axe in 1966.

Chippenham

📷 Museum & Heritage Centre

🕴 Maud Heath's Causeway

Set on the banks of the Avon, Chippenham was founded around 600AD by the Saxon

Maud Heath's Causeway, nr Chippenham

king Cyppa. It became an important administrative centre in King Alfred's time and later gained further prominence from the wool trade. It was a major stop on the London-Bristol coaching run and is served by the railway between the same two cities. Buildings of note include the Church of St Andrew (mainly 15th century) and the half-timbered Yelde Hall, once used by the burgesses and bailiffs of the Chippenham Hundred. This Grade I building now houses the tourist information office.

The recently opened **Chippenham Museum and Heritage Centre** in the Market Place tells the story of the town from the Jurassic period onwards, and the displays focus on Saxon Chippenham, Alfred the Great, Brunel's railway, the celebrated cheese market, Victorian living conditions and Chippenham curiosities.

At Hardenhuish Hall on the edge of town, John Wood the Younger of Bath fame built the Church of St Nicholas; completed in 1779, it is notable for its domed steeple and elegant Venetian windows. Wealth from the wool trade built many fine houses using local stone and Bath stone, which led to Chippenham being called little Bath.

In the flood plain to the east of Chippenham, stands the 4.5 mile footpath known as **Maud Heath's Causeway**. This remarkable and ingenious walkway consisting of 64 brick and stone arches was built at the end of the 15th century at the bequest of Maud Heath, who spent most of her life as a market trader trudging her often muddy way between her village of Bremhill and Chippenham. She died a relatively wealthy woman, and the land and property she left in her will provided sufficient funds for the upkeep of the causeway, which is best seen near the hamlet of Kellaways. A statue of Maud, basket in hand, stands overlooking the flood plain at Wick Hill.

Around Chippenham

CALNE
5 miles E of Chippenham on the A4

🏛 Bowood House 📷 Atwell-Wilson Motor Museum

A former weaving centre in the valley of the River Marden; the prominent wool church reflects the prosperity of earlier times. One of the memorials in the church is to Dr Ingenhousz, who is widely credited with

Bradford-on-Avon

variously as a school, a charnel house for storing the bones of the dead, and a residential dwelling. It was re-discovered by a keen-eyed clergyman who looked down from a hill and noticed the cruciform shape of a church. The surrounding buildings were gradually removed to reveal the little masterpiece we see today. Bradford's Norman church, restored in the 19th century, has an interesting memorial to Lieutenant-

Lawrence, believed to have been founded by St Aldhelm around 700AD. It 'disappeared' for over 1,000 years, when it was used

General Henry Shrapnel, the army officer who, in 1785, invented and gave his name to the shrapnel shell. Another of the town's

---

STILL MEADOW B&B

*18 Bradford Road, Winsley, Bradford on Avon,
Wiltshire BA15 2HW
Tel: 01225 722119 Fax: 01225 722633
e-mail: sue.gilby@btinternet.com
website: www.stillmeadow.co.uk*

You are cordially invited to come to **Stillmeadow B&B** where you will find the seasons pass as gently as a hill farm breeze. Walk through the stunning Wiltshire countryside and gaze upon the distant hills of Westbury White Horse. The aroma of the morning dew upon the landscape in spring awakens your spirit; listen to the melodies of bird songs while you rest in a comfortable chair on the patio area surrounded by tranquil gardens. The accommodation is set in a semi-rural location offering three spacious, modern rooms with en-suite facilities and all other amenities expected of a 5 Diamond guest house. You can expect a very good night's sleep in these warm and comfortable rooms which have the added advantage of the house's position being situated at the end of a private drive some distance from the roadside. The surrounding area is a registered glow worm site and the grounds of Special scientific Interest. Badgers, deer, foxes, rabbits and many birds including Green Woodpeckers, owls and buzzard are often spotted as frequent visitors to the extensive gardens and the wildflower meadow.

For those who enjoy sporting activities there is boating/fishing, cycling, golf, horse riding and motor racing. For the less active there are several National Trust properties within a close proximity, including Dyrham Park, The Courts Holt and Lacock Abbey.

🏠 historic building   🏛 museum and heritage   🏛 historic site   🌄 scenic attraction   🌿 flora and fauna

The Peto Garden at Iford Manor

Bradford on Avon, Wiltshire BA15 2BA
Tel: 01225 863146
e-mail: info@ilfordmanor.co.uk
website: www.ilfordmanor.co.uk

Harold Peto (1854-1933) began his career by training as an architect, and in 1874 entered into parnership with Ernest George which was to last for sixteen years. Among their assistants were the young Sir Edwin Lutyens, Guy Dawber and Herbert Baker. Peto became increasingly interested in garden design after the dissolution of the partnership in 1892. Towards the end of that time he found himself increasingly out of sympathy with current trends in English architecture, his own taste inclined much more towards the style and decorative arts of the Italian Renaissance.

In the late 1880s, as the result of several long visits to Italy, Peto's attention was turned from architecture to the idea of designing house and garden together. He combined a knowledge of practical gardening with an architect's feel for the layout of the garden, and by the end of the century had become well known as a designer both in England and the South of France.

At the time of the break with Ernest George in 1890, he had promised that he would not compete with his former partner as an architect in England so it was in France that he undertook the design of houses and gardens together. It is in the Alpes Maritimes in France that the villas and gardens, for which he is most well known are on the Cote d'Azur at Cap Ferrat, Villa Maryland, Villa Sylvia and Villa Rosemary.

There he was able to concentrate on what he most enjoyed: designing Italianate villas in a garden setting for his clients – wealthy expatriate Americans like Ralph Curtis, for the most part – as well as collecting authentic Italian, French and Spanish fireplaces, doors, sculptures and other fittings to decorate both house and garden. Back in England, in 1899 he found the country house he had been looking for and bought Iford Manor with its attractive 18th century Palladian façade. His challenge was to transform the steep, awkward hillside in conformity with his ideas. He arranged the grounds in such a way – around the grand terrace walk – that they provided an echo of some of his favourite Mediterranean gardens. He was particularly attracted by the charm of old Italian gardens, where flowers occupy a subordinate place amongst the cypresses, broad walks, statues and pools.

The Garden is open: During April & October on Sunday and Easter Monday between 2.00pm – 5pm. From May to September daily between 2pm – 5pm except on Mondays and Fridays.Homemade teas: Available from May to August at weekends and on Bank Holidays. Please note: Saturdays and Sundays are reserved for tranquil visits. Children under 10 years are very welcome during the open week but for health and safety constraints, may not be admitted at weekends. Dogs must be kept on leads.

📷 stories and anecdotes 🐦 famous people 🎨 art and craft 🖊 entertainment and sport 🚶 walks

outstanding buildings is the mighty **Tithe Barn**, once used to store the grain from local farms for Shaftesbury Abbey, now housing a collection of antique farm implements and agricultural machinery. The centrepiece of the museum in Bridge Street is a pharmacy, which had stood in the town for 120 years before being removed lock, stock and medicine bottles to its new site.

Another impressive building is **Abbey Mill**, which was built in 1875 as a cloth mill at a time when the industry was in steep decline. It managed to stay in production until 1902; became a barracks during the Frist World War and then, was taken over by Avon Rubber who used it as a factory until the early 1990s. It is now retirement apartments.

Off the A363, **Barton Farm Country Park** offers delightful walks in lovely countryside by the River Avon and the Kennet and Avon Canal. It was once a medieval farm serving Shaftesbury Abbey. Barton Bridge is the original packhorse bridge built to assist the transportation of grain from the farm to the tithe barn.

Half a mile south of town by the River Frome is the Italian-style **Peto Garden** (see panel on page 421) at Iford Manor. Famous for its romantic, tranquil beauty, its steps and terraces, statues, colonnades and ponds, the garden was laid out by the architect and landscape gardener Harold Ainsworth Peto between 1899 and 1933. He was inspired by the works of Lutyens and Jekyll to turn a difficult hillside site into "a haunt of ancient peace".

Outside Bradford, off the A366, the charming 15th century **Westwood Manor** (National Trust) has many interesting features, including Jacobean and Gothic windows, ornate plasterwork and a topiary garden.

Malmesbury

🏛 Abbey 🌿 Abbey House Gardens

🏛 Athelstan Museum

The Queen of Hilltop Towns is England's oldest borough and one of its most attractive. The town is dominated by the impressive remains of the **Benedictine Malmesbury Abbey**, founded in the 7th century by St Aldhelm. In the 10th century, King Athelstan, Alfred's grandson and the first Saxon king to unite England, granted 500 acres of land to the townspeople in gratitude for their help in resisting a Norse invasion. Those acres are still known as King's Heath and are owned by 200 residents who are descended from those far-off heroes. Athelstan made Malmesbury his capital and is buried in the abbey, where several centuries later a monument was put up in his honour.

Abbey House Gardens, Malmesbury

CAPERS DELICATESSEN

13 High Street, Malmesbury, Wiltshire SN16 9AA
Tel: 01666 824744

The town of Malmesbury is rightly referred to as the "Queen of Hilltop Towns" being England's oldest borough with a rich history over 1000 years. Malmesbury also boasts: medieval architecture, a fine abbey, delightful open gardens and **Capers Delicatessen**.

Capers is the new buzz word in Malmesbury. Proprietor, Jacqui Smith is set to replace a service lost a number of years ago, and aims to complement shops already situated in this beautiful hilltop town.

A food lover's paradise, this fine food delicatessen offers a huge range of regional food, which cover the entire spectrum of culinary delights. The product portfolio is constantly evolving as Jacqui refines the range to provide the very best for her customers. Fresh ranges, local products and organic goods sit comfortably alongside premium British and continental foods.

On the deli counter you will find many different cheeses, a wide selection of olives, sun dried tomatoes, gourmet pies and fresh quiches. It's a beautiful place with friendly staff, loved by local gourmands and the lunchtime crowd as well.

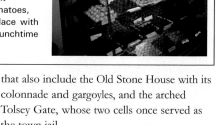

Within the precincts of the abbey are **Abbey House Gardens**, an enchanting place with an abundance of flowers, around 2,000 medicinal herbs, woodland and laburnum walks, fish ponds and a waterfall.

The abbey tower was the scene of an early attempt at human-powered flight when, in the early part of the 11th century, Brother Elmer strapped a pair of wings to his arms, flew for about 200 yards and crashed to earth, breaking both legs, becoming a cripple for the rest of his long life. The flight of this intrepid cleric, who reputedly forecast the Norman invasion following a sighting of Halley's Comet, is commemorated in a stained glass window. Another window, by Burne-Jones, portrays Faith, Courage and Devotion.

The octagonal Market Cross in the town square is one of many interesting buildings that also include the Old Stone House with its colonnade and gargoyles, and the arched Tolsey Gate, whose two cells once served as the town jail.

In the **Malmesbury Athelstan Museum** in the Town Hall, are displays of lace-making, costume, rural life, coins, early bicycles and tricycles, a manually-operated fire pump, photographs and maps. Here, too, are the ceremonial wheelbarrow and spade used to cut the first sod of the Wiltshire & Gloucestershire Railway in 1865. Among the local notables featured in the Museum are Thomas Hobbes, author of *Leviathan* and tutor to Charles II, and Walter Powell, MP for Malmesbury from 1868 to 1881. In December of 1881, the unfortunate Powell was carried out to sea in a War Office balloon and was never seen again.

READER REACTION FORM

The **Travel Publishing** *research team would like to receive readers' comments on any visitor attractions or places reviewed in the book and also recommendations for suitable entries to be included in the next edition. This will help ensure that the* **Country Living series of Rural Guides** *continues to provide its readers with useful information on the more interesting, unusual or unique features of each attraction or place ensuring that their visit to the local area is an enjoyable and stimulating experience. To provide your comments or recommendations would you please complete the forms below and overleaf as indicated and send to:*

The Research Department, Travel Publishing Ltd, Airport Business Centre, 10 Thornbury Road, Estover, Plymouth PL6 7PP

YOUR NAME:

YOUR ADDRESS:

YOUR TEL NO:

Please tick as appropriate: COMMENTS ☐   RECOMMENDATION ☐

ESTABLISHMENT:

ADDRESS:

TEL NO:

CONTACT NAME:

PLEASE COMPLETE FORM OVERLEAF

READER REACTION FORM

COMMENT OR REASON FOR RECOMMENDATION:

....

....

....

....

....

....

....

....

....

....

....

READER REACTION FORM

The **Travel Publishing** *research team would like to receive readers' comments on any visitor attractions or places reviewed in the book and also recommendations for suitable entries to be included in the next edition. This will help ensure that the* **Country Living series of Rural Guides** *continues to provide its readers with useful information on the more interesting, unusual or unique features of each attraction or place ensuring that their visit to the local area is an enjoyable and stimulating experience. To provide your comments or recommendations would you please complete the forms below and overleaf as indicated and send to:*

The Research Department, Travel Publishing Ltd, Airport Business Centre, 10 Thornbury Road, Estover, Plymouth PL6 7PP

YOUR NAME:

YOUR ADDRESS:

RECOMMENDATION

PLEASE COMPLETE FORM OVERLEAF

READER REACTION FORM

COMMENT OR REASON FOR RECOMMENDATION:

READER REACTION FORM

The **Travel Publishing** *research team would like to receive readers' comments on any visitor attractions or places reviewed in the book and also recommendations for suitable entries to be included in the next edition. This will help ensure that the* **Country Living series of Rural Guides** *continues to provide its readers with useful information on the more interesting, unusual or unique features of each attraction or place ensuring that their visit to the local area is an enjoyable and stimulating experience. To provide your comments or recommendations would you please complete the forms below and overleaf as indicated and send to:*

The Research Department, Travel Publishing Ltd, Airport Business Centre, 10 Thornbury Road, Estover, Plymouth PL6 7PP

YOUR NAME:

YOUR ADDRESS:

YOUR TEL NO:

Please tick as appropriate: COMMENTS ☐   RECOMMENDATION ☐

ESTABLISHMENT:

ADDRESS:

TEL NO:

CONTACT NAME:

PLEASE COMPLETE FORM OVERLEAF

READER REACTION FORM

COMMENT OR REASON FOR RECOMMENDATION:

....

....

....

....

....

....

....

....

....

....

....

READER REACTION FORM

The **Travel Publishing** *research team would like to receive readers' comments on any visitor attractions or places reviewed in the book and also recommendations for suitable entries to be included in the next edition. This will help ensure that the* **Country Living series of Rural Guides** *continues to provide its readers with useful information on the more interesting, unusual or unique features of each attraction or place ensuring that their visit to the local area is an enjoyable and stimulating experience. To provide your comments or recommendations would you please complete the forms below and overleaf as indicated and send to:*

The Research Department, Travel Publishing Ltd, Airport Business Centre, 10 Thornbury Road, Estover, Plymouth PL6 7PP

YOUR NAME:

YOUR ADDRESS:

YOUR TEL NO:

Please tick as appropriate: COMMENTS   RECOMMENDATION

ESTABLISHMENT:

ADDRESS:

TEL NO:

CONTACT NAME:

PLEASE COMPLETE FORM OVERLEAF

READER REACTION FORM

COMMENT OR REASON FOR RECOMMENDATION:

....

....

....

....

....

....

....

....

....

....

....

READER REACTION FORM

The **Travel Publishing** *research team would like to receive readers' comments on any visitor attractions or places reviewed in the book and also recommendations for suitable entries to be included in the next edition. This will help ensure that the* **Country Living series of Rural Guides** *continues to provide its readers with useful information on the more interesting, unusual or unique features of each attraction or place ensuring that their visit to the local area is an enjoyable and stimulating experience. To provide your comments or recommendations would you please complete the forms below and overleaf as indicated and send to:*

The Research Department, Travel Publishing Ltd, Airport Business Centre, 10 Thornbury Road, Estover, Plymouth PL6 7PP

YOUR NAME:

YOUR ADDRESS:

YOUR TEL NO:

Please tick as appropriate: COMMENTS   RECOMMENDATION

ESTABLISHMENT:

ADDRESS:

TEL NO:

CONTACT NAME:

PLEASE COMPLETE FORM OVERLEAF

READER REACTION FORM

COMMENT OR REASON FOR RECOMMENDATION:

....

....

....

....

....

....

....

....

....

....

....

TOWNS, VILLAGES AND PLACES OF INTEREST

TOWNS, VILLAGES AND PLACES OF INTEREST

TOWNS, VILLAGES AND PLACES OF INTEREST

TOWNS, VILLAGES AND PLACES OF INTEREST

TOWNS, VILLAGES AND PLACES OF INTEREST

TOWNS, VILLAGES AND PLACES OF INTEREST

TOWNS, VILLAGES AND PLACES OF INTEREST

TOWNS, VILLAGES AND PLACES OF INTEREST

TOWNS, VILLAGES AND PLACES OF INTEREST